TRIQUET'S CROSS

TRIQUET'S CROSS

A Story of Military Heroism

JOHN MacFARLANE

McGill-Queen's University Press
Montreal & Kingston · London · Chicago

ISBN 978-0-7735-3577-0 (cloth)
ISBN 978-0-2280-2639-6 (paper)
ISBN 978-0-7735-7703-9 (ePDF)
ISBN 978-0-7735-7877-7 (ePUB)

Legal deposit third quarter 2009
Bibliothèque et Archives nationales du Québec

First paperback edition 2025

Printed in Canada on acid-free paper that is 100% ancient-forest-free, containing 100% sustainable, recycled fibre, and processed chlorine-free.

This book has been published with the help of grants from the Conference of Defence Associations Institute and L'Association du Royal 22e Régiment.

Funded by the Government of Canada | Financé par le gouvernement du Canada | Canada

Canada Council for the Arts | Conseil des arts du Canada

We acknowledge the support of the Canada Council for the Arts.

Nous remercions le Conseil des arts du Canada de son soutien.

McGill-Queen's University Press in Montreal is on land which long served as a site of meeting and exchange amongst Indigenous Peoples, including the Haudenosaunee and Anishinabeg nations. In Kingston it is situated on the territory of the Haudenosaunee and Anishinaabek. We acknowledge and thank the diverse Indigenous Peoples whose footsteps have marked these territories on which peoples of the world now gather.

LIBRARY AND ARCHIVES CANADA CATALOGUING IN PUBLICATION

Title: Triquet's cross : a story of military heroism / John MacFarlane.
Names: MacFarlane, John, 1963– author
Description: Paperback reprint. Originally published in hardcover in 2009. | Includes bibliographical references and index.
Identifiers: Canadiana 20250148919 | ISBN 9780228026396 (paper)
Subjects: LCSH: Triquet, Paul, 1910–1980. | LCSH: Canada. Canadian Army. Royal Regiment, 22nd—Biography. | LCSH: World War, 1939–1945—Campaigns—Italy. | LCSH: Victoria Cross—Biography. | LCSH: Soldiers—Canada—Biography. | LCSH: Heroes—Political aspects—Canada. | LCSH: Heroes—Social aspects—Canada. | LCSH: Québec (Province)—Biography.
Classification: LCC D811 .T75 2025 | DDC 940.53/71092—dc23

Set in 11/14 Adobe Garamond Pro with Avenir
Book design & typesetting by Garet Markvoort, zijn digital.

McGill-Queen's University Press
Suite 1720, 1010 Sherbrooke St West,
Montreal, QC, H3A 2R7

Authorized safety representative in the EU: Mare Nostrum Group BV, Mauritskade 21D, 1091 GC Amsterdam, The Netherlands, gpsr@mare-nostrum.co.uk

CONTENTS

ACKNOWLEDGMENTS

This work would not have been possible without the encouragement and support of many people. First I wish to thank my colleagues at the Directorate of History and Heritage of the Department of National Defence. Many (Serge Bernier, Paul Lansey, Bill Rawling, and Ken Reynolds) read the entire manuscript, and others (Bob Caldwell, Steve Harris, Michel Litalien, Jean Morin, Charles Rhéaume, and Yves Tremblay) read large parts of it. All provided invaluable comments that have greatly improved the final product.

The team at McGill-Queen's University Press was helpful and efficient. Particular thanks to Philip Cercone, Maureen Garvie, Joan McGilvray, and Joanne Pisano.

I also benefited from the observations and experiences of many people, including Andrea Bélanger, Roch Belzile, Richard Belzile, Michael Boire, Marcelle Cinq-Mars, Hugh Halliday, Yolande (Triquet) MacArthur, Richard Martin, Jocelyne Milot, Marie-Hélène St-Cyr-Prémont, Eric Ruel, Claude and Louise Triquet, the anonymous readers, and all the people who participated in the interviews identified in the bibliography. Warren Sinclair, Valerie Casbourn, and Madeleine Lafleur-Lemire of the Directorate of History and Heritage provided their usual excellent assistance. The research staffs at the archives of Cabano (Fort Ingall and the Legion), the Canadian Postal Museum, the Canadian War Museum, the Citadelle, JAG Library-DND, Library and Archives Canada, Rivière-du-Loup, and the Royal Military College were also all very helpful. In addition, RMC provided a generous research grant, and for this I thank

Colonel Bernd Horn. Generous grants were provided by the Conference of Defence Associations Institute, for which I thank Lieutenant General Richard Evraire and Colonel Allain Pellerin, and L'Association du Royal 22e Régiment, for which I thank Col Jacques Vallières. The Canadian War Museum also generously assisted the project.

Michael Boire conducted three interviews with members of the German Armed Forces and was kind enough to share these.

Mary McRoberts and Douglas Delaney are preparing a book on Bert Hoffmeister's business and military careers and shared helpful information.

Richard Belzile of Fort Ingall as well as Richard Blanchette and Noaline Tremblay of the Paul Triquet Legion all provided helpful comments during my visits to Cabano in 2005, 2006, and 2007.

Finally, I wish to thank my mother and father, sister, Susan, and brother, David, for their support, and above all my wife, Diane, and daughter, Marie-Rose, who make every project worthwhile.

FOREWORD

Serge Bernier

The reader is about to enter into the life of a man who became exceptional thanks to a great feat of arms performed in Italy during the Second World War. We are grateful to John MacFarlane for this biography of the only French Canadian to be awarded the Victoria Cross during this conflict.

The author gives us a story that is much more than a mere recounting of the life of a born leader, Paul Triquet, following his enrolment as a private in the 1920s. For example, we learn how communicators during the war years cultivated a certain cynicism in their reports on the major, decorated in 1944, failing to take into account the man whose exploits they were describing or, even less, the psychological impact of the battles he had witnessed. They put heroic words in Triquet's mouth that he never actually uttered, and they erased from their narratives any mention of the valiant comrades in arms who had made it possible for him to earn his medal. Triquet said and wrote the truth, but in vain. The hero had lost control of the message that his heroic act was shaped to send. On the other hand, it was clear that the media had burdened him with a weight that ultimately became too onerous for his fragile human shoulders to bear.

But with the 1950s came a kind of psychological rebirth of the hero. The model of heroism that Triquet should have represented did not in fact emerge until several years after his valorous deed. In the interim, society adopted a mindset that increasingly saw heroes as simply ordinary people who performed extraordinary acts while remaining essentially themselves. This is exactly what Paul Triquet had been and always wanted to be – this man of action who was ill prepared to play the role of demi-god he had been obliged to take on in 1944. The book's final chapter is especially remarkable on this point.

Dr MacFarlane is opening a window onto a small corner of a vast area of research: military commemoration. This field should attract scores of young people in coming years, and we are all indebted to this bilingual historian who has so ably recounted the life story of Paul Triquet, an ordinary man who became extraordinary.

TRIQUET'S CROSS

INTRODUCTION

In the spring and summer of 1944, Paul Triquet became one of the most recognizable heroes of the Canadian war effort. The nation was told how he had motivated his troops with inspiring leadership and how against difficult German resistance during the victorious battle for Casa Berardi in December 1943, he had shouted: "*Ils ne passeront pas!*" For his actions, at the age of thirty-five he was awarded the highest decoration of the British Commonwealth, the Victoria Cross. Then, so the story went, he returned home for a brief enjoyable rest with his wife and children in his hometown of Cabano, Quebec, near the New Brunswick border, before eagerly going back into action.

There was much truth in the accounts. Certainly Triquet's remarkable bravery is beyond question. But there was also myth.

Although he shouted many colourful words during his unbelievably courageous attack, Paul Triquet never used the phrase "*Ils ne passeront pas!*" He had not lived in Cabano for most of the previous twenty years. He was thirty-three years old, not thirty-five, and legally separated from his wife, who lived in Montreal. He had also been more affected by the shock of his horrific experience than most people knew and would not be returning to action. His real story was modified to fit what comparative mythologists refer to as the typical hero sequence of actions, a cycle that has emerged throughout the world and in all ages to serve specific purposes for the community.[1] His story is thus that of an "ordinary" man singled out for attention that he did not seek. It reveals much about the society of the time.[2]

The first part of this book looks briefly at Triquet's life before he was awarded the Victoria Cross (VC). Growing up in Cabano, in the late 1920s he chose a military career and adapted to the predominantly anglophone environment of the Canadian army before going overseas with his Royal 22e Régiment and distinguishing himself at Casa Berardi. Eighty other members of Canada's Armed Forces, including twelve others during the Second World War, have been awarded the VC, but Triquet's medal is of particular interest because of the purposes for which it was used.[3]

Part 2 explores some of these purposes during the war. For the Canadian government of Mackenzie King, seeking greater autonomy within the British Commonwealth in 1944, Triquet's award provided an avenue to establish in practice some precedent-setting decisions of procedure for recommending, accepting, and announcing a Canadian VC. Triquet's was the first VC awarded to a member of the Canadian Forces who was available for public relations (Cecil Merritt had been awarded the VC for actions at Dieppe, but he remained a prisoner of war), and was awarded after the country had been at war for four and a half difficult years. Inevitably, Triquet's VC was used as much as possible by army public relations officers and the press to communicate their messages to Canadians.[4] As Triquet became a highly visible hero, he would play many roles in the army, but that of a fighting soldier would not be one of them.

Later in the war eleven other VCs would be awarded to men in Canadian uniform, but during the spring of 1944 publicizing Triquet as the face of the Canadian war effort was highly useful, and he knew this. He also knew that fewer francophones than anglophones had volunteered for service and that a francophone "war hero" would help with recruiting. Equally important, it would help convince English-speaking Canadians that francophones were more involved in the war effort than many recognized. So Triquet became a public figure, a kind of diplomat communicating various messages to Canadians. But the role did not come naturally to him, and it caused him considerable hardship in his personal and professional life.

The third part of the book looks at the effect the medal – and his horrific wartime experiences – had on Triquet in the postwar period. Like many soldiers suffering from battle exhaustion – not as well treated with psychological support at that time as it would be today – Triquet developed a serious drinking problem. He experienced difficulties returning home and had to leave his beloved Permanent Force Army in 1947. A network of former soldiers provided assistance, and he in turn was an active member helping others. These vets would have a significant impact on postwar Canadian society.

An epilogue, looking at how and why Triquet has been remembered since his death in 1980, reveals elements of Canadian society today.

Although Canadians may have heard of Paul Triquet, it is probably because of his heroic action – his first sacrifice. Many excellent studies present the Italian campaign; others look at the Royal 22e Régiment; and Triquet receives attention in all of them.[5] Several studies have listed the military exploits of the Canadian Victoria Cross recipients.[6] But none has investigated the many other interesting and important aspects of Triquet's fascinating story after he accepted the role that came with the VC – his second sacrifice.

The theme of military heroism and its socio-political dimensions is now receiving more attention from historians. In Britain, Adam Nicolson's recent book, *Seize the Fire: Heroism, Duty and the Battle of Trafalgar* (2006), explores why and how a certain view of heroism emerged from Lord Nelson's famous battle and in what form that view still exists.[7] In the United States, James Bradley's *Flags of Our Fathers* (2000) details the sad story of Ira Hayes and the heroes of Iwo Jima.[8] In Canada, Hugh Halliday's *Valour Reconsidered* (2006) is one of the rare historical studies to delve into the political considerations involved in the VCs awarded and denied.[9] Several other excellent books consider political and social themes related to individual military heroes of the twentieth century – Brereton Greenhous on Billy Bishop, Brian Nolan on Buzz Beurling, and Pierre Vennat on Dollard Menard[10] – and other earlier figures.[11] A growing body of literature looks at the socio-political dimensions of the commemoration of military events.[12]

This book is an attempt to deal with the effect on the life of one individual of receiving the VC – to look at its political and social contexts and impacts. As such, it is not strictly speaking a military history, although the story of Triquet's experience as a soldier inevitably looms large. Neither is it hagiography, or an iconoclastic attempt to bring Triquet down. It is a book about consequences.

Society has demanded much of heroes, as author F. Scott Fitzgerald realized in 1945 when he wrote, "Show me a hero and I will write you a tragedy."[13] To better understand military heroism, including its challenges, is to better appreciate the sacrifices of those who suffered through it.

PART ONE

From Cabano to Casa Berardi

The first stage of the mythological journey – which we have designated the "call to adventure" – signifies that destiny has summoned the hero … The hero can go forth of his own volition to accomplish the adventure … or he may be carried or sent abroad by some benign or malignant agent … Once having traversed the threshold, the hero moves in a dream landscape of curiously fluid, ambiguous forms, where he must survive a succession of trials. This is a favorite phase of the myth-adventure. It has produced a world literature of miraculous tests and ordeals.

– Joseph Campbell, *The Hero with a Thousand Faces*, 58, 97

1

Call to Adventure, 1910–1942

We have to sleep dressed to be ready for anything. Women cry, men are depressed. As for me, my morale remains good, I know that fear does not prevent danger. Come what may is my motto.
– Florentin Triquet, 1916[1]

Cabano

Paul Triquet grew up in a family with a strong military heritage. His great-grandfather participated in the Crimean War of 1854; his grandfather fought in the Franco-Prussian War of 1870 and joined international forces assisting the Boers in the war in South Africa of 1899–1902. His father, Florentin, received military training during his early life in France. By the time the First World War began in August 1914, Florentin was living in the little Quebec community of Cabano, but he answered the call of the French government for Frenchmen in all countries to join the cause. His daughter recalls Florentin asking her mother whether he should go, and Hélène Triquet replying that it was better to go than to torture himself with worry; besides, he could visit his family in France after an absence of more than a decade.[2]

Florentin's war lasted a grim two years. His children may have inherited the idea of military service as an honourable duty, but they did not receive an idealized image of it. Far from glorifying his experiences, Florentin told his wife and children in one letter: "Pray to God that this terrible war ends soon."[3] He returned to Canada in September 1916 suffering from health problems that would affect the rest of his life: a gas attack had compromised his vision, and trench life left him with painful lumbago.[4] As he recorded in his diary, he was very glad to come home: "Friday, 24 September [1916] … at 9:30, the train arrived at the Cabano station. About fifty of my friends were there waiting for me. I am so moved that I hardly recognize them. Everyone treats me as a hero … I return to ordinary life, happy to be back home, and I thank God to have returned safely."[5]

Paul Triquet, born 2 April 1910, was six years old at the time of Florentin's return, and was undoubtedly impressed by his soldier father's reception. Just over twenty-seven years later, he too would be greeted as a hero, stepping down from the train at the same place to experience for himself the difficulties of a "return to ordinary life."

The town of Cabano, officially established in 1906, is about 60 kilometres southeast of Rivière-du-Loup, near the New Brunswick border. The area was once the site of Fort Ingall, established by Lieutenant Lennox Ingall from 1839 to 1842 to provide a British presence during the border dispute with the United States, but the military presence in the community was not maintained. Few families had colonized this area of the Témiscouata Valley during the nineteenth century until the final decade, when the Fraser Company opened a sawmill and the roads and railways began to link the area to Edmunston and Rivière-du-Loup.[6] The large, 400-metre wooded hill that dominates the landscape provides a constant reminder of the importance of the lumber industry to the region.

While Cabano in the first half of the twentieth century had much in common with the small towns where the majority of North Americans were growing up, the Triquet family was somewhat different from others in rural Quebec. Hélène Pelletier and Florentin Triquet had met in Montreal in February 1905 at the French consulate, where both were then working. They married six months later and agreed to return to the area where Hélène had been raised. For Florentin, who had spent his early life in Caen, adjusting to this isolated area was not easy. Much of his twenty-one years had been spent studying, and he had not developed the physical skills that employers at the sawmill expected in young raftsmen and lumberjacks. One day in 1909 he fell into the icy river and was rescued by his co-workers shouting out the alarm: "The Frenchman's in the water!"[7] Far from hiding his French background, Florentin became a very well-respected member of the community while

Florentin and Hélène Triquet, and children, 1922. Paul is standing second from left, back row. Musée du Royal 22e Régiment, Fonds 43: Paul Triquet.

remaining easily identifiable as "Le Français" with his distinctive beret, accent, and behaviour. Some still remember his ritual before swimming in Lac Témiscouata of entering the water backwards while singing "La Marseillaise."[8]

While Florentin was overseas during the war, and to a lesser degree after his return in poor health, the other members of the large Triquet family helped each other get by. By 1921 there were ten children: three boys and seven girls.[9] Hélène, whose mother had died when she was twelve, had learned early to survive in hard times, and all the children helped out.[10] Paul, the fourth of the ten, was often on his own in his spare time (he preferred his hobbies of woodworking and mechanical repairs to playing with his sisters), but he helped his family however he could. When he was ten he found work with the local baker delivering bread, rising early each morning before school. A year later, in 1921, when Florentin was hired as beadle (the ceremonial officer) of the local church, Paul assisted him. At this time Paul was still recovering from a serious oil-lamp burn to his right thigh that would take eight months to heal, but he got up early to ring the church bell and dig graves. At times he was afraid in the dimly lit, creaking church, and he remembered one evening accidentally opening a coffin as he was digging and seeing a skeleton. He began to run home before deciding that a skeleton could not harm him, and returned to finish the job. For the next three years he contributed to family finances by working on a farm while not at school.[11]

If there was a single lesson that Paul Triquet learned from his early years, it was the importance of helping others. He first made a name for himself during the influenza epidemic of 1918. The rapidly spreading epidemic was terrifying the international community, killing 21 million people worldwide (including about 50,000 in Canada) within a few months.[12] At the age of eight Paul had acted as the messenger to the doctor and priest, visiting families affected by the disease and bringing food supplies from those stores still open. He met many people at this time and made many friends who knew him for years after as "P'tit Paul." Twenty-five years later he remembered in particular a friendship that he developed with a neighbour in his nineties. The ten-year-old Paul enjoyed talking with the man and to encourage this, every morning before school his mother gave him milk to bring to the old man. A few years later Paul took on the job of chopping his neighbour's wood supply, donated by the Fraser Company.[13]

Another important influence on young Paul was the military, to which he was increasingly attracted.[14] His father, despite some opposition in the community, had initiated a cadet school for those interested in military training, and at age eleven Paul became an eager under-aged recruit.[15] Training at a summer camp in Mont Joli for eight days in 1921, he was particularly impressed with Sergeant-Major Bouchard of the 22nd Regiment, and decided to join the army when he was old enough.[16] He left home when he was fourteen for, like his father, he yearned for adventure and wanted to see the world; unlike his father, he was not particularly interested by school (or by the violin lessons that his parents had suggested).[17] As he travelled from job to job in various sawmills and lumber camps of the region, working long, physically demanding hours, he seems to have always maintained his intention to join the army.

Twelve-year-old Paul Triquet leads the cadet corps at Cabano, 1922. Canadian Army photo, Musée du Royal 22e Régiment, Fonds 43: Paul Triquet.

In June 1925 he arrived at the Quebec City Citadelle, ready to begin his career in the Regular Army with the Royal 22nd Regiment. Walking through the main gate, he was impressed by the sentry ordering him to halt. Unfortunately, the recruiting staff were not impressed with a fifteen-year-old applicant and told him to return in three years when he was old enough. Disappointed but no less determined, he went back to work at different mills in the region. He also joined his father with the Fusiliers du St-Laurent in Rimouski for the summer training of the reserve unit in July 1927. Major Florentin Triquet intended to bring him as his batman, but Paul successfully argued to be allowed to join the others in their drills. The training again strengthened his resolve to make the army his career.[18]

On 3 November 1927, he returned to the Citadelle and, although still under age, declared he was nineteen years old and was accepted into the Regular Force.[19]

Home for a Regular Soldier

The Royal 22nd Regiment that Paul Triquet joined in November 1927 had a short but rich history. Formed during the First World War, the 22nd Battalion, as it was then known, had acquired an excellent reputation.[20] It had been honoured with two VCs, awarded to Corporal Joseph Kaeble and Lieutenant Jean Brillant, both posthumously. Georges Vanier, with the battalion from the beginning and its commanding officer in the 1920s, acknowledged the importance of honouring the individual exploits of the VC recipients as representing "a whole legion of unknown heroes."[21] An important aspect of Vanier's philosophy that spread to all the soldiers in his regiment was that "a regiment is not merely a group of men; it is a way of life."[22]

When Paul Triquet was finally accepted into the organization he had wanted to join for much of his life, he was initially disappointed. Most of the unit was in Toronto preparing, with the Royal Canadian Regiment, for a guard of honour to represent Canada in Washington for ceremonies on 11 November. Paul's first duties included scrubbing floors and working in the kitchen. One night he was ordered to prepare a breakfast of beans and toast for the company the following morning. Unfortunately this was not a skill he had learned at Cabano, but the orderly sergeant insisted the meal be ready. At 7:00 A.M. the corporal in charge of the kitchen found the only thing on the table was the "cook," who had stretched out around midnight for a few minutes of rest. Arrested and brought before the company commander, Captain Alex Dupuis, Triquet feared the worst – the end of his military career. Fortunately, the charge of sleeping on duty was dismissed. He made a promise to himself that he would stay out of trouble in the future.[23]

Discipline and tradition are essential to a unit's success, and after experiencing a taste of the first, Triquet eventually began to see indications of the second.[24] At the end of November he was greatly pleased to see the troops return from Washington, marching through the main gate, led by the band playing the regimental march "Vive la Canadienne." He was particularly impressed with their good appearance and smartness on the parade ground. As he got to know the other soldiers, he learned much from more experienced members eager to pass on their knowledge to the younger recruits.[25] As a historian of the regiment has noted, "A small number of decorated men, officers and NCOs were gathered together in a site rich in military history ... These veterans, most of them wounded at least once (Vanier had lost a leg), took the newcomers under their collective wing, inspiring them with their accounts of the unit's glorious exploits."[26] Although Vanier would leave the Citadelle in February 1928 to become military representative on the Canadian delegation to the League of Nations, he left his mark. For many, Vanier embodied qualities that would define the regiment for years to come: extraordinary will, dependability, aggressiveness, camaraderie, fidelity, and loyalty.

The late 1920s were difficult years for the Canadian military. The devastation of the Great War remained fresh in many minds. Prime Minister William Lyon Mackenzie King, reflecting the views of most Canadians, eagerly signed the Kellogg-Briand Pact in 1928 to outlaw war and kept military spending at a minimum through most of the decade.[27] In Quebec the support for the military was even lower.[28] In this context morale at the Citadelle could have been hurt; instead, an even closer bond developed among the small group of troops willing to accept sacrifices – extra work, less pay, decreased opportunities for promotion – for the good of the regiment. There was also the additional pride in the regiment's being the only francophone component of the Canadian regular defence forces. In recognition of this, as of 27 July 1928, the Royal 22nd Regiment was officially redesignated the Royal 22e Régiment ("the Van Doos"), the name it has maintained ever since.[29]

Anxious to begin his training, Triquet was disappointed to be assigned fatigue duties until mid-January 1928, as there were not enough new recruits to begin a course. Hearing of a shortage of trained men for guard duty, he and another recruit, Lucien Richard of Montreal, who had enlisted just five days after Triquet, began to learn the fundamentals of rifle exercises and guard duties from older members in their spare time. The regimental sergeant-major (RSM) agreed to test the two, who had also both trained as cadets. Undoubtedly impressed by their initiative and determination, the RSM agreed after thirty minutes of drills that both keeners could perform guard and picket duties as well as begin

Paul Triquet, Quebec, 1928. Canadian Army Photo. Musée du Royal 22e Régiment, Fonds 43: Paul Triquet, no. 435.

the non-commissioned officer's course. This meant that they skipped the six-month new recruit course, and Triquet was promoted to the rank of lance corporal on 27 July 1928. As he took courses throughout 1928, he became particularly interested in physical training, putting in extra time on the parallel bars and tumbling. In early 1929 he applied to take a physical training instructor's course. He was refused, as he was a year too young (in fact he was three years too young), but again he insisted, was given a short test, and was allowed to take the course.[30]

However, moving so quickly occasionally created problems for him. Skipping the new-recruit course meant much extra work to keep up with the more advanced non-commissioned officer (NCO) course. He was busy as well compensating for the schooling he had missed in Cabano,

Group photo, Valcartier, 1932. Instructor Triquet is in light uniform. Musée du Royal 22e Régiment, Fonds 43: Paul Triquet, no. 435.

taking night classes over a period of four years in subjects required for senior NCOs. In addition, he was trying to learn English, required for the courses he was taking at Ottawa and Kingston. In the case of the physical training instructor's course at Kingston, he had asked if he could write the exam in French and had been fortunate enough to have the officer in charge agree to contact a bilingual civilian to translate the exam; not all of the English-speaking members of the Canadian Army were as accommodating at the time. Another problem was his young age: although he seemed to have no problem giving orders to older men (and all the men of his platoon were older), some were initially reluctant to obey.[31]

On 19 April 1930, two weeks after his twentieth birthday, Lance Corporal Triquet was promoted to corporal and seems to have settled into a fairly regular routine. He continued in the summer with courses in rifle, bayonet, Lewis Gun, fieldcraft, and grenades and was assigned to train recruits of the regiment in physical training. He took an additional physical training course in the fall of 1930 to qualify as an assistant instructor and passed with good marks ("excellent" in physical training, "average" in the combat sports of boxing, wrestling, and fencing, and personality "to be improved").

That November he re-enlisted for three more years. An assignment somewhat out of the ordinary in the summer of 1931 was to organize sports and physical training for the two thousand unemployed men at the Valcartier Camp north of Quebec City. He recalled later that to facilitate relations with the men who helped him organize the games, he would dress as a civilian.[32] He had perhaps not yet developed a strong identification as a soldier, but events a few months later would greatly accelerate this process.

In December 1931 Triquet did something unusual for a man who later claimed to have always dreamed of being a soldier: he left the military. The chief of the Quebec Provincial Police needed qualified drill and physical training instructors and asked Corporal Triquet to join his force, offering higher pay, more rapid promotion, and similar work to what he was doing in the military. For a charge of $75 Triquet was struck off strength of the unit on 12 December, with the comment "Character on discharge exemplary."

Triquet's life outside the walls of the Citadelle, however, was nasty, brutish, and short. His first assignment was at the main entrance of the Quebec Parliament, where he was told plainly by the powerful and angry Liberal member for the riding, who had not approved the appointment, that he would be fired.[33] Officer Triquet convinced the police chief to come with him and explain the situation to the attorney general, but the latter supported the Liberal policy of patronage. Triquet lost his $75 and, despite a week's work, received no pay from his civilian job. He would not forget what he called his first experience with politicians, nor his vow to avoid them in the future, but for the moment his concern was to return to the military.[34]

A New Beginning, 1932–1939

Former Corporal Triquet went to see Major Alex Dupuis, now second in command of the regiment, and much to his relief was accepted back as a private. An officer explained the situation in a letter to Florentin Triquet, who had heard rumours that his son was no longer in the military: "Corporal Triquet quit the regiment on his own to join the provincial police. However, as he was unable to obtain the position he returned to the regiment and, happily, we were able to take him back."[35] Private Triquet realized when he signed on for a new three-year term on 21 December that this was not an easy arrangement for the regiment; a man had to be transferred to make a vacancy. A few days later orders were received from Ottawa that all recruiting was to be suspended.

The situation was not easy for Triquet either. Returning to serve with the older men he had trained and who were now above him, he had at least one confrontation. During a break one day in the canteen, another private announced in a loud voice that he could finally speak to Triquet as an equal and let him know what he thought of him. Triquet reportedly offered to settle things in the gymnasium, but the soldier refused and continued his harangue until Triquet pinned him to the wall, saying that he was glad to be a private again to see the man's true colours. As no one intervened, and the private had nothing more to say, the incident ended peacefully and Triquet had no other problems. Within a month, on 21 January 1932, he was returned to his former rank, receiving congratulations at the mess. He was glad to be back home.[36]

In 1932 he continued with his training and teaching duties. He improved his English, map-reading, and other skills, passed his Second Class Army Education Certificate, and became acting sergeant on 5 October. During his courses at Ottawa in the summer, he became engaged to Alberte Chenier, whom he had met the previous year. The couple set their wedding date for 24 December. They spent the holidays in Cabano and returned to live in Quebec City. For Triquet, who had been living in barracks with the single men of the regiment, married life was a big change in his personal life. The world around him was also going through important changes.[37]

The Depression of the early 1930s did nothing to encourage Ottawa to increase military spending. From 1930 to 1935 the Conservative government of R.B. Bennett maintained the permanent militia force at approximately three thousand members, while cutting back the Royal Canadian Air Force and Royal Canadian Navy. With the return to power of King's Liberals in 1935, spending gradually increased, accelerating from 1937 to the outbreak of war in September 1939. The Munich Crisis of September

1938 was particularly important for convincing the prime minister and the Canadian public that the country was not as prepared as it should be to meet international threats.[38]

From 1933 to 1935 Triquet was increasingly responsible for teaching duties with the Royal 22e and encouraged the use of French in training francophones, having discovered the hard way the disadvantages of not clearly understanding orders. During one of his first courses at the Royal Military College in Kingston, in a swimming lesson, the instructor told everyone that when he gave the command, they would jump into the water. Triquet spoke little English and swam even less. He only understood the word "jump," so he did. After the instructor rescued him from the deep water, he found Triquet a shallow area where he could practise.[39]

His suggestion that candidates for the physical training instructor's course begin in French at Quebec City (and finish at the Royal Military College) was approved by his commanding officer but was strongly resisted at RMC, where the importance of training in the English language was stressed. When Ottawa agreed that the first part of the course be given in Quebec, the first group met a frosty reception at RMC. Even Triquet, who had passed the course five years earlier, was told to repeat it as a candidate. He passed again, with similar scores. The comment that he was "inclined to give up if things don't come easily" was very different from all other accounts of his character.[40]

All ten of the candidates that Triquet had trained in Quebec also passed their RMC exam. He taught medium machine-gun courses at the Connaught Rifle Range near Ottawa as the French-speaking instructor; however, when there were not enough francophone recruits, he agreed reluctantly to teach in English. He enjoyed the experience and improved his English, but increasingly he realized how few resources were available for francophones to teach and be taught in their own language.[41]

Between 1920 and 1939 in the Permanent Force, only members of the R22eR received part of their training in French. Even then, training manuals, and foot drill and arms drill commands were all in English.[42] If Sergeant Triquet wished to make a difference, he would have to do it himself, as so many members of the regular force in the inter-war period were doing. He joined with Quarter Master Sergeant Georges LaBelle and wrote a bilingual dictionary of technical military terms.

Most francophone instructors had been taught in English, and there was some resistance from those who preferred using the technical terms they knew rather than learning the French translations; however, after a few years most believed that French recruits were achieving better results with French-only vocabulary.[43]

Between 1933 and 1935 Triquet continued to expand the dictionary on his own and submitted it to his superiors in Quebec, who forwarded it to Army Headquarters suggesting that copies be printed and distributed. Brigadier J.M. Prower, district officer commanding Military District No. 5, wrote in 1937:

> I beg to request permission to mimeograph and distribute an English-French Military Dictionary. This dictionary has been prepared by C.S.M.I. P. Triquet, Royal 22e Regiment ... Triquet has spent two years, as it were, turning this official French English dictionary inside out ... I estimate that 500 copies of this dictionary will be required ... C.S.M.I. Triquet undertook this work without any idea of being paid for it and he is quite prepared to have it issued without any profit to himself. In view of the amount of work, however, which has been put into it, and its usefulness, particularly in French-speaking units, I consider that he should be paid.[44]

The issue was not a priority with headquarters, as suggested by the reply from the adjutant general, Major General C.F. Constantine: although the work was "excellent" and "of considerable assistance," it would be of greater benefit with terms "relevant to all arms of the Service," and thus could not be paid for with public money.[45] Triquet made a few copies on his own initiative to distribute in the Quebec City area.

During these years he continued to earn good evaluations from his superiors and a reputation among other ranks as a soldier who was severe but fair.[46] In October 1936 he had been appointed as company sergeant major instructor (CSMI). He enjoyed his career, and members of the regiment were growing increasingly close.[47]

Unfortunately the family bonds at the Triquet home were not strong. Paul and Alberte Chenier Triquet had two children soon after their marriage: a son, Claude, born on 28 April 1934, and a daughter, Yolande, on 29 January 1936. But in 1938 the couple separated, with Paul ordered by the courts to pay all legal costs. He paid $35 per month for his wife and children, the CO of the regiment agreeing that the sum be deducted from his military pay as of 1 March 1938. At that time legal separation was not as common as today, while divorce was even more unusual. In Canada there was an average of only forty-two divorces per year during the 1930s, with very few of those in Catholic Quebec. What has not changed is that lawyers were expensive; in addition to his monthly allowance, Triquet owed another $546 for legal costs.[48]

Meanwhile the world was gradually sliding towards war.[49] As events unfolded, francophone Quebecers saw them from a very different perspective than did most English-speaking Canadians; French Canadians were much more Catholic (and more anti-communist) and much less attached to the British Empire.[50] Hitler's deal with the communist USSR in August 1939 helped bring the two solitudes together to a certain degree, but there remained a definite division over support for war.[51] On 1 September 1939 Germany invaded Poland. Britain and France declared war two days later, and a surprisingly united Canada joined the war on 10 September. A crucial element ensuring united support for participation was Ottawa's promise that enrolment for service overseas would remain voluntary for the war.[52]

Paul Triquet was ready to serve. The regiment was mobilized, and all members were to enlist with the Canadian Active Service Force, created for combat.[53] The interwar army was not huge. The Royal 22e Régiment of 1939 included nineteen officers and 165 other ranks in one company stationed at the Citadelle, representing 19 per cent of the Permanent Force infantry and 4.4 per cent of the total Permanent Force of 4,169.[54] Triquet had done his part to increase it in the past decade, convincing many of his friends from Cabano to join him in the R22eR. He returned several times a year to his hometown and vaunted the merits of the army.[55] He had also succeeded in convincing his younger brother Bernard to enrol in 1938 at the age of eighteen, although Bernard was not as enthusiastic as his older brother.[56] Their father, who had received the position responsible for distributing car licences in the area shortly after the election of Maurice Duplessis's Union Nationale in 1936, also enlisted.[57] A retired major with the reserves at fifty-nine years old, Florentin was too old to maintain his volunteer job as company commander of A Company but did take the reserves position with the 2nd (Reserve) Battalion, Fusiliers du St-Laurent, recruiting cadets in the Cabano area.

At the Threshold

The Royal 22e Régiment would not be sent into the fighting until July 1943, three years and ten months after the war began. Some Canadian units participated catastrophically at Hong Kong and Dieppe, but most waited. During almost four years, while other Allied armies fought around the world, some in the regiment became increasingly eager; however, in the fall of 1939 they were fortunate to have a few months of "phoney war" to allow them time to prepare for battle.[58] After years of neglect, orders were placed for new military equipment, and the country converted gradually to a war economy.[59] The huge number of new recruits also had to be trained.

The Canadian Active Service Force of 58,337 men and women that emerged in September 1939 relied heavily on the small nucleus of interwar soldiers trained in the Non-Permanent Active Militia (24,089) and particularly on those, like Triquet, trained in the Permanent Force (4,986).[60] The army would grow to half a million during the war. As the new recruits gained experience, the importance of the pre-war trained professionals diminished; however, the Permanent Force officers and other ranks played a huge role during the first years of war.[61] After two months of preparation, Triquet's regiment left Canada with the 1st Division on 9 December 1939 to continue training in the United Kingdom, arriving at Greenock, Scotland, on 18 December.[62]

Triquet had been promoted quite rapidly during his years of service, at a time when promotions were rare; now the dramatic expansion of the Canadian Army meant more accelerated promotion for regular soldiers with experience. In October he became a quarter master sergeant instructor (QMSI) and in November a warrant officer I and then was appointed as the regimental sergeant major (RSM).[63] The RSM was responsible for the discipline of the regiment and, although he did not do this alone, with so many new recruits unfamiliar with the army, he would have his hands full instructing them on the skills they would need for battle. As RSM Triquet acted as a sort of father figure for many of these young recruits. Reveille rang out at 06:30, the last post at 22:00, and in between there were many drills. Weapons training at night was a high priority in the first month, as was the need to correct the "general laxity" of some men on duty, "lounging with cap on the back of the head and hands in trouser pockets."[64]

The R22eR that trained in the United Kingdom and fought across Italy and Holland from 1939 to 1945 was very different from the group that Triquet had grown up with. Many were new recruits: the average age of men in the regiment during the war was 22.4 years, and only about one-quarter had previous military experience of any kind.[65] From being significantly under strength in March 1939 (with only 184 all ranks instead of the 773 authorized for the peacetime establishment) the regiment grew rapidly to sixteen officers and five hundred soldiers by the beginning of November. When the regiment sailed in December, its numbers had risen to eight hundred, including twenty-nine officers.[66] The battalion joined the Carleton and York Regiment (New Brunswick) and the West Nova Scotia Regiment in the 3rd Infantry Brigade of the 1st Canadian Infantry Division.[67]

1st Canadian Infantry Division

- Royal Canadian Armoured Corps
- The Royal Canadian Artillery
- Canadian Infantry Corps
    - The Saskatoon Light Infantry (MG [machine gun battalion])
    - 1st Infantry Brigade:
        - The Royal Canadian Regiment
        - The Hastings and Prince Edward Regiment
        - 48th Highlanders of Canada
    - 2nd Infantry Brigade:
        - Princess Patricia's Canadian Light Infantry
        - The Seaforth Highlanders of Canada
        - The Loyal Edmonton Regiment
    - 3rd Infantry Brigade:
        - Royal 22e Régiment
        - The Carleton and York Regiment
        - The West Nova Scotia Regiment

The first year overseas was a period of preparations and adaptation to the evolving situation. The regiment performed ceremonial duties: in January, King George VI visited to inspect the division, and from 16 to 21 April 1940 the R22eR relieved the Welsh Guards at Buckingham Palace.[68] While some saw these events as good publicity and morale builders, other officers regretted the loss of valuable training time.[69] In the spring of 1940, with the evacuation at Dunkirk completed on 4 June and the fall of France two weeks later, the commander of the 1st Canadian Division, Major General A.G.L. McNaughton, was forced to revise the initial plans that had proposed several months of individual training followed by divisional exercises in the summer to instead concentrate on "the task of direct defence of the United Kingdom."[70] As Germany focused its attention on Britain during the summer and fall and a squadron of the Royal Canadian Air Force fought in the crucial Battle of Britain, protecting the coasts against invasion became an important activity for the Canadian Army, laying minefields and preparing anti-tank ditches and barbed wire.

For Triquet, and most French-Canadians in the army, living in Great Britain was a cultural shock and the language barrier was an important obstacle. As the population prepared for invasion and rumours of spies circulated, speaking with an accent was not always an advantage. The deputy commanding officer of the Van Doos, Major P.E. Poirier, was arrested and held by local authorities suspicious of his accent. But along with the problems, the Canadians also witnessed the British people during their finest hour, and many soldiers were impressed with the people's courage and determination as German bombs fell. One soldier remembered, "During the bombing of London, I had an opportunity to observe and admire this traditional discipline and calm. The ruling people we French-Canadians have frequently known only through our local anti-British propaganda became a people to be admired."[71]

Triquet having now attained the highest non-commissioned rank, his superiors decided his experience and talents would be more effectively employed as a commissioned officer. After a brief course at a British training centre where he received accelerated officer training, in the fall he returned to Canada for a year. In November 1940 he was in Valcartier, where he continued training and was promoted to lieutenant on

18 March 1941. On 24 July he was assigned to an all-purposes Advanced Infantry Training Centre (AITC), where he had the opportunity to familiarize himself with his new role. After a brief holiday from 14 to 28 August, he returned to the UK, leaving on 17 September and arriving, an officer ready to rejoin his regiment, on 7 October 1941.[72]

During his absence, international events had continued to move quickly. The USSR, after being attacked by the Germans, had entered the war in June. The United States would join the war in December after the attack by the Japanese at Pearl Harbor, and in 1942 the tide would begin to turn in favour of the Allies.[73] There was much fighting to be done to liberate Europe from the well-installed and determined Nazis, and Asia from the Japanese, but the final result became increasingly predictable.[74]

At this time Canada faced its most serious domestic dispute of the war. Prime Minister King asked Canadians to release his government from the promise not to apply conscription for service overseas. King had recently lost his Quebec lieutenant, Ernest Lapointe, who had guided him through such minefields with success, and on his own King made the serious miscalculation that francophone Quebec would not mind a plebiscite on the question of conscription for service overseas.[75] Quebec opposition to conscription had deep cultural roots not fully appreciated by all anglophones.[76] Far from encouraging francophone Quebecers to enlist, the results of the plebiscite of April 1942 (supported by 80 per cent outside Quebec and opposed by 72. 9 per cent of Quebecers) highlighted the divisions of Canadian society and reminded francophone Quebecers of their minority status.[77] Whether Triquet voted is not known. He had vowed to avoid politicians in 1931, but he was certainly consistently opposed to the idea of conscription.[78]

Knowing that their time to join the battle was approaching, Lieutenant Triquet and the R22eR continued training in the UK in 1942, with increasingly large and complex exercises.[79] Triquet's Canadian Training School report of 11 October to 4 November 1942 noted that he "worked very hard," was quick to learn, had a good knowledge of weapons, and was "a good and energetic leader." He had a minor accident on 23 November 1942 when he was slightly injured in his left eye during a grenade exercise. He described the incident in his injury report: "Being in charge of a Grenade throwing exercise had to destroy a dud grenade which was lying in the field. I was about 15 feet away from the grenade when the explosion occurred and a shrapnel of Bakelite struck me in my left eye."[80]

It was in 1943 that the 1st Canadian Division would finally see its first action together. The time in England had been of great advantage for training and, perhaps even more important, for arming.[81] One observer described a parade in December 1942, on the third anniversary of the 1st Division's arrival:

> To those who had witnessed the development of the Canadian military force in Britain from those early days, when it consisted of a single infantry division and a few ancillary troops, armed mainly with the weapons of last war, into the powerful mechanized force of which a cross-section paraded on this winter day of 1942, the demonstration was a most heartening experience ... The day's proceedings served to symbolize the fact that the three years since 1939, though they have brought the Canadian Army Overseas little contact with the enemy, have nevertheless been years of intense activity and remarkable expansion.[82]

Another important consequence of the time in the UK was the building of the esprit de corps of the 850 men in the R22eR.[83] References to the glorious past were frequent, particularly to the two regimental recipients of the VC during the First World War as models of courage.[84] As the soldiers of the regiment prepared for battle, the older leaders who had trained them ceded their place to a new generation: in January 1941 P. Flynn was replaced by P.E. Poirier ("the old man"), who was replaced in October by the popular and efficient thirty-year-old Lieutenant Colonel J.P.E. Bernatchez.[85] He shared the same background as most of the men, was born in the francophone village of Montmagny, and had experienced their problems going through the required army courses while learning English.[86]

Triquet was as prepared for battle as he would ever be. For most of the first thirty-three years of his life, he had defined himself as a soldier. He had an independent character that made it difficult for him to take orders from politicians, civilians, or the church, and was thus to some degree a social outsider, particularly after the split with his wife, rare at that time. But he had found his place with the R22eR, and he was glad to give and take orders in the military environment. He had acquired many skills during his years of training by older soldiers and had great respect for Bernatchez, whom he would follow with his company for their first major tests in the summer of 1943.

2

The Road of Trials, 1943

Le courage, ça se cultive comme autre chose.
– Lieutenant Colonel J.P.E. Bernatchez[1]

First Months of Combat

In 1943 many Canadians were eager to see their forces in action, anywhere. Prime Minister King and Minister of Defence J.L. Ralston, pushed by Canadian public opinion, both encouraged British Prime Minister Churchill to use Canadian troops if at all possible in the campaign being planned for Sicily. In January 1943 at the Casablanca Conference, British and American leaders had decided that this was where their next major operations would be.[2]

Certainly the troops, particularly those waiting in the UK since 1939, were anxious to fight. An intelligence report of April 1943 suggested that morale would be increasingly affected if their waiting continued another year, when the major operations in northwest Europe were now planned to begin: "Notwithstanding the long period of waiting, the Canadian Army appears to be in excellent condition on the whole, and ready and anxious to move. There are still a number of comments which indicate restlessness and boredom due to this inactivity, but there is much evidence of a great desire for, and anticipation of, action in the near future. The chief desire is to get on with the job, for which they came over, and then get back to their homes."[3] In late April space was made in the British Eighth Army for a Canadian division. Canadian leaders had been

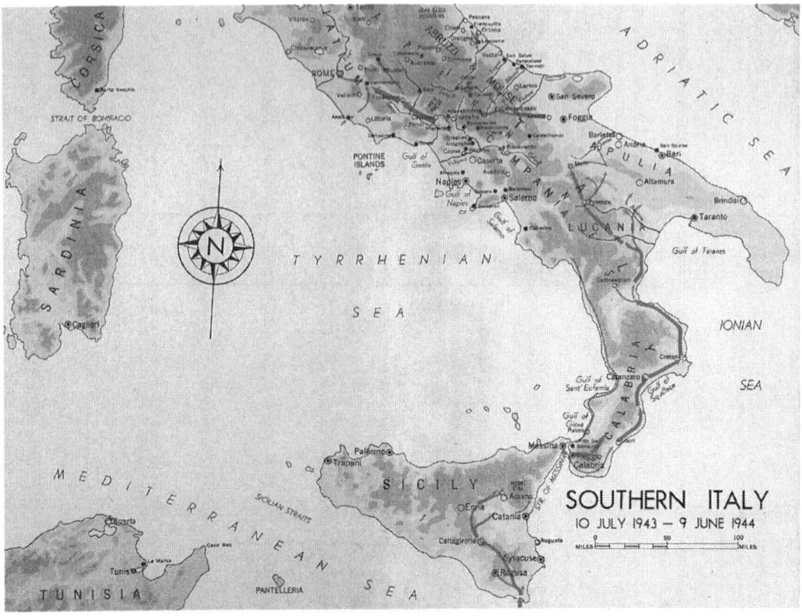

Southern Italy. Map compiled and drawn by Historical Section, National Defence. Originally published in G.W.L. Nicholson's *The Canadians in Italy, 1943–1945*.

planning to keep their army together under their commanders, but (as with the plan to form a francophone brigade) the objective of action proved more important.[4]

The Allies would land in Sicily on 10 July. Leaves had been cancelled on 27 April as preparations accelerated for the participation of the 1,851 officers and 24,835 other ranks of Canada's 1st Division, led by Major General G.G. Simonds.[5] It would be part of Lieutenant General Oliver Leese's 30th Corps, which was part of General Bernard Montgomery's Eighth Army.[6] The United States Seventh Army led by Lieutenant General George Patton was to land simultaneously further west. When the Eighth Army landed on D-Day in Sicily, the 1st and 2nd Brigades of the 1st Canadian Division led, with the R22eR and 3rd Brigade in reserve. With overwhelming superiority of forces in the air and on land, the Allies quickly succeeded in establishing their objectives, and the battle was underway. Although Ottawa was certainly pleased to see the

Canadian contribution to the Allied effort, several incidents revealed that having these efforts acknowledged would not be easy.[7] Publicizing the role of Canadians would remain an important consideration as the major operations of the war in Europe began.

The R22eR, led by Lieutenant Colonel Bernatchez, took the lead of the advancing 3rd Brigade, led by Brigadier M.H.S. Penhale, on 17 July. Bernatchez's four company commanders were Captain Léo Bouchard (A Company), Major Gilles Turcot (B), Major Charles Bellavance (C), and Captain Bernard Guimond (D). Their first action was at Grottacalda on 18 July, where they lost thirty-one men (including seven killed) but accomplished their objective. According to the regimental war diary, the men in their first battle fought like veterans.[8] General Montgomery was eager to advance but adapted his plans when faced with increased German reinforcements, as he did not wish to risk heavy losses. The regiment fought a particularly difficult battle at Catenanuova from 25 to 30 July. They lost eighty-nine men, including twenty-two killed, and also lost company commanders Bouchard (killed 27 July) and Bellavance (wounded 30 July).[9]

For Triquet, his responsibilities had evolved. Landing in Sicily as a lieutenant, he became acting captain on 30 July 1943, and officer commanding C Company to replace Major Bellavance. He would be confirmed captain on 29 October 1943, but in the meantime, only a week after becoming acting captain, on 5 August 1943 he became acting major, to be major on 5 November 1943.[10] He led C Company through some relatively minor engagements with the Germans, who continued their retreat but not without resistance. He and his company were singled out in press reports back to Canada for their role in crossing the Simeto River in early August.[11] Overall, by most accounts the Canadians in Sicily performed very well before receiving the news that on 16 August they would be taken out of action and given a chance to rest and reorganize.[12]

Having emerged through the ranks and spent time as RSM, A/Major Triquet played an important role in cementing the social cohesion of the regiment. As new recruits were added to replace casualties, these replacements had to learn quickly, under difficult conditions, and their casualty rates were often higher. Their integration into the close-knit regiment that had trained in Britain was also difficult at times, as a group known as the "original veterans" emerged. Such feelings were apparent with soldiers on both sides of the fighting in Italy.[13] One newcomer to the R22eR remembered arriving shortly after the Sicilian campaign: "All the officers are watching us, the last to arrive. Some of them have a condescending smirk as if to say: 'just wait, you haven't seen anything yet'; others shake our hands, and some welcome us warmly."[14] Major Gilles Turcot, who led B Company at this time, remembers that Triquet "was very popular; he was a nice guy and he was a good soldier so people admired that."[15]

One newcomer who was far from green had been transferred to the R22eR in August as the second in command. Major Jean V. Allard remembered his first days: "I knew no one in the R22eR, with the exception of Captain Ovila Garceau, a native of Trois-Rivières and a childhood friend. Nor did I expect to receive an enthusiastic welcome from a group of officers who had lived together for more than three years ... There was, within the R22eR, a sort of Lower St. Lawrence chauvinism which created barriers to my relationships ... I chose discretion and felt my way slowly and very politely among the officers, the NCOs and the men. Finally, when Captain Paul Triquet broke the ice, I knew I had chosen the right approach. From that day on, I felt I was part of the group."[16]

After Sicily, British and American planners agreed that Italy would be the next theatre of operations. The initial objective in Sicily – to seize the island to be used as a base for future operations and for airfields – was later expanded to include knocking Italy out of the war. Allied planners hoped that this would compel Germany to reinforce the area with even more troops from other theatres.[17] The 1st Division landed in Italy on 3 September and saw relatively light fighting during the month. The R22eR landed at Catania and began the march north. The division, which had moved from Leese's 30th Corps to Dempsey's 13th Corps on 10 August, suffered 178 casualties during the month, thirty-two fatal. The Italians, led by Marshal Pietro Badoglio since Mussolini's fall on 25 July, capitulated on 8 September. Hitler, increasingly concerned about the European situation, sent more divisions to Italy at the end of September. His orders were still to delay the Allied advance and continue retreating, but only to the Gaeta-Ortona line, south of Rome. He insisted that "this line will be held."[18]

In October the 1st Division continued its advance, with somewhat more action than it had found in September or would find in November.[19] The main engagement for Triquet's C Company was at Gambatesa in the second week. The R22eR attempted to establish a foothold across the Fortore River but were pushed back before the Carleton and Yorks and West Novas joined them and the Germans withdrew. The incident is of some interest in revealing Triquet's decision-making under orders to advance while minimizing casualties. Below is his account of the initial contact with the enemy:

> Around 16:00 on 5 October, the Battalion advanced through the mountain towards Gambatesa ... Our company was sent in front to scout the area and path to the city ... The patrol returned, reporting that the path to the bridge was guarded by what looked like about twenty German soldiers. Report was made to commander and a plan of attack prepared with the artillery ... Platoons 13 and 15 were in position for the attack at 06:00 on the 6th. The platoon advanced ... the Germans opened intense machine gun fire ... Platoons 13 and 15 were surrounded by machine gun fire unable to advance or retreat. It was then that the commander ordered the retreat; during this time Platoon 14 found itself in a dangerous situation ... In order to win time and confuse the enemy, the commander of the company asked for a concentrated artillery fire followed by some smoke bombs ... During this time, there was perfect order in the platoons and sections, each maintaining his position and waiting for the order to return.[20]

To hold their position, the company spent two more nights in shell scrapes without food, water, or communications. The battles were unspectacular but effective, in the words of the official historian of the campaign: "The skill and persistence with which the 1st Canadian Division had harried the enemy ... and kept him continuously in retreat were now to be rewarded" with a relatively easy final phase of the advance. German records confirm their "deep respect" for the artillery and advancing troops of the 1st Canadian Division. After the division had established a secure area at Campobasso in the last week of October,

Triquet appreciated a short break. He wrote to his sister, "We have made pretty good progress since we landed in this country."[21]

The Canadians resumed their march in November, with the Germans continuing to resist and retreat. In early November Major General Simonds was replaced by Major General C. Vokes in command of the division; a few weeks earlier Brigadier Penhale had handed the 3rd Brigade over to Brigadier T.G. Gibson. Triquet's company was involved in several relatively small actions, and he continued his cautious approach, backed up by plenty of artillery fire. During this period Triquet came to see more and more that the Italians appreciated seeing the Allies – one group prepared his company a meal he considered "worthy of the best restaurants." Arriving at San Pietro on 18 November, he saw why the Italians were so glad to see the end of the German soldiers: they had burned the buildings and houses of the two thousand inhabitants and were burning more villages as they retreated.[22]

By the end of November the regiment had been in Italy for almost five months. During this time Triquet had become known as an ordinary commander following orders of his superiors, not a reckless daredevil leader taking unnecessary chances with his life or the lives of his men. With experience he had learned to anticipate danger and acquired the skills to minimize losses while achieving his objectives.[23] Brigadier Hoffmeister, commander of the 2nd Brigade in November 1943, had organized a training session for his company commanders, emphasizing the importance of setting an example for the troops, showing enthusiasm, encouraging team spirit, and demonstrating loyalty to the chain of command "irrespective of [their] own opinion of [the] plan or arrangement." Triquet seemed to follow this model, except in one characteristic of Hoffmeister's ideal company commander (but then, Hoffmeister didn't follow it either): Company commanders "should not lead [in the attack and risk] jeopardizing the leadership of [the] Coy."[24]

December would be different. The number of 1st Division soldiers killed and physically wounded greatly increased, as did the number of cases of psychological trauma. Major A.M. Doyle, the divisional psychiatrist, had treated a few cases earlier; during the last three weeks of December, he was overwhelmed with 587 cases.[25] One reason for the increase in the number of casualties was that the division had reached the position that the Germans were determined to hold. A second reason was that British and American planners were exerting pressure to move more quickly. They had agreed that priority for resources would be given to preparations for the landings in northwest Europe over operations in Italy; however, in October and November 1943, it appeared that withdrawal of resources, particularly LSTs (Landing Ships, Tank: i.e., naval vessels carrrying vehicles, cargo, and troops), could compromise the Fifteenth Army Group objective of attaining Rome in the near future. Several delays were granted to allow the LSTs to remain in the area, but on 8 November General Eisenhower instructed the Allies to secure Rome as quickly as possible. After this important objective had been achieved, the armies would pause, regroup, and prepare for the next advance. General Montgomery prepared a message to be read to all troops in November: "The time has now come to drive the Germans north of Rome."[26] The task was complicated by poor weather and rising rivers that made hills and gullies particularly muddy. The rush seemed to be a departure from previous Eighth Army tactics, which had been characterized as moving deliberately, in limited steps, with the aid of as much firepower as possible. With Germans reinforcing the area, the ratio of defenders to attackers became roughly one to one along the Eighth Army front – a great difference from the three-to-one advantage preferred by Montgomery for an attack.[27]

The 1st Canadian Division was moved in to replace the 78th British Division in Lieutenant General C. Allfrey's 5th Corps.[28] With the advantage of hindsight, it seems clear that Major General Vokes, like General Montgomery and Lieutenant General Allfrey, was overly optimistic about how far and how fast the division could move. All decision-makers were perhaps overly influenced by the relatively light opposition of the previous months and unaware of how determined the Germans were to hold the line south of Rome. On 4 December Allfrey informed Vokes that "Indians are in Frisa with some tanks over river. New Zealanders held up at Orsogna and Guardiagrele ... You must get over River Moro as soon as possible."[29] But, as would soon become apparent, the Germans were no longer retreating. German veterans of the Italian fighting remember well the change in December 1943 from moving around for short but intense fights to remaining in the front lines to the end. Vokes would write in the war diary after the fighting was over that "everything before Ortona was a nursery tale."[30]

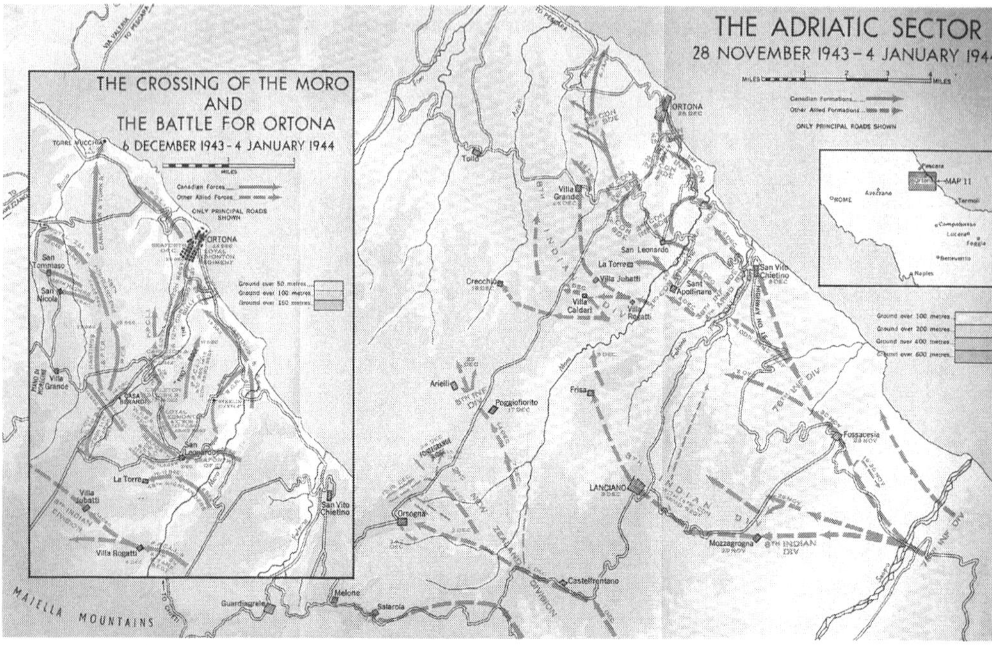

The Adriatic Sector. Map compiled and drawn by Historical Section, National Defence. Originally published in G.W.L. Nicholson's *The Canadians in Italy, 1943–1945*.

On 6 December the Canadian 2nd Brigade moved north across the Moro River, with the Edmontons in reserve, the Seaforths attempting to establish a bridgehead at San Leonardo, and the Princess Patricia's Canadian Light Infantry (PPCLI) at Villa Rogatti. The PPCLI had success against the increased enemy resistance, which was noted in the war diary of the Eighth Army:

> Enemy has dug his heels well in along the road running from Ortona to Guardiagrele, a position which is strengthened by the obstacle of the River Moro to the East. However, Cdn tps who have arrived in the coastal sector have effected a crossing in the face of stiff opposition from the new 90 Lt Div and have held their ground against several counter-attacks in which five enemy tanks were KO'd. This crossing is all the more meritorious in view of the

appalling weather conditions which caused the R. Sangro to rise 6 ft in two hours.[31]

For the next three days the 2nd Brigade was joined by the RCR, Hastings and Prince Edward Regiment, and 48th Highlanders of the 1st Brigade (as well as the usual invaluable support of the artillery, armour, engineers, and other vital units of the division) in the attempt to secure San Leonardo. After this objective was achieved, the war diary of the 1st Division recorded that it had been the Canadians' "first real battle on a divisional level with the Germans."[32]

The Canadians were tasked with securing Ortona to clear the Germans from the coast. They could now cross the Moro, but they met an important obstacle known as "the gully" on the way to their next immediate objective, the Cider Crossroads on the road from Ortona to Orsogna. From 10 to 13 December the 1st Division sent battalion after battalion into the action, as the West Novas and Carleton and York regiments of the 3rd Brigade joined in.

But the gully provided an excellent defensive position for the dug-in Germans. Vokes had sent the Edmontons on 10 December, the West Novas the following day, and the Carleton and Yorks on 13 December, but without success. As casualties grew, so did anxiety at all levels of command. Montgomery was pushing Allfrey and Vokes to move more quickly, and this led Vokes to push Gibson and his other two brigadiers to move without taking the time for reconnaissance and planning that they had in the past.[33]

Artist Charles Comfort, who had been following the headquarters of the 1st Division, remembers that the atmosphere became extremely tense as Vokes ordered Gibson to commit the last remaining regiment in reserve, the R22eR. Despite the repeated setbacks, there was hope. A gap had appeared briefly in the German defences, but advantage was not taken, as the 1st Division war diary for 13 December explained: "Reports in the battle were confused and it was very difficult to get a clear picture of what was happening."[34] What was clear was that air strikes on 29–30 November had hit German morale, and the constant pounding continued to take its toll: 5th Corps' intelligence reported on 13 December that the Germans had "indeed fought well, but they have paid dearly for their stand, and it is a badly mauled force that now stands in front of us."[35]

Reports later confirmed that the Germans were badly wounded, but the Allies had not realized that during the night a fresh new battalion of parachutists had reinforced the position.[36] Again with the advantage of hindsight, it would seem highly unlikely that the R22eR would have been sent if time had been taken to assess the situation, but in fairness, Vokes has also been criticized for not moving more quickly.

The atmosphere in the regiment had been tense during these difficult days of heavy 1st Division losses. The regiment's priest brought everyone together on 12 December to give them their last rites.[37] Lieutenant Colonel Bernatchez realized the need to keep everyone's spirits up and made several jokes before beginning the presentation of his plan. In private he confided to Allard, "It's a big risk, and if my command post is destroyed, you'll have to take over."[38]

The next evening Triquet was called in to see Bernatchez and told that his C Company had been selected to lead the battalion into battle. With the aid of a squadron of Ontario Regiment tanks, they were ordered to take Casa Berardi and the crossroads to allow 3rd Brigade to continue on to Ortona. Triquet later remembered being surprised, almost shocked with the news, but he quickly accepted the important assignment that would put into practice what he had been training for: "As he gave his orders, the commander mentioned that he had chosen 'Triquet' to attack with the support of the tanks, due to my experience working with them. I did not protest but knew well that my experience was mostly theoretical, from teaching infantry-tank tactics to many officers and NCOs while we trained in England. I accepted the task; I would finally be able to prove that what I had been teaching in theory applied in practice – this explains my great determination to succeed."[39]

A Long Day

Major Triquet led eighty-one members of C Company, already under strength, to their start line in the very early hours of 14 December.[40] Around 03:00 they saw a German patrol but were not seen. Some slept as they waited in silence for the 07:30 signal to go, remembering the final advice of Triquet to never leave enemy automatic weapons behind as they advanced and to eat well, as it was not known when they would have their next meal.[41] Captain Garceau's D Company was also in place, ready to proceed along the south side of the gully after Triquet's group had crossed over a culvert, turned right, and begun to proceed along the north side. Also waiting to accompany C Company were the seven Ontario Regiment tanks of Major "Snuffy" Smith, whom Triquet had just met the night before, and the Royal Canadian Horse Artillery (RCHA) forward observation officer (FOO) Captain Bob Donald with a soldier carrying a radio for communications.[42]

At 06:00 the artillery opened fire for an hour on the German positions, with such ferocity that Triquet remembered that even some of his troops were close to panic. C Company began their advance at 07:30 and, running over the gully, immediately met a platoon of Germans, who surrendered with little resistance under the shock of the artillery. Triquet remembers taking a young officer's P-38 pistol, which he brought back to Canada as his only war trophy.[43] The prisoners were sent back, but all knew that the fighting was far from over. Those early minutes are described in the regimental war diary account written by Triquet and Garceau with Lieutenant Claude Châtillon of D Company:

> Walking down the track, the men could see clearly the [junction] with the lateral highway and two large [houses] which were near by. There was still no further sign of the enemy. But they had all "been there" before and were not optimistic; and they glanced warily from side to side. No one was much surprised when the roar of a [heavy] engine starting was heard and first the long gun then the low snout of a Mk. IV Special pushed around the right of a house about 200 yds S.W. of the [junction] on the near side of the main road; and at the same time [heavy] MG and mortar fire was opened by enemy positioned among houses 1,000 yds to the South along the lateral.[44]

Jean Allard, who had just gone to see the two companies off, wrote in his memoirs that after only a few minutes "it soon became apparent that the day would be a long one."[45]

Of most concern was the tank that had appeared, as the Ontario Regiment's seven Shermans were still well behind, crossing slowly through the mud. Lieutenant Marcel Richard, commanding No. 13 platoon, called for his two-man PIAT (Projector, Infantry, Anti Tank) group and their anti-tank weapon, but the PIAT malfunctioned. While signalling to No. 14 platoon for a new PIAT, Richard was wounded, and Sergeant J.P. Rousseau stepped in. He ran across the open ground with the thirty-two-pound weapon, positioned himself, and fired a bomb that "hit the tank squarely between the turret and engine hatch. The blast must have penetrated to the 75mm shells stacked within the turret for the tank literally blew apart. Later more than thirty pieces were counted."[46]

The action was good news not only for the company but also for officers who had been trying to maintain the confidence of increasingly sceptical soldiers in the effectiveness of the PIAT, which had suffered numerous failures. The 1st Canadian Division issued an account of the incident in a training memorandum, pointing out, "This quick, resolute and well thought out action demonstrated clearly that enemy tanks can be dealt with effectively by infantrymen who have confidence in their weapons and the ability to use them."[47]

Working forward section by section, Triquet led his company, applying the battle-drill tactics learned in theory on the training fields of southern England and perfected during the past five months of practice. One of his lasting impressions of this long march was the moment when both sides stopped firing to allow an Italian woman with two young children to run towards the Canadian line. After only a few hours, casualties had been heavy. Triquet took the time offered by a brief pause to reorganize his forces, now roughly fifty, with two platoon commanders wounded. It had become obvious that movement in the open could not be long endured. He sent the injured back and reported his situation to Bernatchez. His radio was out, so he relied on those of Major Smith and Captain Donald, telling his commander that he was ready to continue. At one point, with Casa Berardi still a mile away and the Germans firing from both sides, he told his company in a phrase that became famous: "We are surrounded, the enemy is in front, behind and at our sides – the safest place is the objective."[48]

Triquet would often repeat how vital the contribution of the artillery was for the advance. An account of a corporal in the company noted, "Our artillery hammers continuously the German positions; the enemy doesn't seem to like that too much. If we escape from here we will owe it in large part to the work of our artillery."[49] The gunners were equally impressed with Triquet's work. One gunner remembered that Triquet,

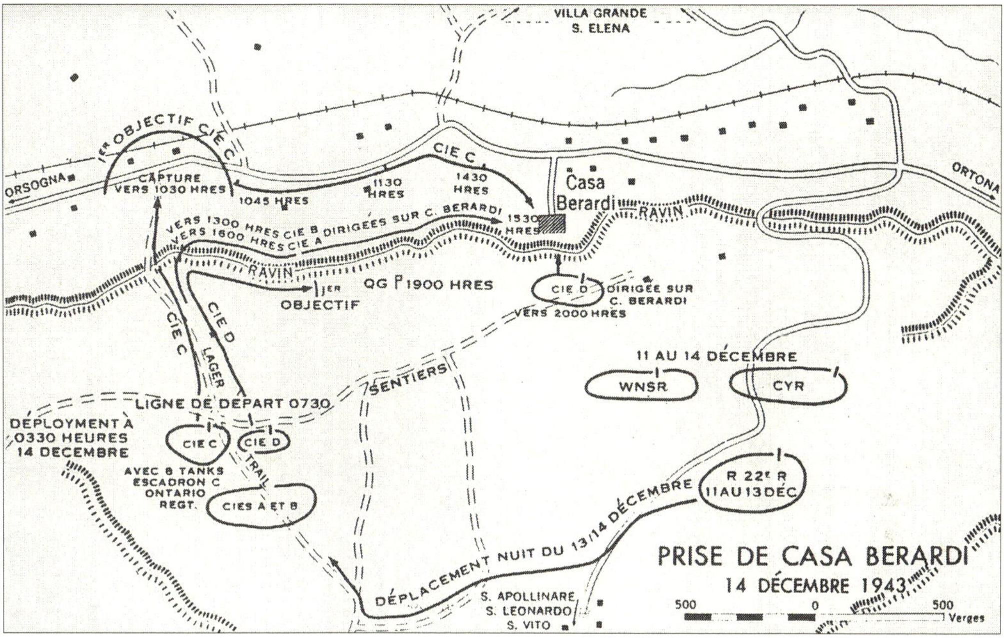

Casa Berardi. Originally published in Boissonnault's *Histoire du Royal 22e Régiment*, 199. Musée du Royal 22e Régiment, Fonds 2e Guerremondiale.

with the help of FOO Bob Donald of the RCHA, helped direct gunfire on the enemy and that the cooperation between the arms, under difficult circumstances, remained superb.[50] Donald's role, often overlooked, was an essential element in Casa Berardi's capture.[51]

The support of Major Smith's tanks remained crucial to the advance. After Rousseau had knocked out the first German tank early in the day, the Ontario Regiment had taken out another and encouraged other MK IVs to withdraw. But they soon returned.[52] A historian of the regiment has noted that "throughout the day, the Ontarios out-gunned the enemy by a wide and heartening margin. The Germans held well concealed defensive positions. Had their shooting been of as high a caliber as that of the Canadian tank men, 'C' Squadron's losses would have been very high." As they advanced together down the road, Triquet saw much that Smith could not and let him know where the Germans were hiding by repeatedly jumping on his tank to get his attention, or dropping a handful of gravel through the open turret on his head and pointing.[53]

"Casa Berardi, South Exposure," painting by Charles Comfort, ca. 1944–46. Beaverbrook Collection of Military Art. CWM 19710261-2164.

The officer leading 16 Platoon of D Company on the south side of the gully, Claude Châtillon, remembers seeing this final approach to Casa Berardi with his binoculars. "What a show! On the left of the Casa the Germans retreat, hiding behind trees, some firing as they withdraw. Rifles and machine guns are firing. Germans are falling, others rolling and hiding behind hay stacks, several run to the cover of the building's backyard." As the Germans were retreating, the Canadians were advancing, protected by two tanks.[54]

In the afternoon German tanks pulled back, closely followed by their infantry. Triquet noted that "on viewing the sudden departure of their [tank support], about 15 enemy [infantry] leaped from doors, windows and out-houses of the [buildings] and set off at a fast pace in the same direction. Others, slower, were just beginning to abandon dug-in [positions] between the houses as our [infantry] approached and [these Germans] were killed or surrendered."[55] Casa Berardi, a large house surrounded by a few scattered buildings, was attained around 15:00 by C Company, which continued on the way to their objective at the Cider Crossroads but soon returned to the house, under orders to hold that position until reinforcements arrived.[56] Triquet's company had been reduced to fourteen men accompanied by four tanks; ammunition (as well as water and food) was running dangerously low. He was, however, "agreeably surprised" to note that almost all of the survivors were armed with automatic weapons.[57]

Holding the house would not be easy. C Company had cleared the surrounding buildings, but lacked sufficient numbers to occupy them. The Germans quickly moved back in. Harassed by German snipers, artillery, and tanks, Triquet met with Smith and Donald just before dusk to discuss their defensive plans. As they heard the whistle of incoming mortar fire, Smith recalled, "Paul and I managed to duck in time, but Bob was hit." Triquet's orderly, who was bringing him a can of food, was also killed. The death of the FOO, an invaluable link in communication, hampered the efforts of the artillery, which continued to fire with less guidance.[58] Luckily, B Company arrived to help beat off the German counterattack.

Triquet was still waiting for the arrival of his friend Major Garceau and D Company, advancing on the south side of the gully. The official historian of the battle writes that "'D' Company on the right had become lost in the confusing terrain, and straggled into the West Nova's area later during the afternoon," but Châtillon insists that this impression was due to a misunderstanding in communication with the West Novas after D Company had reached its objective.[59] Triquet grew increasingly concerned for their arrival: the Germans remained very close, exchanging insults and invitations to surrender; supplies were low, and fatigue was setting in. He found another use for the invaluable tank support: "In order to remain standing I had to lean up against a tank or I would have fallen asleep." At 03:00 he heard noises, and asked who was there. The familiar voice of Major Ovila Garceau replied, "Don't worry, Paul, we're here to help you."

Triquet recalled, "Never in my life would I feel an emotion as strong as the one I felt hearing in the dark the voice of my best friend, with his company, bringing reinforcements to our small, exhausted group."[60]

Approaching the Crossroads

The next day would be a tense one on the north side of the gully. On 14 December all three brigades had continued to attack without substantial gains against the determined German opposition. The Canadian commander became convinced that the key to success lay in exploiting the favourable situation around Casa Berardi.[61] The objective for Triquet's C Company, now supported by the regiment's other three companies, remained the Cider Crossroads, but they also had to be sure to maintain enough men at the house to secure their vital foothold.

At 06:00 on 15 December the four companies of the R22eR headed out, again heavily supported by artillery, hoping to advance the thousand yards to the crossroads. C Company, reinforced with a platoon from A Company, took the left, D Company straight ahead between the road and the gully, B Company the centre, and A Company in reserve on the road. This would be a very active day for the artillery, as it received many urgent calls from all infantry groups, and preparing ammunition in the mud was not easy. The day was also long for the Van Doos, as they again suffered heavy losses, particularly B Company, and they barely moved from their start lines. The 3rd Brigade war diary recorded that all its units were "tired, under strength, and nervous from the day's very heavy fighting and shelling they had been through," and that the rate of casualties was twice as high as the number of reinforcements. Loss of confidence was a problem in some units; however, the brigade intelligence officer reported, "By contrast the R. 22e Regt, who were similarly shaken had all the confidence in the world."[62]

Maintaining morale was not easy during the day. After the morning setbacks, Brigadier Gibson and Vokes informed Bernatchez to wait for reinforcements and hold the house for forty-eight hours. The Germans were determined to dislodge them and began with artillery fire throughout the day followed by a counterattack with an estimated two hundred men at 15:00. Suffering heavy casualties, the Germans were turned away in an hour; but the Van Doos were now down to seventy-nine men in all four companies.[63] Unable to evacuate their wounded, the regiment turned part of the house into a first aid station. Throughout, Triquet played an important role, inspiring his young men, mostly with his actions but also with his words:

> All day on the 15th, the Germans continuously bombed our position ... Men were tired and tense and to maintain morale, after each intense bombardment, I called out the names of the men still with C Company ... [Later I was left with not] one man from my company headquarters and I spent the rest of the day jumping from hole to hole. After leaving each hole enemy machine gun fire was heard but as I always made it to the next hole I said, to take my men's minds off the danger: 'they don't know how to shoot.' This continual movement was very important for my men and even more so for me; in the state of mind I was, seeing all those dead bodies strewn over the area, and being unable to bury them, I had to, in order to hang in there, be able to speak with the few survivors that remained.[64]

This was one of Triquet's very rare references to the psychological trauma he suffered. On one other occasion, years later in a television interview, he referred to the emotional shock he had experienced. As he described the events, seeing so many friends killed and wounded, he talked of the noise – the noise of the guns firing from all sides, "the noise of the mind." He quickly moved on to the next part of his story. He noted that in December he had to bury thirty-three of the men from his regiment who had started out, and that "was quite a heavy percentage."[65] Certainly any company commander would be affected by seeing seventy-two of his eighty men go down. Jean Allard later commented on the strong relationship between officers and men in the Van Doos: "The officers were chosen from among the men because they had the same spirit and the ability and courage to refuse meaningless adventures and to embark upon only those actions, regardless of the risks involved, in which they themselves were prepared to participate. This willingness on the part of the officers to share everything and to command by exam-

Capt Bernard Guimond, Major Gérard Charlebois (second in command), Major Paul Triquet, VC, Capt Pierre Chassé, Capt P.F. Potvin, Capt Ovila Garceau. Photo taken at the front in headquarters of the commanding officer of the R22eR, Lt Col J.V. Allard, 1944. DND, DHH, Allard Collection.

ple created a unity of spirit which was, and still is, the strength of the R22eR."[66] Triquet would perhaps have been especially affected, having served as RSM for so many of the men.

Around midnight seven more tanks arrived with much-needed ammunition. A few hours later the second-in-command, Allard, arrived with about one hundred LOBs (men usually Left Out of Battle, including cooks, administrative services, maintenance, as well as the doctor and priest) from his echelon B. They brought mules packed with water, arms, and rations.[67] Triquet remembers this as an important turning point: the arrival of the reinforcements greatly improved the fighting strength, but above all it raised the morale of the troops. All were now convinced that they could hold the house until the other units of the division arrived: "Everyone that lived through that night will never be

Maj Gen Chris Vokes (left), Lt Gen Charles Allfrey (right), and Lt Gen Kenneth Anderson review the campaign on maps near Ortona, 17 March 1944. DND-31132-N.

able to forget it; the comradeship, the spirit of solidarity was felt by each and every one of us."[68]

The position as well as the morale of the troops was much more secure on 16 December. Triquet, who received word that day confirming his promotion to the rank of major, continued to inspire everyone with his inimitable words of encouragement. The regiment's doctor, Major Guy Latour, remembers seeing a tired, unshaven Triquet at his emergency post asking for rum. With sparkling eyes and a wide grin, Triquet boasted, "They'll never get this old soldier."[69] He wrote in the regimental account that a cold-blooded determination had set in with the 22e: "Hold out or Die. That was our motto. The old spirit of Vimy and Courcelette had been breathed into the 22e."[70] Ironically, the expression for which he is most famous Triquet attributes to one of his men: as he bounced from hole to hole on the previous day, he spoke with a young recruit in his first action: "He told me in a determined voice: 'Don't worry, Captain, they won't pass here' [*ils ne passeront pas ici*]."[71]

Lieutenant Colonel Bernatchez, who now had enough reinforcements and supplies to occupy all the buildings in the area, met with his company commanders to establish a defensive plan to hold the area for the next two days. However, later in the day Major Allard replaced Bernatchez, who was to take over 3rd Brigade three weeks later. According to Triquet, "Each officer and soldier of the Royal 22e Régiment was sorry to see this commander, who had done so much for our battalion, leave; he had trained us, in Scotland, led us during the invasion of Sicily and had commanded us from then to Casa Berardi. Major Allard, his successor, was already highly esteemed by the regiment and from his arrival all realized that once again we were in very good hands."[72]

During the third night, 16–17 December, Triquet finally had a chance to examine the German P-38 that he had liberated from the surrendering enemy officer three days earlier. By accident he fired a shot that just missed his friend, Captain Bernard Guimond. At this point Major Allard, "in a paternal tone," suggested that Triquet was tired and should try and get some sleep. He agreed, undoubtedly much to the relief of Capt Guimond, and slept for the next twenty-four hours.[73] While he slept, the exchange of artillery fire continued, but the regiment held its reinforced position.

On 18 December the brigade was ready to advance to the crossroads. Operation Morning Glory began at 08:00 with the heaviest fire to date from 1st Division artillery. The gunners continued to play a crucial and costly role; during the seven days from 11–12 to 18–19 December, the RCHA suffered more battle casualties (twenty-four) than any week before or after. As had now become clear, the Germans were not retreating and remained determined to hold the area despite mounting casualties.[74] However, the extra two days taken to prepare the details of the advance had been well spent: the initial stages of "Morning Glory" set a standard of cooperation between artillery, infantry, and armour for

Canadians in the Italian campaign.[75] All infantry battalions of the division were involved with the advance, led by the 48th Highlanders, who reached their objective at 10:30.

A few hours later the next phase, "Orange Blossom," did not go as well. The Royal Canadian Regiment suffered heavy casualties. But the next afternoon, on 19 December, the RCR continued and this time attained its objective before nightfall as the gully and Cider Crossroads were finally in Canadian hands.

In winning the long 2,500 yards from San Leonardo to the Ortona Road, each brigade of the Canadian Division had played an important and costly part. For Triquet's C Company, of the eighty-one who had set out on 14 December, nine remained in action on the evening of 19 December. He wrote later, "On 20 December, the dead of the RCR were also buried not far from the soldiers of the 22e; Canadiens-Français and English-Canadians rest there, side by side, testimony of the furious and heroic fighting that went on in this place."[76]

Evaluating Casa Berardi

On 20 December the Canadians had arrived at Ortona, a city of seventeen thousand. But clearing out the Germans would be far from easy. The Seaforths and Edmontons of Hoffmeister's 2nd Brigade suffered heavy casualties in the difficult house-to-house fighting, as the other two brigades moved north towards the Riccio and Arielli Rivers. Some have suggested, with the advantage of hindsight, that it might have been preferable to bypass Ortona or to pin the Germans down so they could be bypassed. But once in, it became important to win. As casualties continued to climb, Vokes asked Brigadier Hoffmeister if he would like to stop. The reply, based on the importance of the objective and occasional glimmers of hope, was "Absolutely not, to quit at this time would be letting the brigade down and the effect on morale of the brigade would be such that it would be just shocking."[77] The Canadians took Ortona when the Germans left on 28 December.

The advance continued for another week, but on 4 January the march towards the Rome-Pescara line ended just short of the Arielli River. Corps Commander Allfrey remembers visiting Division Commander Vokes, increasingly worried about casualties, and receiving a letter from

Officers of the Royal 22e Régiment, San Leonardo, Italy, 26 January 1944: Lt J.A. Girolani, Major Paul Triquet, Lt F. Hogan, Lt J. LeClerc, Lt Y. Beaulieu, Lt P. Larochelle, Lt R. Larin, Lt M. Couter; Capt Y. Dubé, Capt P. Potvin; Lt P. Fuchette; Capt C. Châtillon; Lt J.P. Chautte, and Lt R. Dussault. DND-LAC-PA-130590.

the Canadian commander, "the gist of which is that his division, owing to loss of leaders, casualties, no specialists, and the high sickness rate, has made it desirable for the division to go right out of the line and re-train."[78] Allfrey agreed, as did Gibson. The 3rd Brigade war diary noted that as a result of numerous battle casualties and wastage through sickness, the standard of training in units had "deteriorated very noticeably ... This [formation] has been on the move or in action practically continuously since Sep 43. The turnover in personnel within some rifle coys has been as high as 100% in one month. The standard of training of [reinforcements] arriving from England is variable."[79] The rest was also welcomed by the R22eR, which had suffered 191 casualties in December (thirty-three fatal) – a number roughly equal to the losses of the other nine infantry battalions of the 1st Canadian Division.[80]

Evaluations of the importance of the fighting had already begun. The first short descriptive account of the battle at Casa Berardi was prepared on 22 December by Triquet with Garceau and Lieutenant Châtillon of D Company.[81] This account notes that the objective for the day was not attained: "'Ortona x-rds' was NOT reached." However, the objective was established without appreciation of the large number of Germans that had reinforced the area. The account did note that the enemy withdrew and that "there can be no doubt that the existence of the Quebec [battalion] astride [the German] line of [communication] contributed greatly to this decision. And 'C' Coy by its energy, effective leadership and willingness to act against tanks with [infantry] weapons, which enabled its supporting tanks to cross successfully a disadvantageous stretch of ground, was in no small degree responsible for this success."[82] The Allies had cleared the gully and controlled the road that allowed them to clear Ortona and its ports.

Certainly the Germans considered it a crucial defeat, as suggested by the number of soldiers they had deployed. The war diary of the 76th Panzer Corps recorded gloomily on 14 December that the enemy would bring up further forces and "in the exploitation of today's success, will presumably take Ortona." Generalfeldmarschall Albert Kesselring was furious.[83] A German veteran of the fighting remembers that "it was after Ortona, at the beginning of 1944 that we in the Fallschirmjaegers [parachutists] realized that the war was lost."[84] The official historian has noted that the "conclusive German testimony to the significance of the blow delivered along the Ortona road on 14 December by the hard-fighting force under Captain Triquet strikingly endorses the recognition which this gallant officer received for his achievement."[85]

Related to the question of how important the fight at Casa Berardi was is the question of how important Triquet's role and leadership in general were. There is much truth in the statement that all members of his company had been heroic; one account of the battle in the regiment's newspaper refers to the company winning the VC for their commander.

Lt Gen Charles Allfrey (right), speaking to Major Paul Triquet (left), San Leonardo, Italy, 26 January 1944. DND-LAC-PA-130592.

And the company was well supported by the entire regiment. One historian praises Triquet as well as "the equally deserving Major Smith."[86] In addition to the armour and artillery, many other units were involved, each playing vital roles. But in extraordinary situations some people perform extraordinary acts that inspire, and there is little doubt that Triquet inspired his men that day. In an interview for a CBC documentary in 1972, he and Allard remembered "their Springtime of Life." Allard emphasized that Triquet's lack of regard for his personal danger greatly moved the men, and without that "they would have never made it" to Casa Berardi.[87]

Triquet was undoubtedly aided by his many years of training and five months of battle experience. His athletic abilities developed from his training as a gymnastics instructor also helped at times, as when he was standing with Major Smith, Captain Donald, and his orderly; he and Major Smith were able to hear and react quickly enough to escape the incoming shell and were lucky enough to survive uninjured. Another account of the battle in the regiment's newspaper focuses on Triquet's role during the battle, describing the company commander as the perfect example of a courageous leader and accomplished soldier.[88]

An interesting final note on the first part of Triquet's life, before he became a mythical hero, concerns his experiences during the two months following his trials. It is clear that on 6 March, when he learned of the award, he was in hospital, but the reason why he was there is less clear. The first story to emerge indicated that he was suffering from nervous exhaustion. Allard told journalists on 6 March that Triquet "wouldn't rest and finally I had to order him to hospital. He didn't want to go but I insisted for he was exhausted." The Canadian Press story specified that "Major Triquet himself is in hospital, victim of his own devotion to duty. Never content with carrying the normal task of officer, he worked himself into a state of nervous exhaustion." Soldiers who saw him at the time remember his being agitated and "needing rest."[89]

However, two weeks later the story that emerged in the press was different. According to a journalist, "The 'Van Doos' were out of the line following the battle and Triquet was training some new recruits in the use of mortars. One of the recruits fumbled a smoke shell, which barely popped out of the muzzle of the gun. Triquet leaped out and seized it, to throw it to a safe position from his men when the mortar shell burst and burned his thighs above the knees." He remained with his unit for six weeks before entering the hospital.[90]

It is possible that the second story emerged to gloss over what was seen as a less heroic element of his story. There is no accident report in

Triquet's file, and he had been badly burned on the thighs as a child which would account for any scars. It is also possible that this second story and the first are both true; the record is unclear. But what would become increasingly clear after March 1944 is that presenting the real story of Triquet as an ordinary soldier would not be a high priority. His life as a hero would be told, and modified, by many different people with many different messages to communicate.

PART TWO

Cross Purposes: Medals, the Media, and an Army at War

A hero ventures forth from the world of common day into a region of supernatural wonder: fabulous forces are there encountered and a decisive victory is won: the hero comes back from this mysterious adventure with the power to bestow boons on his fellow man … The original departure into the land of trials represented only the beginning of the long and really perilous path of initiatory conquests and moments of illumination. Dragons have now to be slain and surprising barriers passed – again, again and again.

– Joseph Campbell, *The Hero with a Thousand Faces*, 30, 109[1]

3

A Canadian Victoria Cross, March 1944

In the case of the VC the act must be so outstanding as to provide an example to the Army for all time.
– Major General Guy Simonds[2]

Politics and the VC

News of the 1st Division victories and heavy casualties of December 1943 reached Canadians slowly. Assuring the country that the accomplishments had been worth the sacrifices was easier for the Canadian government and military after the announcement on 6 March 1944 that Paul Triquet would be awarded the Victoria Cross.

Triquet's VC was of particular interest to Canadian political and military authorities involved with honours and awards, because it was in several important ways a test case for Canadian VCs in the post–Statute of Westminister era. Triquet is usually listed as the fourth VC of the thirteen given to men in Canadian uniform during the war, after John R. Osborn, Charles Cecil Merritt, and John W. Foote; however, the awards for Osborn and Foote were not announced until after the war. (Another early VC recipient, Frederick T. Peters, was born in Prince Edward Island but served in the Royal Navy and so was not at this point considered a Canadian VC.) Only Cecil Merritt's award (which Ottawa insisted was not to be regarded as "a precedent") had been announced, on 2 October 1942, and so Triquet was referred to at the time as the second VC. Consequently, during the period between December and 6 March 1944 there was much political interest in the procedures for recommending and announcing Triquet's Canadian VC.

Although military honours and awards, as strategic decisions, are sometimes more affected by politics than is openly admitted,[3] they recognize bravery, "the highest attainment of the human spirit in adversity."[4] The VC, instituted in 1856 (retroactive to 1854), quickly became known as the ultimate recognition for courage on the battlefield by soldiers of the British Empire.[5] When Queen Victoria decided to establish the award as the highest of all honours, the intent was for the award to be bestowed regardless of rank, concerns for boosting morale, or politics.[6] The intention of the original warrant was that "conspicuous bravery was to be the only qualification for the award"; the odds of survival had to be small; the recipient had to show leadership, providing an example for others; and there had to be some influence on the tactical situation.[7] However, by 1939 standards had evolved, and the admirals and generals signing the recommendations for the king did consider politics and morale.[8]

In the twentieth century the number of VCs awarded to each part of the empire became one of the considerations given increasing importance. In 1901 Lord Roberts had supported VCs to an Australian and a New Zealander because he believed it "desirable to show the Colonials that we appreciate their gallantry and their coming forward to help us. We may require them to do so again perhaps ere long."[9] During the First World War the award to British Second Lieutenant W. Leefe Robinson in September 1916 for shooting down the first Zeppelin destroyed over England is considered to have been politically motivated, "handed down by an intensely relieved bureaucracy fearful of a restive population suddenly and painfully exposed to the horrors of aerial bombardment."[10] The case of Billy Bishop, the great Canadian First World War flying ace whose great bravery has never been questioned, is another where political considerations played an important role. Bishop was encouraged by his superiors, who were eager for a Canadian hero, and his VC remains the only one awarded without a single witness to corroborate the action.[11] B.L. Montgomery considered that "though other considerations have their importance, the one, dominant factor in winning a battle is morale; and the VC is the outcome, as well as the outward symbol, of a high state of morale in the individual and nearly always in the unit also. Men who win the VC certainly help to win battles."[12]

British Empire honours policy had been established in London throughout the nineteenth and early twentieth centuries. Between the wars Canadian autonomy within the British Empire evolved rapidly, particularly with the Statute of Westminster in 1931. Although by 1939 the Canadian government was still a long way from having developed its own system of honours and awards (that would begin in 1967), it was increasingly interested in exercising greater political control over awards to Canadians, despite the characteristic caution of Prime Minister King.[13] King had replied in private to Minister of Defence J.L. Ralston in December 1940 that he was in no hurry to alter the status quo: "Situation re honours remains exactly as it was when you left. Not a question raised or word said in House about subject. Quite clearly members generally believe Nickle Resolution will be held to, and wish to have it so. My personal view is it would be well for all to let sleeping dogs lie until we are a little more certain of new order for which war is being fought."[14]

The Canadian government on 22 May 1919 had passed the "Nickle Resolution" asking Britain to stop conferring titular honours upon Canadians, but this did not extend to military decorations. A report of 1944 commented, "Owing to the fact that no awards were made to Canadians during the twenty years following the peace of 1919, the British Government at the outbreak of the present war were not altogether clear as to the policy which Canada would wish to adopt, and attempts were made to clarify the situation ... A draft telegram was provided, suggesting an approach to Dominion Prime Ministers to obtain their authority at least for 'immediate' awards to Dominion personnel serving with United Kingdom units." The commander in the field recommended immediate awards such as the VC, and committees in the War Office, Air Ministry, and Admiralty forwarded those they accepted to the king for final approval. Ottawa asked that it be made clear that such decisions involving Canadians were made "with the concurrence of HM Government in Canada."[15]

Ottawa eventually sought even greater control over periodic awards, presented to a certain number of individuals at given times. Representatives of Buckingham Palace again noted the importance of the commander in the field, to which a Canadian official unofficially replied that "it was improbable that the Canadian Government would accept a situation which permitted a Commander In Chief In The Field, other than a Canadian, to reject recommendations of a Canadian commander for operational and periodical awards."[16] On 31 July 1942 Ottawa in part lifted its ban to allow Canadians to receive awards of British orders of chivalry, in grades not involving titles, and also considered establishing a Canadian order.[17]

As Canadians had not been receiving periodic awards for some time, political considerations were involved with the preparation of an honours list for New Year's 1943. Major General H.F.G. Letson, the adjutant general, telegraphed Lieutenant General McNaughton, commander of the First Canadian Army, to draw his attention to the lack of French-Canadian representation in the proposed list: "I fully realize that merit must be a prime consideration and also that total quota was extremely limited but in these circumstances there must be many deserving in the same degree … I feel that public reaction to publication [of] this first list may largely influence whole future policy both civil and military. It is therefore extremely important that this first list should receive most favourable possible public reaction throughout Canada."[18] McNaughton and Major General P.J. Montague (at CMHQ in London) replied that they had considered this and that the percentage of French-speaking Canadians (eight of seventy-five on the list) was "in excess of a mathematically due proportion." What would be an appropriate number was not made clear. Although precise statistics were not recorded, it has been estimated that French-speaking Canadians made up 20 per cent of volunteers in the three services, but there would not be this many on the proposed list as they were largely under-represented at the higher levels.[19] The question attracted increased attention, and a committee was created in 1943 to recommend guiding principles, which included "the desirability of adequate representation of French-speaking Canadians."[20]

In 1943 Canadian officials at the Department of National Defence created Canada's first operational award. They had waited for King George VI to announce the first British stars (the Africa Star and the 1939–43 Star) in the summer of 1943. Many Canadians, who had not yet met the enemy, would not qualify, and Ottawa's Canadian Volunteer Service Medal was therefore intended to go to all Canadian volunteers serving for eighteen months or longer.[21] The day the CVSM was issued in January 1944, one Canadian remembers bumping into British Corps Commander Allfrey, who asked about the medal ribbon. After being informed, Allfrey replied "Well, I think it's a damn good idea. The Americans are simply plastered with ribbons, even before they get to the front. Jolly good show, this Canadian ribbon, I would say."[22]

Appeals by Canadian authorities for greater input into the procedures for recommending and awarding the highest honour of the British Empire system had not been as well received. Before March 1944 the Canadian government had intervened directly in at least two cases involving Canadian VC candidates, with disappointing results. First was the recommendation of Chief Petty Officer Max Bernays of the RCN for his actions on 6 August 1942. When the British Admiralty hesitated to pass the recommendation up the chain of command, the Canadian cabinet intervened on Bernays's behalf, but the Admiralty again refused.[23] A second intervention was in support of Cecil Merritt's recommendation for his actions at Dieppe on 19 August 1942. Although this VC was awarded, the Canadians expressed concerns with the procedure. British authorities had arranged for a Canadian, Major General J.H. Roberts, who had been the military force commander, to be responsible for recommending awards (to Canadians as well as British and Allied personnel) for consideration by the War Office. However, there were several complications.

Minister of National Defence J.L. Ralston had understood that names and proposed awards for Canadians should be passed through Ottawa and then the governor general would "submit recommendations by cable directly to Buckingham Palace." When Canadian Military Headquarters (CMHQ) suggested that this might cause delay and compromise some awards, Ralston accepted that it was preferable under the circumstances not to insist, noting that "the Government wishes it to be understood that their concurrence in the procedure to be adopted for DIEPPE should not repeat not be regarded as a precedent. This should be made clear to the War Office."[24] Roberts recommended two VCs: one to Major Patrick A. Porteous of the British Commando force that landed with the Canadians, and the other to Lieutenant Colonel Cecil Merritt, who was "believed to have lost his life." When it was learned that Merritt was a POW, there was concern that he would be ineligible, as British policy permitted VCs to recipients still in captivity in only very rare cases; Canadian authorities intervened with success. Major General H.F.G. Letson, the adjutant general, told Major General P.J. Montague at CMHQ in London that the award for Merritt would have a good effect on army morale. It should be added that awarding a VC to one of eight hundred British commandos with none to the five thousand Canadian soldiers had the potential to harm morale.[25] Shortly after, on 31 December 1942, an amendment to the Victoria Cross warrant allowed direct submission of recommendations from Dominion ministers to the king, bypassing the British chain of command.[26]

Recommending Triquet

Given this context, the administrative procedure involved with Triquet's VC had a surprising beginning. Initially he was recommended by his commanding officer for the Distinguished Service Order (DSO), an important but lesser recognition.[27] It should be remembered, however, that Allard was still new to the job, in his first week of command, during an exceptionally busy period of fighting. He won a DSO himself for actions on 30 December 1943.[28] His decision may also have been affected by the case of another member of the regiment recently recommended for the VC: Lance Corporal Gerard Gagnon, who had been killed in action on 30 July 1943 in Sicily. After the regiment went through the significant procedures required to recommend Gagnon, the VC was not approved. This was not uncommon, but Gagnon received no recognition, not even a posthumous Mention in Despatches, suggesting that the file may have been lost.[29]

What is perhaps even more surprising than the regiment's decision to recommend Triquet for the DSO is that neither Canadian superior at brigade or divisional level (Gibson or Vokes, who were better placed to appreciate the importance of Casa Berardi in the larger picture) suggested a higher award. This was proposed by British General of the 5th Corps Sir Charles Allfrey: "I won't recommend the man who broke the crust on my front for a Military Cross or a DSO," Allfrey told Allard – "Make it a VC, he deserves it."[30] Although many recommendations for the VC have been reduced for lesser awards, it is not as common – particularly during the Second World War – that a recommendation for a lesser award be increased to a VC at that stage.[31]

Canadian officers of the 1st Canadian Division had only three months previously been provided with the guidelines of Major General Guy Simonds. He began by noting: "The correct allocation of honours and awards is of great importance, since it affects morale. If decorations are distributed too freely they lose their value in the eyes of the Army as a whole and to the recipients. Conversely the recognition of valuable service by the award of a decoration is a just encouragement to others and in the best interests of the Service." Simonds's main points were that "A proper allocation of honours and awards should: a) give recognition to exceptional acts, or duties performed with outstanding ability, or recognition of exacting duties performed unfailingly during a difficult or long period; b) encourage aggressiveness and skill and the offensive spirit; c) discourage foolhardiness or the unnecessary and useless risk of lives and equipment. I look to every Commander and Commanding Officer to strictly discourage any forms of 'medal hunting'; d) to give recognition to acts of such outstanding gallantry that they are an example to the Army for all time."[32]

The first written account recommending Triquet for an award came on 22 December, a week after the action, when Major "Snuffy" Smith wrote a letter to Allard:

> I wish to submit the following report on the commendable work done by Capt Triquet, P., who commanded "C" Company of your Battalion, with which I worked in close contact on December 14th and 15th. Throughout these two days, despite severe casualties this officer set an example of leadership which was of the highest caliber. During the advance, despite heavy enemy opposition and fire, and with the loss of all his Officers and the greatest percentage of his NCOs, he kept the Coy organized as a fighting unit and pushed home the attack. The following day when the enemy counter-attacked he again took command of the situation and gathered the remnants of the troops, organizing them successfully in a defensive line. At all times his cheerfulness and personal disregard of danger were apparent.[33]

A month later the campaign for a VC was definitely underway. As part of the screening process for the award, Allard took statements of two more witnesses to the act. Both praised Triquet's work and, for the first time, using suspiciously similar language, both credited him with the phrase "*Ils ne passeront pas.*" Lance Corporal R. Comeau provided a statement in the field, on 20 January 1944, to Allard:

> I was in Number Fifteen Platoon acting as number three on Number nine Section Bren gun ... Upon arriving near the main road ... we were engaged by tanks, machine guns and mortars and suffered many casualties. Major Triquet encouraged us telling us "Never mind them, they can't shoot." By this time I was the only one left, in my section. So I joined number fourteen platoon. Major Triquet ordered us to move forward shouting to us that there was enemy all around us and that the only place to go was with him on the objective ... The enemy attacked us heavily several times before night, but Major Triquet encouraged us crying out repeatedly "They will not pass, with our tanks we will stop them." All the attacks were repulsed. During the whole of the advance Major Triquet was a great example to all of us. He encouraged us and cheered us on repeatedly [when] we were under heavy fire, and did not seem to mind the danger. We all felt what a splendid officer he was.[34]

The third witness was Lance Corporal J.R. Ducharme, again in the field, on 20 January 1944, to Lt Col Allard:

> On the 14th of December 1943 I was runner in "C" Coy. when it put in an attack on CASA BERARDI ... We lost quite a number of men but Major Triquet told us not to mind the fire as the Germans couldn't shoot. We could see some of the enemy running down the gully on our right side. So I went to Major Triquet and asked him who was on our right flank. He told me that "D" Coy was supposed to be on our right and, at the same time he ordered the company to move towards the objective, shouting to us: "there are enemy in front of us, behind us and on our flanks. There is only one safe place, that is with me on the objective ..." He went to place the tanks with Major Smith [and repeated] "We are only a few but they won't pass; with our tanks we will stop them." At that time I think there were only about eleven of us left

in the company ... Major Triquet did a wonderful job. He did not think of his own life but in spite of the fire was everywhere telling us what to do and cheering us up. His bravery was a wonderful example to us all and encouraged us to fight on. I do not think we could have done it without him.[35]

Allard's recommendations went up the chain of command. Brigadier T.G. Gibson, commanding the 3rd Brigade, gave his approval during this process on 17 January. He signed the following statement:

> I certify that I have personally examined the ground and have discussed the action with Major H.R. Smith, OC "C" Squadron 11 Cand Armd Regiment, who was in support of Major Triquet's Company. From my knowledge of the action, from my observations of the ground and from information I have obtained from eye witnesses I consider the achievement of Major Triquet and his company truly extraordinary ... This was, in my view, a remarkable feat of arms and was undoubtedly due to the incomparable courage, determination and leadership shown throughout the action by Major Triquet. Herewith letter from Major Smith and also sworn statements of further eyewitnesses [Comeau and Ducharme].[36]

Vokes, commander of the division, stated on 24 January: "I have seen the ground on which Major Triquet fought this action. In view of the difficult conditions then prevailing and the strength of the enemy [position] I consider it was an outstanding deed of heroism."[37]

Canadians had become convinced that the recommendation satisfied the high standards, and the file quickly passed through the British chain of command. Lieutenant General C.W. Allfrey, Commander 5 Corps, approved on 28 January, Lieutenant General O.W.F. Leese, GOC Eighth Army, on 4 February,[38] and General Officer Commanding-in-Chief H.R. Alexander, Fifteenth Army Group, signed and, following previous procedures for British Empire VCs, forwarded it to the War Office on 11 February.[39]

Twelve days later, on 23 February, Montague informed Letson that the War Office had received the recommendation. Triquet's recommendation, like Merritt's, had not followed the procedure preferred by

Ralston, but as the action being recommended had occurred ten weeks earlier, Montague urged Ottawa to accept: "Since award recommended in consultation with Canadian Major-General for act in December recommend you agree [Canadian officials] place before VC Committee for approval and submission to the King." Unofficially, he added, all considered it a "good case," that the king's approval could be obtained in four days at most if recommendation passed committee, with "First release Canada and Gazette announcement to be coordinated by [NDHQ]. Advise urgent."[40]

Ralston accepted that the procedure continue through the War Office as "a special case." He asked Montague to inform CMHQ authorities and the VC committee "that minister has approved of the submission of the name of A/Major Paul Triquet for consideration for the award of VC as recommended by CinC 15 Army Group in consultation with the Canadian Major-General in the Field. Also ask Canada House to inform Sec. of State for War that Minister of National Defence Canada has approved of this VC submission being made in this manner as a special case."[41]

Triquet's case seemed to meet all VC standards. One important criteria was the chance of survival.[42] As with the George Cross, the chance of death had to be greater than the chance of survival, and Triquet was undoubtedly aware of the risks during his action.[43] Another consideration was discipline. While honouring bravery, the award was clear that commanders should not encourage reckless behaviour contrary to discipline, and again Triquet showed leadership and example but only to carry out the objective assigned him by his superiors.[44] Another important consideration was whether the cause had been advanced, but this did not mean that the VC was only to be awarded in victory. Great bravery is often shown in adversity.[45]

In the past, several VCs had been awarded for costly losses (particularly in cases when decisions of commanders had been questioned), when it appeared that the loss might have put the morale of the men in jeopardy. The first VC to a Canadian was awarded to Alexander Dunn in 1857 for his brave actions during the unsupported Charge of the Light Brigade at Balaklava in 1854. There were three VCs to Canadians for actions at Leliefontein, a successful withdrawal during the South African War, but none for the more strategically important action at Paardeberg. Canadians received two VCs for Dieppe but none for the D-Day landings on Juno Beach. In the case of Triquet, there was the possibility that morale of the soldiers was suffering as casualties mounted with little visible results during the very slow December advance to Ortona. Montgomery and Vokes had misjudged German resistance and diverged from previous tactics of careful reconnaissance and massive artillery power in favour of attempting to move more quickly. Triquet himself had written in the regimental war diary that his company had failed on 14 December to attain their objective, the Cider Crossroads. However, their capture and holding of Casa Berardi was undoubtedly a great success and a very important advance for the Canadian Division. It was a well-earned VC.

Finally, the unofficial political considerations also favoured Triquet. While a VC is awarded to one individual for one isolated incident, it very often represents the contribution of many. In the words of the British secretary of state for air, considering a case in August 1945: "There are many cases of men who may have earned a VC who inevitably go unrecognized, and the VC must in fact be regarded as a token award given to a few in recognition of the bravery of the many."[46] A letter supporting the VC of Flight Lieutenant David Hornell in July 1944 pointed out "that no award of the Victoria Cross has been made to any officer or airman engaged in anti-U-boat duties. I feel that, apart from the outstanding heroism displayed by this officer, some recognition of the gallantry by the crews of the anti-U-Boat squadrons in Coastal Command is well deserved ... it would be some small recognition of the very great part played by Dominion squadrons and Dominion air crew personnel in Coastal Command's successful war against the U-boat."[47] Triquet's actions provided a good opportunity to highlight the contribution of the 1st Canadian Division's work in Italy. The VC committee in the War Office accepted the recommendation and sent it to the king for final approval.[48]

Announcing a Canadian VC

By March other individual awards had already been distributed for actions at Casa Berardi. Included were Major "Snuffy" Smith, awarded the Military Cross, and Sergeant J.P. Rousseau, who received the Military Medal for his action with the PIAT.[49] The number of awards available to be distributed to Canadians in Italy was limited, and some Canadian officials argued it was insufficient.[50] But the British did not want to increase these numbers.[51] Rumours had been circulating that, with the delay, the award to Triquet had to be the VC.[52] The official announcement came on 6 March 1944.[53]

The citation read:

> For determined leadership and example.
>
> The capture of the key road junction on the main Ortona-Orsogna lateral was entirely dependent on securing the hamlet of Casa Berardi. Both this and a gully in front of it had been turned by the Germans into formidable strong points defended by infantry and tanks.
>
> On 14th December 1943, Captain Triquet's company of the *Royal 22e Régiment* with the support of a squadron of a Canadian Armoured Regiment was given the task of crossing the gully and securing Casa Berardi. Difficulties were encountered from the outset. The gully was held in strength and on approaching it the force came under heavy fire from machine-guns and mortars. All the company officers and 50 per cent of the men were killed or wounded. Showing superb contempt for the enemy, Captain Triquet went round reorganizing the remainder and encouraging them with the words, "Never mind them, they can't shoot." Finally when enemy infiltration was observed on all sides shouting, "There are enemy in front of us, behind us and on our flanks, there is only one safe place – that is on the objective," he dashed forward and with his men following him broke through the enemy resistance. In this action four tanks were destroyed and several enemy machine-gun posts silenced.
>
> Against bitter and determined defence and under heavy fire, Captain Triquet and his company, in close co-operation with the tanks, forced their way on until a position was reached on the outskirts of Casa Berardi. By this time the strength of the company was reduced to 2 sergeants and 15 men. In expectation of a counter-attack Captain Triquet at once set about organizing his handful of men into a defensive perimeter around the remaining tanks and passed the *mot d'ordre, ils ne passeront pas*. A German counter-attack supported by tanks developed almost immediately. Captain Triquet, ignoring the heavy fire, was everywhere encouraging his men and directing the defence and by using whatever weapons

were to hand personally accounted for several of the enemy. This and subsequent attacks were beaten off with heavy losses, and Captain Triquet and his small force held out against overwhelming odds until the remainder of the battalion took Casa Berardi and relieved them the next day.

Throughout the whole of this engagement Captain Triquet showed the most magnificent courage and cheerfulness under heavy fire. Wherever the action was the hottest he was often seen shouting encouragement to his men and organizing the defence. His utter disregard of danger, his cheerfulness and tireless devotion to duty were a constant source of inspiration to them. His tactical skill and leadership enabled them, although reduced by casualties to a mere handful, to continue their advance against bitter resistance and to hold their gains against determined counter-attacks. It was due to him that Casa Berardi was captured and the way opened for the attack on the vital road junction.[54]

A consideration involved with announcing the award to a Canadian officer still serving in theatre was identifying his unit. The practice had been that when honours and awards were published in Canadian Army Routine Orders (CARO), for reasons of security no units were shown. Thus the possibility was raised that the name of the regiment might have to be left out.[55] Canadian Corps Commander H.D.G. Crerar had argued in mid-February 1944 that this should be changed, as it "particularly affects the infantry, who are all shown as Canadian Infantry Corps. It is considered that a definite contribution to morale would be made if units could be shown."[56] NDHQ told CMHQ that of the sixty immediate awards to be published in the *London Gazette*, "names of units will not be released or promulgated except in the case of Capt (acting Major) Triquet."[57]

The official announcement caused other concerns. Triquet, perhaps appropriately, received the news of the award from a military journalist. He described how "One Sunday [6 March], as I was walking back from Church [to the hospital] ... some [journalist] friends walked over to me to extend their congratulations, I asked them what for and they answered that I had been awarded the VC."[58] Triquet replied, "Are you quite certain of what you are saying? If what you say is so, I find it astonishing that I have received no official word of any kind."[59]

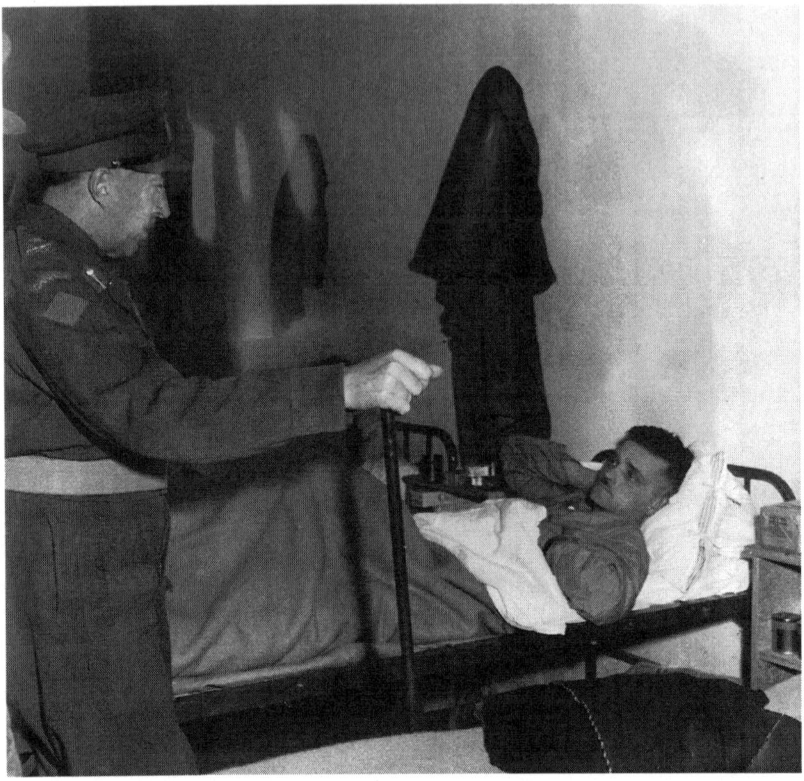

Lt Gen H.D.G. Crerar, GOC, 1st Canadian Corps, from 6 April 1942 to 19 March 1944, visits Triquet in hospital on 8 March 1944 to congratulate him on the first Victoria Cross of the Italian campaign. DND-31070-N.

Confirmation arrived shortly after when a colonel from the 1st Canadian Division visited him in the hospital "carrying a rectangle of purple ribbon and a letter of congratulations from Maj-Gen Chris Vokes."[60] While Triquet was surprised about how he initially received the news, Canadian officials were even more concerned about how the Canadian public learned of it.

On 1 March the War Office had informed CMHQ that the king had approved Triquet's award and asked CMHQ to "inform this Department of a date for the announcement of this award in the London Gazette which will be convenient for a simultaneous announcement in Canada. Arrangements will be made by the War Office with the BBC that no announcement will be made on the Wireless prior to 21.00 hours on the evening of the publication of the London Gazette and no announcement will appear in the Press until the following morning." CMHQ told Ottawa that it was "most desirable" that the news of the award be announced simultaneously in Canada and the UK. The date agreed upon was 6 March.[61]

All did not go as planned. The BBC announced the award at 12:00, and Defence Minister Ralston was forced to give his statement to journalists rather than make his initial announcement in Parliament. Ottawa sought explanations. There had been earlier problems of coordinating the release of information as journalists overseas were frustrated to have stories they could not announce while others were announcing them in Canada from British sources.[62] Ottawa told CMHQ: "Repeated breaking of release dates and times unexplained and requires drastic remedial action. Present good relations with Press jeopardized and in present case Canadian Newspapers were not advised in advance of Victoria Cross award as it had been arranged that minister would make first release in House of Commons. Situation created by lack of control over releases in UK so serious it may be necessary to discontinue any advance advice to UK of Date and time for publication."

Montague replied that his investigation revealed that information had been released to the press with "not for use before published in a special supplement of the London Gazette," but this had not been respected overseas by a "broadcast ... regularly heard and relayed in Canada." He concluded, "There is no assurance that BBC will not broadcast before agreed time. Alternative is to make first announcement and publication in Canada and defer publication in London Gazette until subsequent day and personally I recommend this as it should obviate any future problems."[63]

Canadian and British officials had much work to do to coordinate in practice the principles of Canadian autonomy in the post–Statute of Westminster British Empire. The recommendation and announcement of Triquet's VC had revealed some difficulties; however, the occasion was undoubtedly a very happy one for Canadian political and military officials and one with many future possibilities.

Triquet's life, present, future, and past, was about to change in important ways.

4

Army Public Relations, April 1944

"Paul, you generously offered your life to the service of your country and your country accepted it, it no longer belongs to you."
– Jean V. Allard to Triquet, March 1944[1]

Messages for Canadians

The announcement of Triquet's VC was the beginning, not the end, of his public life. The media and those responsible for Canadian Army Public Relations had messages to communicate to the Canadian public, and the voice of a war hero was an invaluable resource. This did not mean that formulating and presenting such messages to English- and French-Canadian audiences would be easy.

Attempts to increase Canadian public support for the war effort had so far not been very successful. The top priority in March 1944 was to improve relations between English-speaking and French-speaking Canadians to provide a more united war effort. This objective was a great challenge, complicated by political hesitation to address the issue. There were two main reasons that Prime Minister King was reluctant to allow representatives of his government to try to improve francophone-anglophone relations. First, King had spent his political career following, not leading, public opinion. King's biographer notes, "There could be no fireside chats, no public discussion of controversial issues, no campaigns to shape public opinion because King's approach forced him to resolve all controversies within the confines of the party."[2] The prime minis-

Triquet posing for Army photographers, 9 March 1944, three days after the announcement that he had been awarded the VC. DND-30809-N.

ter was uncomfortable with the idea of any government organization attempting to influence how people thought and acted.

The second reason was that King did not believe there was a problem. He had always been convinced that he understood French-Canadians, and during much of his time in office he enjoyed overwhelming support in Quebec. But his past support in Quebec, much more than he would admit to himself, had been due to his leading Quebec minister, Ernest Lapointe. On key issues dividing anglophones and francophones, a pattern had repeatedly emerged. King would propose a policy based on his English-Canadian background and assume that French-Canadians agreed; Lapointe would oppose – often strongly, occasionally threatening to resign; King would reluctantly bend to Lapointe's advice and then convince himself that the successful compromise policy had been his idea. When Lapointe died in November 1941, King was left on his own. Within a month he had decided to unite Canadians with a plebiscite (which Lapointe had strongly opposed) on conscription for service overseas. King felt sure French-Canadians would vote yes and the conscription issue would be resolved.[3]

French-Canadians did not vote yes. Anglophones in cabinet had debated conscription during the war in largely (often exclusively) military terms. Up to the time of his death, Lapointe had stressed the cultural aspects – the symbolic importance for the minority group of forced participation in what many saw as Britain's war. The debate was less about soldiers than about recognition. King attempted to replace Lapointe with Louis St-Laurent, who had not opposed conscription.[4] Quebecers' confidence that their voice was included in the Canadian war policy was deeply shaken. A month after the plebiscite, King, to his credit, began to have doubts and to consider that public information efforts had been insufficient.

Public relations had not yet developed into the coordinated systems led by specialized personnel that would be more common after the war. RCN programs of the 1950s emphasized the importance of specialists dealing with the press.[5] RCAF programs were much larger and emphasized the importance of public support for recruiting and even for the existence of the Air Force.[6] The Army program of the 1950s and 1960s was bigger yet.[7] However, these increasingly elaborate postwar programs had all begun during the war. There had been some very limited initial PR attempts made during the First World War, but the focus had been more on censoring press stories than actively shaping public opinion.[8] The Defence of Canada Regulations applied on 3 September 1939 included a "Censorship Coordinating Committee," and soon after, other agencies emerged, most notably the Bureau of Public Information under the Ministry of National War Services. Newspaper circulation increased and remained high during the war, and most Canadians listened to a daily radio broadcast about the war; Ottawa tried to ensure that information in the media would reinforce feelings of patriotism, duty, and support for the war effort. The goal was to spread an optimistic message promoting Canadian achievements.[9]

In May 1942 King asked Charles Vining, his friend and a public relations expert, to study the situation. This report led, in the words of an authority on the subject, to "the establishment of a comprehensive information policy for the first time during the war."[10] In September the Department of National War Services' information function was transferred to a new Wartime Information Board (WIB) responsible to the prime minister. The methods proposed throughout 1943 by the increased WIB to achieve its objectives were wide ranging, particularly considering that the whole idea of government intervention in such matters was very new.[11] Press cooperation was vital and largely achieved; even the resistance in right-wing circles to any government action was fading. The Canadian press and the Army both wanted to help win the war, and this cooperation was recognized when journalists were recommended for awards by H.D.G. Crerar, commander of the Canadian Army.[12] But the media sought news value, which occasionally meant they pressured the Army to move more quickly, as in December 1943. The Army focused on military success, which occasionally meant keeping journalists away (as Major General Chris Vokes did).[13] The WIB consulted not only with journalists but also with advertising agencies, academics, and pollsters, and it established links with the National Film Board.[14]

Most believed that the main target should be to improve the war effort in Quebec. Vining suggested as well that Canada had not promoted its wartime contribution effectively in Washington, leading Americans to be less sympathetic to Canadian concerns. One of Vining's proposals to improve Canada's image in the United States, that Ottawa apply conscription for service overseas, suggests that he was not as concerned with the objective of convincing Quebecers to do more for a united war effort.[15] But the perception in Quebec of Ottawa's war effort was a major concern, and some were not too upset when Vining resigned in January 1943.[16] His successors began to implement the plan that had been prepared to more effectively promote the highlights of Canadian military accomplishments.[17] Much time and energy were devoted to some helpful initiatives: a "coordinated plan for increasing and improving French-speaking representation in the Army" had been approved on 5 August 1941. Progress reports informed of developments on translations of manuals and a Directorate of Public Relations with French representation. The WIB also published 45,000 copies of the magazine *Nouvelles*

Catholiques every two weeks and supported a group that prepared fact sheets to send to Quebec newspapers refuting rumours such as the one claiming that things at Dieppe had been "arranged that the Fusiliers Mont-Royal bore the brunt of enemy fire."[18]

There were two problems that had to be solved. The first was the relatively weaker support for the war in Quebec (requiring a PR campaign in the province); the second was a misconception about Quebec participation in the rest of the country (requiring a PR campaign there). When the public affairs machine attacked the problem of perception in the US of the Canadian war effort, the focus was not only on convincing Canadians to do more but also on illustrating to the US what was being done. Had the WIB put more energy into this approach in English-speaking Canada, relations might have improved.[19] Instead, the Quebec war effort, often measured by support for conscription, continued to be portrayed as much weaker than it was.[20] Incredibly, the official historian of the Canadian Army wrote that the war, which had "moved English-speaking Canada to great sacrifices, moved French Canada only slightly." He maintained in one book that statistics showed that "whereas in British Columbia, the province that made the greatest contribution to the war in terms of military manpower, just over 50 per cent of the male population from 18 to 45 was in the forces during the years 1939–45, in the province of Quebec the parallel figure was only 25.69 per cent." Using the same statistics, Quebec's contribution of 175,441 men (compared with BC's 90,976 men) represented 17.04 per cent of the 1,029,510 men in the Canadian Armed Forces. Even though the 25.69 per cent figure was below the Canadian average of 41.15 per cent, it was still an important contribution. Anglophones and francophones were different, but the difference should not be exaggerated.[21]

That being said, francophone Quebecers' support for the war effort was undeniably less. The number believing that they were not affected by the war was amazingly high. As noted by his biographers, Pierre Elliott Trudeau, known for his intelligence and internationalism, would later be "called upon to justify" his less than enthusiastic support for the Allies' cause during the war.[22] Historians Béatrice Richard and Serge Durflinger have recently provided increased detail that helps us better understand how and why francophone Quebecers saw the war differently.[23] Certainly events (the fall of France in 1940, the battle of the St

Lawrence, etc.) affected their views. But it seems clear that government efforts to convince them to do more failed.

The first reason these efforts failed is that they began too late. During the crucial period from 1939 to 1942, no serious attempt had been made to influence opinion in Quebec, despite repeated requests from francophone leaders.[24] Any PR campaign that began after the 1942 plebiscite would have been met with scepticism, no matter how effective. A second reason that Ottawa's efforts failed is that they were not particularly effective, being largely directed by anglophones: Norman Mackenzie, Arnold Heeney, Brooke Claxton, and Norman Robertson made most of the decisions, with a staff that included few French-Canadians.[25] When the few francophones involved attempted to formulate messages targeted to a French-Canadian audience, anglophones insisted that Ottawa not allow different messages in different parts of the country, Protestants opposed references to the Catholic Church, and what increasingly emerged was a program of English-Canadian material translated into French. The result was an increased scepticism about all information. Francophone leaders supporting the war effort – including Premier Godbout, Lieutenant Governor Fiset, and Cardinal Villeneuve – preferred not to have Ottawa's "help" unless all interventions were approved at the provincial level. A poll in mid-1944 revealed that almost two-thirds (62 per cent versus 28 per cent) of Canadians outside Quebec believed that they received generally truthful media accounts about the war, while only one-third (30 per cent versus 57 per cent) of Quebecers agreed. By the end of 1944 the WIB would give up trying to increase support in French Canada for the war.[26]

Initial Reactions to a French-Canadian VC

Although there were problems and certain risks involved in using medals in public relations strategies, in this context Triquet's award represented a golden opportunity and a last chance for the WIB's efforts to encourage a more united war effort. A story such as Triquet's VC was an obvious good news story to promote.[27] However, the campaign did not begin well. The message to English-Canadians that participation of Quebec volunteers should be recognized was hampered when several anglophone sources identified Triquet as a Frenchman from Normandy.[28] The mes-

The Triquet family, with Florentin pretending to receive the news of his son's VC as his wife Hélène listens with grandchildren Claude and Yolande. DND photo, Claude Triquet Collection.

sage to French-Canadians that this was their war was hampered when the Army sent unilingual anglophone PR writers and photographers to Cabano on 6 March to provide a story on the town and Triquet's family. In addition to problems of communication, this limitation also affected how the story was told. For example, a francophone might not have written the following, referring to Paul's older brother, Louis, for a francophone audience: "The eldest of the family, he was helping keep things going at home. From his expression when he looked at pictures of Bernard, the youngest son, and Paul, it was easy to guess he wished ardently to be where they have been." Journalist H.R. Martin described his conversation with ten-year-old Claude Triquet, Paul Triquet's son: "'Don't you speak any English at all,' I pleaded, 'un peu' was the laconic reply ... 'What do you think of your Dad's award,' I asked. 'Un peu' was the phlegmatic answer."[29]

The job of promoting the war was complicated for the PR team by the return of Paul's brother at almost the same time. Bernard Triquet had been seriously affected by the war and after his return to Canada in early 1944 would spend the rest of his life in the military hospital Sainte-Anne de Bellevue near Montreal. His sister Florence remembers: "I had difficulty recognizing him. I was used to seeing him full of energy and humour and now his look was indifferent and his movements slow. To my questions he replied with single syllables or not at all."[30] She found the cameras intrusive: "A horde of journalists came down on us. They were everywhere they could find a Triquet! My military father was very happy with the news; but my poor mother remained deeply concerned about Bernard ... They forced my parents to pose with big smiles for the photos. All the other members of the family also. They even came to Sainte-Anne de Bellevue ... I was ordered to go to the hospital for a photo with Bernard. Only in front of the camera did I realize how cynical these people were."[31] She adds that they made the teacher at the school attended by Paul's children "furious" with their presence.

Accounts detailing the exploits of Triquet and his regiment at Casa Berardi, closely watched by military authorities, did not begin to circulate until late January, seven weeks after the battle and about the time that the process began for his VC recommendation.[32] Common themes, once Triquet began to be identified with the action, included his courage and leadership. "We were sure of him ... we all had confidence," said one of his men, and another said, "We were all glad to stay. He is gallant and a gentleman."[33] A sub-theme was his modesty. One journalist wrote, "No genuine hero – and Major Triquet is one of these – looks for public plaudits."[34] Foster Barclay wrote that when Triquet attended a memorial service in January to honour his fallen comrades, "army photographers attempted to follow him but he turned and said softly: 'Please go away. This is personal.'"[35] Ralph Allen added that Triquet "is the kind of man Canada would like. It is standard journalist practice to say that heroes are modest, but the description would fit Triquet even if he were not a hero."[36]

When Defence Minister Ralston presented the first official Canadian announcement in Ottawa, repeated in the House of Commons, he read the citations of both Triquet and Merritt and said that Canada was proud of both VC winners. He added that both had inspired their comrades in the Army and "they are equally an example and a challenge to those at home; they have brought great honour to Canada."[37] The MP for Vancouver Centre, Ian MacKenzie, immediately pointed out that Merritt came from Vancouver, while the leader of the opposition in the House, Gordon Graydon, after congratulating Ralston for drawing attention to the heroism of the two who had shown that Canada was playing a part in the war, mistakenly reported that a third Canadian VC of the war had been awarded to a soldier born in his constituency.[38] It took three days before MP Jean-François Pouliot of Témiscouata rose to remind everyone that Triquet came from his riding. He congratulated Merritt and Triquet and suggested that citations describing their exploits be sent to schools across the country and also that a tax-free parliamentary grant be given to all living VCs to allow them to live independently.[39] At this point the speaker, fearing a precedent, suggested that in the future only the government call attention to bravery and decorations of soldiers.

The theme of francophones and anglophones working together was repeated in many news stories.[40] A series of press releases referred first to the three VCs earned by French-Canadians, then to Cabano, and then to Triquet's family and how his father had taught him military skills. One Army PR release highlighted a musical composition dedicated to Triquet called "Ils Ne Passeront Pas."[41] The *Maple Leaf* had several stories on Triquet. One front page story described an event, probably motivated by the objective of seeking to increase Canadian visibility in the United States, of a meeting between Triquet and an American sergeant who had earned the US Medal of Honour.[42] An army brochure, "Mission à Casa Berardi," written by a francophone, emphasized the praise of religious, civil, and military authorities of Quebec and Canada for Triquet and others who, "despite many obstacles, accomplished their mission."[43] And the army produced a radio program dramatizing the exploit of the "tall, quiet-spoken man."[44]

Triquet's desire to return quickly to action was also widely reported.[45] The first stories in the anglophone press, on 6 and 7 March, followed Army Public Affairs releases and referred to the proud reputation of the

R22eR and the role French-Canadians were playing in the war. One reported that "Major Triquet said he knew that French-Canadians of his own bn ... and other units fighting in Italy were 'sure' that they were being backed by 'the people at home in Quebec.'"[46] Another stated, "Major Triquet has proved that all Canada can depend on him and his gallant company in the battle for freedom."[47]

Many reports in the francophone press were translations of anglophone ones, but there were some differences. Francophone reporters had not been in Italy with the initial landing, but Marcel Ouimet had begun following the 3rd Brigade through Italy in September 1943, and others joined him later.[48] At least one francophone soldier had expressed concern that the French-Canadian press would minimize or even criticize the heroic act.[49] But almost all recorded with pride the R22eR exploit at Casa Berardi, and some with additional pride noted that it had been recognized by the anglophone press: "This participation of French-Canadians in one of the greatest military success of Canadian and British Forces was, very happily, recognized in all the Canadian press."[50] Just as English-Canadians were eager to have their contribution acknowledged in Washington and London, French-Canadians were also pleased to see recognition of their efforts.[51]

Maurice Desjardins, a war correspondent for the French language press, described how, following the VC announcement, he was suddenly bombarded with questions from British journalists about French-Canadians in the war. He reported how his reply emphasized that they were all volunteers. He added that they were mostly in good physical condition, "the result of living in the fresh air of the country," often full of imagination and initiative; "they have no equal when it comes to improvising and getting themselves out of even the most difficult situations," and they were very Catholic.[52] All newspapers emphasized to some degree the importance of family, but again the francophone press had more on Triquet's wife (and her work as a secretary at la Société Radio Canada), their children, and Triquet's parents.[53]

The British press mostly repeated the report of a war correspondent that Triquet was "almost embarrassingly self effacing ... of medium height, broad shouldered and wiry and every inch a professional soldier."[54] It is interesting to note that most British newspapers also quoted Triquet's comments that his men had won the VC for him and that the press should focus on others, such as his batman: "He brought me food saying 'but sir you must eat' and a second later he dropped dead at my feet ... [and] there was another private into whose slit trench I crawled for a few minutes. He was alone there and utterly exhausted but he whispered 'don't worry sir. I'm all right. They won't pass.' He died later that day. They're the heroes you want to write about not me."[55]

The Canadian press did not write about the young private who had whispered "they won't pass," as Triquet had asked. Only the first part of this story was reported, all the Canadian papers crediting Triquet with the phrase, adding to his discomfort. It is also interesting that "*Ils ne passeront pas!*" was repeated in headlines despite the reference to Maréchal Pétain, who had used the phrase in the First World War but had become somewhat less popular in 1944, particularly in English Canada. One even more embellished version that did not catch on with other francophone newspapers maintained that Triquet had called out, "*Les salauds, ils ne passeront pas*" (the bastards, they will not pass).[56]

After the obvious news blitz of a week or two, one public affairs officer refused to invest in a proposal to distribute copies of a Triquet portrait, as the story "had no more news value."[57] However, others saw many more opportunities in it. Lieutenant General J.C. Murchie, chief of the general staff in Canada, informed his predecessor, now chief of staff at Canadian Military Headquarters in London, Lieutenant General K. Stuart, "Strong representations received that Major Triquet VC be returned to Canada for short period to take part in Victory Loan Campaign. In view importance our assisting Loan Campaign to fullest extent possible may necessary arrangements be made for return Triquet if operational requirements permit." Stuart approved, asking Lieutenant General E.L.M. Burns (who was taking over command of First Canadian Corps) to proceed "if you agree and operational requirements permit," noting it was "an excellent idea which would help not only Victory Loan but Canadian Army as a whole."[58] Continuing to publicize Triquet's VC helped Army PR by encouraging Quebecers to contribute more to the war effort and convincing English-Canadians that Quebecers were involved more than acknowledged.

Returning to Canada to begin the next phase of his PR work, Triquet was no doubt aware that it would not be easy. Dollard Ménard, a hero of Dieppe, and Major Abbé Sabourin, who accompanied the Fusiliers Mont-Royal at Dieppe, had recently participated in public relations campaigns. Their comments, and the way they were interpreted by some anglophone journalists during speaking tours, had created some controversy.[59] One French-Canadian friend warned Triquet about the need to avoid the previous problems of WIB publicity campaigns: "Be suspicious ... They will try and use you for propaganda ... Do not do as [Major Abbé Sabourin] during the 5th Victory Loan: MAKE A MOCKERY OF FRENCH-CANADIANS, in order to give yourself more weight with military authorities." He recommended that Triquet "be himself," as Ménard "had been himself" when he spoke with his own French-Canadian message specifically targeted to a French-Canadian audience.[60]

A Hero of Our Own

On his way home Triquet stopped in London to receive his VC from King George VI. Triquet recalled their two previous meetings during ceremonies in 1939 and 1940, and the king replied, "I thought I had seen you before."[61]

Many others recognized something familiar in Triquet. When the news of Triquet's VC was made public on 6 March 1944, many groups celebrated, identifying to varying degrees with the heroic action. The pressures on well-publicized award recipients to be examples to the broad range of groups identifying with the inspirational act were heightened for Triquet by the large amount of publicity. One author who has studied the VC suggests that all men receiving the award were models: "With few exceptions, they are men of quiet, composed dispositions, wearing with the utmost modesty the halo that inevitably surrounds them. Nearly all are men of fine character and personal integrity."[62] Triquet would have preferred to remain the ordinary guy from Cabano. A fellow soldier remembered that when he was assigned to drive the older, higher-ranking hero, Triquet was like a friend; as they talked and learned that they came from the same region in Quebec, they spoke as if they were back home. But Triquet was well aware that many were watching.[63]

As he left Buckingham Palace, he told reporters that his award recognized more than one individual's actions.[64] But the number of groups identifying with him and hoping to meet him was perhaps more than he expected. Catholic newspapers in Europe were proud of the "12th

Triquet after leaving Buckingham Palace where he received the VC from King George VI, 27 March 1944. DND-31150-N.

Catholic to win VC;" Scottish papers recalled his time training there; papers (and letters from individuals) throughout Canada found local connections to his past experiences.[65] The leader of the Opposition in Quebec, Maurice Duplessis, joked that Triquet's association with the Union Nationale (when the government had hired him as an instructor) had led to such high heights.[66] Even before he left London, Triquet's engagement book began to fill up. After telling a journalist that he was on leave and had the day off, almost immediately the phone rang and CMHQ asked him to drop by for a few photos; then a press conference

Triquet speaking with Lt Col F.J. Fleury (centre), and Capt Edmond Bissonnette afer receiving the VC at Buckingham Palace. The one-man investiture took place in the king's apartments only a few hours after Triquet had flown from Italy, 27 March 1944. DND-31152-N.

was arranged and "two radio engagements emerged out of thin air – one to speak to Canada and one to speak to France."[67]

The military units he had served with were pleased with the award to Triquet and to French-Canadians. Oliver Leese, commander of the Eighth Army, wrote: "Your splendid citation will be read throughout Canada – and with especial pride by all French-Canadians … The people of Canada will realize something of the deeds which are being carried out by their men."[68] On behalf of the corps he had served under,

(*left*) Triquet in 1944. DND -2754-N; (*right*) Triquet posing in 1944. DND photo.

Lieutenant General Allfrey sent his congratulations for the "thoroughly earned decoration."[69] Lieutenant General H.D.G. Crerar, commanding the Canadian Corps in Italy in March, wrote to tell Triquet that his action would "inspire all Canadians, particularly those of French descent ... I am sure your name and deeds will be long remembered in our homeland. May you live long to wear the Victoria Cross you so gallantly won."[70] The War Diary of the First Division recorded "great rejoicing in the Division today when news came out that Major Paul Triquet of the R22eR had won the Victoria Cross. It is our first such award and everyone is pleased."[71] Lieutenant Colonel J.A. Calder, temporary Brigade Commander of the 3rd Brigade, extended "on behalf of all units of the Brigade hearty congratulations to all ranks of the R22eR on the distinction which has been won by a member of the Battalion, and which reflects great credit upon the unit ... All members of Third Canadian Infantry Brigade may well be proud of this achievement ... For all of us this award to a member of the Brigade can be an inspiration

(*left*) Maj Gen Georges Vanier, with Lt Gen E.L.M. Burns, commander of a Canadian Corps, during a visit to Canadians in Italy, 27 April 1944. DND-32609; (*right*) Lt Col Paul Bernatchez, Commanding Officer, Royal 22e Régiment, reading his mail while en route to Campobasso, Italy, October 1943. LAC-PA-190821.

and we can all conduct ourselves both in and out of battle in a manner consistent with the high tradition of devotion to duty which accompanied the gallantry for which this award has been made."[72]

Triquet clearly had a particularly significant relationship with his regiment and, by extension, French Canada. During the First World War, a strong feeling of solidarity had developed within the French-speaking unit, and that was increasingly shared by many French-Canadians.[73] Georges Vanier visited the regiment shortly after the announcement of Triquet's award and described his speech to the troops in a letter to Major General Tremblay, also an ex-member of the unit: "I spoke of the old 22nd, and of the confidence we had in the 22nd of today which had already proved itself. I made a comparison between Triquet, Brillant and Kaeble. I told them (as I said so often in Quebec) that the French-Canadians at the front were not only soldiers, but the representatives of a people; that all eyes in Canada were fixed on them; that the French-Canadians were proudly counting on the 22nd to maintain our finest military traditions."[74] As with Maurice Richard and the Montreal

Canadiens, Triquet and the Van Doos represented their people at a time when recognition was particularly important.

After offering his congratulations, Triquet's former commanding officer, J.P.E. Bernatchez, emphasized to him that he was now, more than ever, an ambassador for the Regiment:

> I am of course extremely pleased to see that your devotion and great bravery have been recognized by the King … [I was still commanding and] I know perfectly well how much you deserved this high distinction. You have been working to improve the regiment for years and have always brought us honour. Today you become a source of pride for the regiment and for all French-Canadians. Tomorrow and forever your exploits will remain an example for those that follow you in the 22e … Paulo, if you will allow me, as your friend (and type of father figure that I have been for all my guys) I would emphasize that it might be a good idea, that you would do a good thing if you could arrange everything with your wife – it seems to me that you would be much better off, that you would only be happier – especially now that you have become a "*figure Canadienne française.*"[75]

Allard, Triquet's new commanding officer, was even more direct: "Paul, you generously offered your life to the service of your country and your country accepted it, it no longer belongs to you."[76]

Triquet arrived in Montreal increasingly aware of the importance of his political role in public relations. A journalist recorded that "Major Triquet smiled slightly, perhaps resignedly, as he appeared in the doorway of the Lancaster and saw the group of high ranking army officers, civic officials, reporters and photographers waiting to greet him … [He was a] little ill at ease during the press conference." That afternoon he visited Sainte-Anne de Bellevue's military hospital to see his brother Bernard, who had little to say during their ten-minute meeting.[77] His agenda again filled up quickly with new requests in addition to the many already planned.[78] En route to Quebec City, he dropped by Trois-Rivières "to say hello to Mme Jean Allard." Jean Allard had asked Triquet to do this, and Public Affairs was glad to accommodate and publicize the visit.[79] The mother of Ovila Garceau in Louiseville

Major Paul Triquet greeted as a hero on his arrival at Dorval Airport, Montreal, 30 March 1944. Canadian Army photo. Musée du Royal 22e Régiment, Fonds 43: Paul Triquet.

asked him to stop by if he had time, and Triquet replied that he would with pleasure.[80] Snuffy Smith's mother asked him to pay a visit to Dauphin, Manitoba, while he was touring the West, and Triquet said that he would arrange it.[81]

Arriving for ceremonies in Quebec City, he must have been greatly pleased to return to the Citadelle. However, when he crossed the street for a ceremony in the Quebec Assembly, he undoubtedly felt less at ease; he still remembered a decade earlier being yelled at and fired from his

Major Paul Triquet, VC, at Quebec City, 12 April 1944. DND-LAC-PA-157376.

police security job by an angry politician. Premier Adélard Godbout highlighted the role of the family and the importance of Mme Triquet's encouragement, and concluded that the whole Canadian family paid tribute to him. J.A. Beaulieu, Liberal MPP for Témiscouata, and others, hit the notes sought by the WIB, affirming that Triquet proved that French-Canadians were doing their duty and that his qualities of heart and mind should serve as an example to the whole French-Canadian race to do their duty. Opposition leader Maurice Duplessis suggested that Triquet's actions illustrated that he was the son of a proud race. Anti-

Triquet arriving with Brig Gen E. Blais at one of his many heroic welcomes, April 1944. DND photo.

participationist nationalist MPP René Chaloult admitted he admired military heroism; it was just the cause served that he opposed. Triquet must have been moved.

As Triquet sat at the side of the speaker's throne listening, MPP Jonathan Robinson, a veteran of the First World War, suggested that the acclaim was probably "a worse ordeal for the hero than that which he had faced so gloriously in Italy." Triquet later had a private audience with Cardinal Villeneuve, and Mayor Bourne announced that 17 April would be a civic holiday to celebrate "the hero of Casa Berardi."[82]

Cabano was glad to receive its hero back home. This type of event was not unique – earlier celebrations had welcomed the return home of Quebec heroes such as Dollard Ménard and Buzz Beurling – but the media attention now was much greater.[83] After the announcement in March, *Le St Laurent*, a newspaper of the Lower St-Laurent region, noted that the honour for Triquet was received "with enthusiasm throughout Québec, and particularly in his hometown of Cabano and the region ... [it] places him henceforth among the greatest heroes of our history."[84]

Hero's welcome at Cabano, April 1944. DND photo.

Although Triquet had not lived there for almost twenty years, reporters encouraged the impression that he was a typical small-town boy. One observed that although Triquet had greatly appreciated all the messages of congratulations, "the one he made you feel gave him the deepest pride of all was a simply worded cable from Cabano, Quebec, signed 'Isidore Bérubé, mayor.'"[85] The local press expressed its gratitude to officials who brought "our hero" home so that all the country was watching Cabano and the region of Témiscouata.[86] The welcome included a parade through the streets attended by most of the town, followed by a reception and brief speeches. Triquet spoke again more of his men than of himself and, as he did on several occasions, began by asking for a moment of silence for those who had fallen.[87] Several residents remembered the welcome home as the biggest event in Cabano ever, not just during the war, and one acknowledged that the story of Triquet "certainly" influenced his

Paul Triquet posing during Easter 1944, with parents, estranged wife Alberte Chenier, and children, Claude and Yolande. DND photo.

decision to join the Army. Triquet's son, Claude, remembers that his father was "very well received."[88]

After the ceremonies in Cabano, Triquet was granted a few days rest in his hometown with his wife and family. For the Triquets it was a time of happiness – to have Paul home with a hero's award – but it was also a time of sadness, as they were concerned about Bernard, who was suffering serious mental problems diagnosed as schizophrenia.[89] Medical staff found him confused, depressed, and disinterested. The only bright spot in the very gloomy reports came the day after Paul had visited on 29 March, when Bernard seemed "much brighter and more active" and apparently had been emotionally awakened by meeting his brother.[90] But the improvement did not last. The following week the staff "strongly advised against" taking him home to Cabano, but the family "was quite insistent" and Bernard returned for a week. After this short reunion the family agreed that the hospital was the best place for him, and he returned there for the rest of his life.[91]

Triquet's return to Alberte and his children was also awkward. Following the advice of Bernatchez, he and Alberte agreed to pose together, pretending to be still happily married. Their son Claude recently remembered that even though he was only ten years old, he was well aware of how uncomfortable both were with the situation.[92] The media reported how glad Triquet was to return "into his wife's arms."[93] Alberte Chenier was even more uncomfortable answering questions: "'Was I glad to have him home?' She laughed. 'I was so excited I couldn't sleep all last night ... I know he loves it, so it's not so bad when he's overseas."[94] Knowing the situation, these comments may be interpreted in different ways. One comment that could only be taken one way was whispered by his eight-year-old daughter, Yolande: "*Nous sommes tous fiers de toi, Papa*" – We're all proud of you, Daddy.[95]

5

Hero in an Army at War, May 1944 to August 1945

> I understand your disappointment with not serving directly in the Royal 22e; however, I admit frankly to you that we are eager to keep alive our only Victoria Cross winner.
>
> – Major General T.L. Tremblay to Triquet[1]

Bond Tour Sacrifice

After a brief rest to catch his breath in Cabano, where he celebrated Easter with his family, Triquet prepared for the main reason he had been brought home: the publicity tour for the Sixth Victory Loan Campaign. Ottawa spent over $30 million promoting these campaigns, which became the focus of its public relations efforts.[2] After the tour Triquet presumed he would return to his unit overseas, although his role had yet to be determined.

Public speaking is not what soldiers are trained for and Triquet was particularly uncomfortable.[3] Even before the speaking tour began, he developed a mild case of laryngitis. He told a doctor that it was painful for him to speak and he continued to feel very tired.[4] His former commanding officer encouraged him in his uncomfortable but important role representing his regiment and French-Canadians, and Allard sent him another reminder: "Just a few lines to let you know how proud we are of you, and how your actions have become a model for all who are called into combat. [The bond tour will be] for the best for all French-Canadians ... my only desire is that you come back to us very soon. Allow me to remind you what I said before: 'Paul, you generously offered your life to the service of your country and your country accepted it, it no longer belongs to you,' and today all your actions reflect upon the regiment and all French-Canadians. So remember our conversation and accept, as you always have, the sacrifice that is asked of you."[5]

The pressure on Triquet was even greater because of several controversies surrounding his participation. Some opposed using military heroes for fundraising and publicity campaigns at home.[6] One journalist suggested that it was "like asking a hunting leopard to come and address a Sunday school."[7] Another minor controversy involved the use in army PR of Triquet's friend, "the beautiful and glamourous" Maria Teresa Berardi. After she announced that Triquet had come "not only as a friend, but as a saviour," possible suspicions were raised about the relationship between the married hero and his Italian friend, who lived in the now-ravaged home. The *Globe and Mail* complained that a soldiers' paper went overboard for Maria Teresa, devoting to her hundreds of words, a two-column picture, and the title "uncrowned Queen of the Moro Valley.'" Of greater concern was that some people from Ortona were arguing that she had been a fascist supporter of Mussolini.[8]

Triquet became entangled in a much more important controversy concerning his involvement with a pre-tour "recruiting campaign." Major General Pearkes asked him to come to address a French-speaking unit of National Resources Mobilization Act (NRMA) men in British Columbia. Triquet told of his experiences, encouraged the men to volunteer, and had good results.[9] Soon after, Mayor David Howrie of Vernon described the recruiting trip as "prostitution of the Victoria Cross" and argued that "the humiliating duty imposed on a good soldier ... is in very poor taste."[10]

Major General Pearkes replied that he had asked Triquet to come to tell the young soldiers about conditions in Italy: "Major Triquet, who served with me in the 1st Canadian Division, is a splendid officer and at once accepted my invitation. After telling of his war experiences, he appealed to those whom he was addressing to volunteer for active service, pointing out that this was a critical year and that the need was urgent. I have spoken along the same lines many times myself. I see nothing humiliating in trying to do my duty or encourage others to do theirs. I did not win my V.C. by keeping my boots clean at Passchendaele, nor has any other officer recipient of that decoration won it by leaving things to the sergeant-major."[11]

This "recruiting campaign," if it was that, was done without the knowledge of the Directorate of Army Recruiting: "At no time during [Triquet's] visit to this country were his services requested by this directorate or within the knowledge of this Directorate by any District for recruiting duties. [He did make appeals to NRMA men] but this is not recruiting in the accepted sense."[12] Ralston also replied that "to call this either humiliating or the prostitution of the VC is nothing less than sabotage of Canada's war effort and will no doubt be read with the greatest satisfaction in Berlin."[13] He said that all Triquet did was talk to soldiers, "indicating what the needs of the army were and what had been his experience overseas." While it was not considered humiliating when people talked of the need for money, "recruiting seems to be something which must be disparaged, and I can only think it must be because there is some sort of fetish on the part of some people for conscription."[14]

Conscription was indeed a sensitive issue, particularly in francophone Quebec. In that context, instead of focusing on Triquet's achievements and seeking opportunities to recognize and encourage Quebec volunteers, Ralston joined others in using Triquet to attack the other side in the increasingly emotional debate. Anti-war French-Canadian nationalist René Chaloult, according to a news report, "criticized authorities for sending Maj. Paul Triquet ... to recruits' training camps 'to incite them to join up.' He said he did not blame Maj. Triquet personally, but that Maj. Triquet was being used 'to spread imperialism.'"[15] The Quebec parliament's praise of Triquet and support for Canadian volunteers overseas received less attention in the English-speaking media than did its motion two weeks later opposing conscription.[16] One journalist argued that "Quebec's Legislature's almost unanimous vote expressing disapproval of any move to send conscripted men overseas is a condemnation of Major Paul Triquet, Quebec's VC winner, who at the Pacific Coast urged men in home-service units to join Canada's defenders overseas."[17]

The journalist added that Triquet favoured conscription, which he did not. In fact, Triquet had been uncomfortable even sharing the same platform with the conscriptionist Pearkes. Triquet's sister Florence remembers his saying when he returned from BC, "I would have given anything to avoid crossing [Pearkes's] path."[18] But he was far from opposed to encouraging others to volunteer; as he expressed it in a letter from London during the war to another sister, Cécile, who was a teacher: "Try

Major Paul Triquet, VC, speaking at the opening of the Sixth Victory Loan campaign, Ottawa, 24 April 1944. DND-LAC-PA-181259.

to clean up our young Canadiens. Today more than ever we need good men."[19] In public Triquet refused to comment on conscription, because "it is not for a soldier to talk about politics."[20] As a hero, however, his voice was important, and others were willing to speak for him. His commanding officer, Brigadier E. Blais, CO of Military District (MD) No. 5, announced that "these comments from Western Canada are sickening ... He will go anywhere in the interests of the war, but his greatest aim is to rejoin his comrades of the Royal 22nd Regiment overseas. That is all he wishes to say – and you can quote me as saying this for him."[21]

A preliminary ceremony for the campaign was held on Parliament Hill on 24 April 1944. Prime Minister King recorded in his diary that "the main feature was the presentation of shields by Triquet, VC (a fine young fellow) to couriers to take from Parliament Hill to the different provinces."[22] Triquet delivered the plaque himself to Sir Eugène Fiset, Quebec's lieutenant governor, who then officially opened the campaign

Triquet began most of his speeches with the warning, "I am not a speaker, so don't expect a long speech." He always emphasized the contribution of others, particularly those buried in Italy. DND photo.

in Quebec.[23] A five-mile-long parade through the streets of Montreal marked the occasion, and, according to one journalist, 300,000 persons attended as Triquet, the "central figure of the parade ... received an ovation all along the route as he stood in an open car" with his father.[24] It should be added that not all, and quite probably not the majority, of the crowd in Montreal were francophones, as the English-speaking community there were particularly strong supporters of the war effort. Triquet's photo was published in papers across French-speaking Canada, along with the following message: "All French-Canadians are proud today to loudly praise the bravery of the great hero who has just received the Victoria Cross, Major Paul Triquet, VC who so valiantly defended us at Casa Berardi. But all those who voluntarily left in 1940–41–42 and 1943 to fight the enemy of our freedom, they are all also deserving of our praise ... and of our support."[25] The message emphasizing that the war was fought by volunteers to defend Canada – not Britain – was what francophone members of the PR effort in Quebec had been urging, and the results were good.[26]

Ottawa had limited objectives for the three-week campaign as there had been five previous drives and the war situation was improving. Triquet provided a much-needed boost to motivate those buying bonds for patriotic reasons (as opposed to an investment).[27] The *Globe and Mail* reported: "Soon after the campaign was underway yesterday seven municipalities in the Quebec district reported they had topped their objectives ... Cabano claimed the honor to be the first village in the [Témiscouata] county to have topped its objective [$35,000]. Témiscouata County also topped its $110,000 objective."[28] Triquet also toured Ontario, participating in ceremonies and events including a rally on 9 May at Maple Leaf Gardens in Toronto attended by a crowd of 15,406.[29] The assistant chairman for the National War Finance Committee informed Lieutenant General J.C. Murchie, chief of the General Staff, that the Victory Loan campaign would be ending on Saturday, 13 May, and that "the visits of Major Triquet to many communities in Quebec and Ontario have been a very great stimulus to the Victory Loan."[30]

Triquet also thought that it had gone well. He later told his son Claude, "If I had ten cents for every bond I sold I'd be a millionaire."[31] Triquet was given a few weeks of rest, and Murchie refused other public relations requests for his appearance: "The reason for not agreeing [to a request from the RCA Victor Company for a ceremony] was that it was considered desirable that all ranks who had returned from Overseas for duty with the National War Finance Committee be relieved of all duties for a period of three weeks from 13 May 44, after which those of suitable category will be returned overseas."[32]

Immediately after the successful bond tour, another incident suggested that Army Public Affairs did not handle messages (and possible messages) to Quebec very well. Triquet was made a knight of the Legion of Honour by Dr Jules Abadie, representative of Charles de Gaulle, leader of the French National Liberation Committee. Abadie told Triquet, "I am happy to bring this decoration to a valorous Canadian warrior who is representative of the alliance existing in this war between Canada and France." De Gaulle's citation read: "For his courage, his audacity and his gay spirit in action which have been the admiration of all the Allied nations." The Army published a news release, emphasizing that French and English were united in the same fight,[33] but more PR mileage could have been gained. When Vanier, the Canadian representative to free France, asked Ottawa if Triquet could receive the award, permission was quickly granted; however, permission to wear it took much longer.[34] While authorities had previously authorized the reception and wearing of British awards to Canadians, awards from other countries were clearly in a different category.

The VC was well known in English-speaking Canada but not as well known in Quebec where the British Empire's system of honours and awards did not have the same power to inspire.[35] For many English-speaking Canadians, their nationalism was essentially linked to Britain and its symbols, while for many French-Canadians the French award was as impressive as the VC.[36] One journalist wrote: "With the Victoria Cross, the highest decoration of the British Empire presented to him by the King of England ... Major Paul Triquet will now wear on his chest another decoration that he should particularly cherish, since it comes to him from his former mother country, France."[37] Triquet said that it would be his father who was particularly pleased, as he was the "real Frenchman."[38] But Triquet was not allowed to wear his decoration. Vanier asked Ottawa in August 1944 and again in November for officials to authorize permission for Triquet and other Canadian recipients of French awards to wear them, noting that the War Office in London had already replied that it had no objection. "I would greatly appreciate anything you may be able to do to speed up the announcement of these decorations in order that we may grant permission to the recipients to wear the appropriate ribbon."[39] However, Triquet's award was not recognized by the Canadian Army until June of 1946.[40]

By June 1944 Triquet had been out of action for half a year and had been separated from his regiment for three months. Being presented as a hero, an exceptional individual, he could not help but feel even more detached from his friends and their war effort. He was increasingly eager to return. In addition to the D-Day landings on 6 June, the Canadians were entering Rome as they continued to help give the German Army the boot from Italy. But the fighting was intense, and the R22eR continued to suffer casualties. Triquet received the sad news that his friend Ovila Garceau had been killed.[41] He was probably not cheered up by the news that his wife was robbed of $60 in a store on D-Day.[42] He was ready to go back to rejoin the fight as an ordinary soldier.

Certainly Triquet was uncomfortable in his PR role, but many were glad to see him home. Along with the critics of the Army's use of him, there were also strong supporters. One journalist suggested that if Triquet was (understandably) uncomfortable in his role, he should accept his important mission as a soldier and a positive example of national pride. "We could not give our people a more lively lesson of courage and generosity then by multiplying the triumphant demonstrations around one of its own sons who, by his bravery and skill, was able to carry out, with his comrades of the same blood, an enormous feat. After having admired the heroes of ancient times, why hide the glory of one of our own?" He added that Triquet's presence provided a great lesson of national pride that would be more striking than any fiery speech or propaganda booklet. Triquet was being asked to perform a second heroic gesture "by accepting with the same courage the weight of unceasing honors and interminable ceremonies. If the two heroisms serve at the same time the cause of the country and of the civilized world, why should we be upset? ... We can regret it as much as we like but war, the great plague, is not won without real sacrifices. And the least of all sacrifices, in war time, is to tolerate that people speak about you and an event of interest to all civilized people."[43]

Can Canadian VCs Return to Battle?

The Canadian Army was glad that Triquet had been awarded the VC, and he received good PR assistance for recruiting and selling Victory Bonds, particularly in French Canada where effort was most needed. But did a VC recipient have other uses for the Army? Specifically, could he return to battle? If he could, were there any unique conditions, and if he could not, what would he do for the rest of the war?

Triquet's situation again served as a test case, as he was the first Canadian VC of the Second World War whom the Army could send back into action. Initially there was no clear policy in place. British VCs had been returned in the First World War, and two had even received bars to their awards.[44] The New Zealand 2nd Lieutenant Charles Hazlett Upham had also been returned to action after his 1941 VC action and had a bar added for actions in 1942 when he was captured. But what would be the Canadian policy? When General Murchie had asked General Stuart in March 1944 if Triquet could return to Canada to help with the loan campaign, he had added, "if operational requirements permit,"[45] indicating that it was not yet clear or even a consideration that a VC would not return to action. After Stuart approved, he left the decision to General Burns to proceed "if you agree and operational requirements permit."[46]

Triquet's status was complicated during the bond tour. There were indications that he would be returning to active service, and certainly he did all he could to encourage this impression. A central theme he constantly repeated was that he was eager to "return to my regiment wherever it may be" as quickly as possible.[47] He said one time that, after his bond tour, "I want to return to my unit, anywhere. And if they want to keep me in Canada, I'll find some way to return."[48] He often added that he planned to remain in the Army after the war: "I have been a professional soldier since I was seventeen. The professional army has been good to me and I think it has proved its value to Canada."[49] His superiors encouraged this impression, since suggesting that a war hero would be on PR duty for the rest of the war would not be good PR. There were occasional references to "an important post in Canada" that never materialized.[50] The Army was also looking to fill a bilingual instructor position at the Canadian Training Centre in Brockville, and Triquet's name was suggested, but CMHQ preferred that he return overseas after the Victory Loan tour.[51]

Triquet returned to the United Kingdom on 5 July. He would rejoin his unit by the end of the month, but only for PR purposes. He wrote to his father, according to an Army press release, that he was "back with my soldiers. Am in best of health and spirit."[52] And he told reporters, "It's good to be able to come back and resume the job."[53] On 30 July Triquet officially became temporary deputy commanding officer of his unit while Major G. Charlebois was away.[54] The following day King George dropped by to review the troops, and, a journalist wrote, "when he reached the 'Van Doos' His Majesty asked the colonel whether Major Paul Triquet, new VC from Cabano QC, was with the unit and the commanding officer presented him."[55] Their meeting was widely reported in the Canadian Press.

During the ceremony with the king, John Mahony was presented with his VC for actions in Italy, becoming the third Canadian VC of the war and the second who could return to his unit. Immediately after the

HM King George VI meeting Major Paul Triquet, VC, during a visit to the Royal 22e Régiment, 31 July 1944, in Raviscanina, Italy. DND-LAC-PA-189918.

ceremony, in the words of a journalist a few years later, "One of the first people [Mahony] met was another VC. Major Paul Triquet of Cabano Quebec, just back from Canada and 'browned off' over bond tour soldiering. 'Where are you going?' asked Triquet. 'Back to my unit' said Mahony, 'That's what you think,' said Triquet." Mahony tried – even going AWOL on a truck for the front – but did not return to battle during the war.[56] (It is interesting to note that the recommendation for Mahony again went to the VC committee through the War Office, and

Ralston again accepted it "as a special case." Canadians repeated the preferred channel of submission.[57])

Triquet became increasingly frustrated and vocal.[58] Placed at a training centre in the United Kingdom, he complained about the lack of recruits to train. In September he wrote to his CO at 1 Canadian Base Reinforcement Depot (CBRD), Colonel J.H. Christie: "I herewith request that I be returned to the R22eR as soon as possible. I am 34 years of age Category A and fit for Field Services, and have served in the above unit for eighteen years. If this request is impossible, could I be posted to an appointment in some theatre of operations, such as Liaison, etc. I feel I am being discriminated against on account of my decoration, and if such is the case, it would be the end of my military career. I also believe that I can be of greater service in some other appointment than my present one."[59]

Triquet sent a copy of the letter to his former CO, Bernatchez, saying he had been glad to be able to visit recently at No. 5 General Hospital to see some of the boys and receive news of the regiment. He appealed for Bernatchez's help and also let him know how he really felt: "Mon cher Colo … I read in the *Maple Leaf* today that the French-Canadians are fighting well in the Adriatic area. I am a bit jealous of you all. As I am fed up being a Chief Instructor at a school without students, I have sent a request to return to the battalion. I am forwarding you a copy of the letter I sent my current commander. If they don't want me they can send me back to Canada where I can at least find something to do. I know very well that they sent me here only to get rid of me. I'm not at all pleased."[60]

Triquet also sought help from Major General T.L. Tremblay at the Citadelle. Tremblay was understanding and direct: "I understand your disappointment with not serving directly in the Royal 22e however I admit frankly to you that we are eager to keep alive our only Victoria Cross winner."[61] Tremblay also seemed to suggest that Triquet should realize that others were having difficult times: "You remember my son Jacques who has been at Debert for some time and is very disappointed at not being able to go further. In addition, he had to be hospitalized for a knee accident he suffered while training, and, I understand that he will be there at least one month. His main problem is that he is low on the list of priorities and you know how anxious he is to rejoin the 22e as soon as possible. If, at your end, you can do anything, I know that he will be grateful."[62]

On 21 November Brigadier Edmond Blais, CO MD No. 5, announced that Triquet would command a R22eR unit in Canada. Triquet had been helping with training at a Reinforcement Battalion in Italy and, despite sending letters trying to return to the R22eR and saying he was unhappy, continued to perform his task and receive good evaluations.[63] Newspapers reported that Blais had "ordered the mustering up of two regiments destined to reinforce overseas the Royal 22nd Regiment and le Régiment de la Chaudière. Brigadier Blais added that Major Paul Triquet ... will command the new Royal 22nd unit. He said he had cabled overseas to ask for the immediate return to Canada of the hero of Casa Berardi. He will be promoted to the rank of Lieutenant Colonel."[64] However, the next day the plans of many people were changed.

On 22 November 1944 Prime Minister King bowed to pressure from conscriptionists and allowed the Army to send NRMA men overseas. There were many social and political consequences.[65] Attempts to encourage NRMA men had not produced the numbers some felt necessary, but the announcement came as a surprise to francophones. Only the day before Major General Laflèche had encouraged French-speaking NRMA men to go active as the situation was serious and "the honour of the French-Canadians is at stake." But he also assured them that "if reinforcements are required we will find them. And we will find them by our own means, and not by insult ... We must find the solution between ourselves."[66] With the surprising announcement Quebec Minister Chubby Power resigned, explaining to a journalist that the actual consequences on Quebecers were not serious (few were actually sent overseas),[67] but it was a powerful symbol of domination by "*les maudits anglais*." Power added that he believed that many French-speaking Quebecers would not forgive and forget: "They have a deep sense of injury and of betrayal. They will nurse this, harbour it, nourish it, by so-called patriotic speeches ... [leading to] a French party, a Quebec bloc, wallowing in grievances, and gloating in non-cooperation."[68]

Much was changed, and one of the military consequences was that the training structure was reorganized. A week later Army officials announced that Triquet would remain overseas.[69] Exactly what he would and could do overseas still had to be clarified. In December there were more training positions available, and also more Canadian VC recipients. There were now six (eight, including the two in British uniforms). In addition to Mahony, David Currie (announced 27 November) and Smokey Smith (announced 20 December) increased the number of VCs eligible to return to battle to four.[70] Triquet sent his congratulations to Smith, who replied that he warmly appreciated the letter and was "proud to be included in the team of which you are a prior member." Smith also replied to Prime Minister King's telegram, noting that he trusted "that I may render further service alongside my comrades until victory is achieved."[71] Currie was sent home in December 1944 shortly after his award had been announced, according to historian Don Graves, "because the policy was that VC winners were sent back to Canada." NDHQ suggested to CMHQ that it would be "desirable as future policy that all winners of VC be granted 30 days leave in Canada [and remain] on command and not [Struck Off Strength] overseas." Slowly, a policy began to emerge on employing VC recipients in the Canadian Army.[72]

On 22 December 1944 Triquet's case brought to the attention of the authorities the issue of employing VCs. Brigadier W.G.H. Roaf, commanding officer, Canadian Secretariat General Headquarters 1 Echelon, wrote to Major General Weeks at CMHQ:

> 1. By virtue of having won the V.C., the m/n officer is precluded from further service in the [field], leaving only [administration] and [training] employment available for him.
> 2. He has had no staff [training], nor has he any [administration] experience within a HQ; consequently, in view of his rank, it would be inefficient to attempt to employ him in either of these manners.
> 3. Comd [1 Canadian Base Reinforcement Depot] has pointed out that, while Maj. Triquet is doing a reasonably satisfactory job, he is not particularly happy in his present appt as [2nd in command] of the [reinforcement battalion]; and could in fact, be replaced by a more appropriately qualified officer.
> 4. It is felt that consideration to the return of this officer to the UK should be given. It might be possible to suitably employ him in an

> instructional capacity, either in the UK or in Canada; or because of his language, his services might be of value in a Liaison [or translation role] …
> 5. In any event, there is little chance of efficiently utilizing Major Triquet in this theatre; and it is requested that his proposal for his return to the UK be given favourable consideration.[73]

When the letter arrived, the first paragraph was not questioned at CMHQ. Major C.P. Lailey wrote beside it: "I understand this is an Eighth Army regulation. Ireland [an officer in the department] states the [War Office] are considering recalling their VC winners to [training] employment." He therefore recommended Triquet's return to the UK. Brigadier Booth agreed but the chief of staff did question the paragraph and insisted that Triquet remain in Italy for three months, followed by a further report.[74] Thus Weeks replied to Roaf:

> 1. In para 1 of your letter under reply it is stated that the officer named in the margin is precluded from further service in the field, leaving only adm and trg employment available for him. There appears to be no Canadian order or instruction to support this contention and further information referring to any such order or instruction is required.
> 2. In para 3 of your letter you quote Comd 1 CBRGroup as saying that Major Triquet is not particularly happy in his present appointment as 2 IC at a Reinforcement Battalion. Further information and details are requested as to the reasons why Major Triquet is not particularly happy in order that the question of his return to the UK can be given consideration. In this connection it is pointed out that if Major Triquet is not particularly happy while he is employed in a Reinforcement Battalion in Italy, there is little reason to believe that he would be happier in similar employment in the UK.
> 3. It has therefore been decided that Major Triquet will not return to the UK at present, but the case will be given further consideration, if desired, on 31 Mar. 45. In this event, a detailed report covering the points raised will be submitted.[75]

Further correspondence raised other issues showing how Triquet's personal case was complicated. Triquet had shown that he was an excellent fighter and could do a reasonably good job as a trainer, but concerns were raised about his interest and competence with administrative duty. Another consideration was that he was more comfortable in French than English, which was a slight disadvantage for a position with anglophone troops but a great advantage for a posting with francophone troops. Finally, he was being considered for a position at the rank of lieutenant colonel, at a time when many NRMA men were arriving from Canada, and it was important to ensure he would do a good job.[76]

Gibson and Roaf discussed instructional employment for Triquet and came to the following conclusions: "Triquet is fighting soldier with battle experience and ability to instruct in inf trg however is employed [as second in command at] 1 CBR GP, consequently almost entirely concerned with ADM." By all accounts he had been working hard, performing adequately and "not repeat not really unhappy in active sense"; he simply felt that he was unsuitably placed. His poor English was a "minor embarrassment to him" and the percentage of French-speaking soldiers with which he had contact was minimal, meaning that the drive and prestige of an instructor such as Triquet was to a degree wasted. Roaf's impression of Triquet after personal contact was that he had "improved personality and presence considerably and appears to have understanding of his position and rank." He saw no evidence that Triquet would be unhappy or unsuitable in a training role and again recommended him for command of a French-speaking reinforcement unit in the UK. General Roberts of the Canadian Infantry Training Regiment (CITR) in the UK confirmed that he was "prepared to try him out," and this arrangement was approved.[77]

Aside from the peculiarities of the Triquet case, the general question of whether a VC could return to battle was now being faced, and a Canadian position was being established. In January those looking at Triquet's case were informed: "Policy in respect to employment of VC winners in combatant roles sought of [Allied Forces Headquarters (AFHQ)] and reply awaited."[78] By the end of the month Canadians were told "that no ruling to the effect that a VC may not be engaged in combatant duties has been given by that HQ although it was understood by them that such a ruling had been given by [Lieutenant General Richard McCreery, commander of the Eighth Army, who had replaced Leese in October]." AFHQ therefore asked General McCreery and received the following reply: "It was the practice of the late Comd Eighth Army, General Sir Oliver Leese, to withdraw winners of the Victoria Cross from front line of duty. Although it will often be desirable to give a change of employment to the winner of a Victoria Cross, I do not consider it desirable to lay down any such rule. I consider that the matter must be left to the discretion of the formation comd concerned."[79]

As the reply of Tremblay and others had indicated, the regiment was not eager to return Triquet to action.[80]

The End of the War

On 27 January 1945 Major General J.H. Roberts, commander of the Canadian Reinforcements Unit, officially requested that Triquet be posted in his present rank to command 17 Canadian Infantry Training Battalion of No. 9 CITR.[81] He arrived in the UK from the Italian theatre on 4 February 1945.[82] He would have liked to remain in Italy, as he occasionally visited the regiment there,[83] but he accepted his situation.[84] The new minister of national defence, General Andrew McNaughton, told reporters that Triquet was "doing a very important job training behind the lines."[85] In his new position Triquet held the rank of acting lieutenant colonel as of 7 March 1945, and Roberts stated that if he proved satisfactory, he would be recommended as lieutenant colonel but that this was not automatic. Triquet continued to have good evaluations and was later confirmed in the rank with effect from 12 June 1945.[86]

His role in public relations did not end. In April 1945 his comments were widely reported from England that he found "there is absolutely no friction between volunteers and drafted men." He said he had one thousand men in his camp and hundreds were NRMA (National Resources Mobilization Act draftees) "and they get along famously well with the volunteers." He added that he told NRMA men "that all Canadian soldiers, whether they be draftees or volunteers, are over here united for the defense of the same noble cause." He also said that reporters should tell the troops that well-trained francophone reinforcements would soon be going to the front to help them.[87]

A trip to France proposed by Triquet was encouraged by an Army Public Relations officer. However, the request was denied, again suggesting that some in the Army underestimated PR possibilities involving France. Triquet had hoped to visit his aunt there, as he explained in his request for leave. As she had "lost all personal belongings during the attack on Caen," he said, "it is my wish to see if some help could be afforded her by my visit." His father was pleased at the prospect. However, a letter from Colonel Spankie indicated that no exceptions were to be made to the army "policy presently in force covering the granting of leaves to France [which] does not permit leave being granted under the circumstances set out in your letter."[88]

Two weeks later the war in Europe was over. On that day Major Léo Gratton, a priest of the R22eR who had served with Triquet in Italy, wrote to remind him that his PR role as representative of the regiment and of French Canada's war effort would continue into peacetime: "Dear Paul, always remain a good soldier, good Christian, and never forget that all of French Canada is proud of the hero of Casa Berardi." At the same time, Major Gratton warned him that he could receive a rocky welcome when he returned to Quebec society, and that even Quebecers in the Army who did not serve overseas had not fully appreciated the sacrifice of those who had served: "I assure you, friend, the mentality of soldiers, not to mention others, is very different from that of our 'boys' overseas. Too bad, damn politics in the Army ... Forget it ... as we say in the Regiment."[89]

The return home would be another stressful change for Triquet who, like so many soldiers of the time, had been experiencing significant stress for years. However, his psychological problems remained hidden from the public. He liked to drink with his comrades and on occasion would have one too many, but accounts by his friends of this period indicate that he had not developed a serious problem with alcohol.[90] When Paul Bernatchez married a Toronto nurse, Joan Ward, in May 1945, Jean V. Allard maintained that Miss Ward "showed courage in meeting her fiancé's friends. The gang, of which I was a member, along with Paul Mathieu, Paul Triquet and a few others of the same stripe, was not particularly reassuring. The stag could have been a problem. Joan managed to control the situation, apparently, because Paul [Bernatchez] arrived on time for the ceremony."[91]

Although the war in Europe had ended, Triquet was in no rush to return to Canada. He volunteered to join the Canadians going to the Far East, where the war would continue for another three months. He asked that "approval be given and application forwarded so as to take part in Far East Force which is apparently in the early stages of formation … It is strongly felt and desired by the undersigned to see this war through to the end including the Far East campaign."[92] As the 9th Canadian Infantry Training Regiment was disbanded in early June, with only some soldiers being absorbed into 4 CITR, Triquet became surplus to that unit. Brigadier E.W. Haldenby, commander of the 14th Canadian Infantry Training Brigade, did not rule out the possibility of Triquet going to the Far East:

> He has been a reasonably satisfactory Trg Bn Comd where his experience in action was useful in the trg of inf rfts. There is, however, only one French speaking Inf Trg Bn within Cdn Rft units. This officer is NOT considered suitable for emp in a Repat Dep, as his experience and temperament are more suited to ops and trg than to adm. He is very anxious to obtain an appointment with the Cdn Far East Force and I consider that he would be of much more value to the service in such a capacity than in repatriation or adm work. It is therefore recommended that he be returned to Cda for suitable emp while his application for service in the Pacific Theatre is under consideration.[93]

Haldenby's recommendation was accepted by the commander of the Canadian Reinforcement Units and forwarded to CMHQ.[94] Triquet was struck off strength from Canadian Army Overseas for thirty days leave in Canada.[95]

He returned home on 20 June 1945 with eight thousand others, five thousand from the Army and three thousand from the Air Force.[96] An article in the *Halifax Herald* reported that Triquet "believes Japan will be defeated comparatively quickly and at the same time thinks a happy choice was made in the selection of General B.M. Hoffmeister as leader of Canadian Army forces which will enter the Pacific conflict. Obviously pleased with his personal prospects of action in the Far East, the 35 year-old hero … returned to Canada yesterday on the *Ile de France* … He volunteered for service in the theatre at the first opportunity and is razor-keen to help black out the Rising Sun. Colonel Triquet doesn't know when he will be going to the East or what his duties will be when he gets there, but for the time being the fact he has well-founded hopes of Pacific action is in itself sufficient." Triquet may have been hoping that the selection of General Hoffmeister would help his chances, as the two had become friends in Sicily when Hoffmeister was the officer commanding the Seaforth Highlanders. "The choice will be very popular among the Canadian troops," Triquet added.[97]

Dick Ryder, the journalist writing about the returning men, provided some interesting insights into Triquet's personality and how he appeared to others:

> No lover of interviews, the Quebec officer steered clear of newsmen during the day. But when a reporter found him late in the afternoon, standing beneath the protection of a gun turret mounting on the liner's top deck as he watched rain slant into the harbour, Colonel Triquet shrugged, laughed, then answered questions freely and affably … Chain-smoking cigarettes as recollections erased his friendly smile, Colonel Triquet recalled the five days of December 14–19, 1943 … His face a healthy tan, beret cocked at a jaunty angle, Colonel Triquet looks every inch the soldier he is. Erect beneath the gun mount, he gave the impression of force temporarily leashed and of restless impatience which will give him little peace until he is back and on an active front, this time against the Japanese.[98]

But he would not go to Asia. None of the Canadians volunteering for the Pacific from the European theatre made it, as Japan surrendered in August. In July, shortly after his return to Canada, Triquet had the news that he would not go when army officials again disqualified him from fighting because of his having received the VC. Brigadier W.A. Bean wrote that he was "of the opinion that this officer should remain in Canada and not be used in active operations again in view of his excellent record. I have so advised [Chief of Staff, 6th Canadian Infantry Division]."[99]

Triquet had been treated as an exceptional hero for the last year and a half of the war, and it had been a difficult battle. His struggle to be treated as an ordinary soldier would continue into the postwar period.

PART THREE

The Warrior in Postwar Society

This brings us to the final crisis of the round, to which the whole miraculous excursion has been but a prelude – that, namely, of the paradoxical, supremely difficult threshold-crossing of the hero's return from the mystic realm into the land of common day … if the monomyth is to fulfill its promise, not human failure or superhuman success but human success is what we shall have to be shown. That is the problem of the crisis of the threshold of the return.

– Joseph Campbell, *The Hero with a Thousand Faces*, 207, 216

6

Last Attempt at Being a Regular Soldier, 1945–1947

> Who knows but the waters of peace may well be more troubled than those of war.
> – Major General Georges Vanier to R22eR soldiers[1]

Return to Canadian Society, July 1945–July 1946

For returning soldiers, postwar Canada was "no paradise," in the words of historian Desmond Morton. "Returning veterans faced families and communities that could never understand their problems."[2] Reintegration for all men and women in uniform into this society would be difficult; for an ordinary soldier like Lieutenant Colonel Paul Triquet, singled out as a hero – "a man of superhuman qualities, favoured by the gods; demigod"[3] – it would be particularly difficult.

The number of individuals leaving Canada's Armed Forces and returning to civilian life was enormous: 395,013 were discharged in 1945, and they were joined by another 381,031 in 1946.[4] After the First World War, the return home had caused serious social and economic problems; the government had learned from the experience and put into place a series of measures known as the Veterans Charter. As a result, the reintegration of troops this time went much more smoothly.[5] The major difference was that, with the help of government intervention, jobs were available for men looking for work, and opportunities were provided for those wishing to further their studies.[6] One veteran said that the returning men were "ready to forget all we've gone through."[7] The success integrating troops and the dramatic drop in military spending over the next five years help explain why the nation could so quickly forget about the war and turn its attention to future projects.[8]

French-Canadians were particularly eager to put the war behind them. In Verdun, a bilingual city in Quebec, the Legion branch and most local veterans opposed erecting a new war memorial, preferring more practical projects such as an educational or job-training facility over commemorations.[9] Throughout Quebec the desire to commemorate heroic individuals and events, very strong at the start of the century, had faded. The majority of Quebecers did not have the same appreciation as did Canadians in other provinces for those who had volunteered; they remembered the war less for the united struggle for freedom that changed the world and more for the divisive conscription debate. Catholic Quebec at this time was very socially conservative, and many were eager to return to the traditional family model with women "homemaking" and men working close by to provide a role model for their children. Most did not want to see war heroes or be reminded of the struggle they hoped to leave behind.[10]

In English-speaking Canada the conscription debate (and WIB public information failures) also affected views of participation. In general, the sacrifice of French-Canadian soldiers was less appreciated than that of English-Canadian soldiers. Much of the anglophone population, when they thought of French-Canadians, focused on those who had not served rather than recognizing the remarkable achievements of those who had. It is interesting to note that English Canada's image of Aboriginal Canadians improved during the war due to their participation in the war effort, while the image of francophones deteriorated because of a disproportionate focus on the opposition to conscription.[11] Chester Bloom wrote in the *Winnipeg Free Press*: "It does not seem to the writer that the fighting French-Canadians have been given the public acclaim that they deserve. Certainly a man who braves not only death and wounds and hardship but also the disapproval of large elements of his own countrymen must carry a double dose of courage within him."[12]

Differences between anglophones and francophones in this period should not be exaggerated; they had much in common, sharing most economic and social objectives.[13] Many Quebecers welcomed the soldiers of the R22eR home. Although not, as in the Great War, the only francophone regiment to participate in the fighting, the Royal 22e remained well aware of its role as representative of French Canada. Major General Georges Vanier emphasized the responsibilities of those young men to continue, despite the obstacles, building a better world by playing an active part in postwar society: "When the war ends, we will be in the front ranks, and our voice will be heard and respected. I want us to have a positive, idealistic, young, generous, broad and audacious program ... Those of you who will occupy the bridge during the storm, who will save the ship of state, must maintain your command after Victory. You must keep your hands on the wheel and guide the ship to a safe harbour on the waters of peace ... Who knows but the waters of peace may well be more troubled than those of war."[14]

No French-Canadian soldier represented the Canadian war effort more than Triquet. By being the most recognizable hero promoting the war effort for over a year, he had also become the most recognizable symbol for those opposing the war. His sister remembered his being insulted in hotels in Quebec and "everywhere he went." In Cabano, at a restaurant owned by another sister, a visitor commented, "So this is Cabano, town of that hoodlum Triquet."[15] Not even all residents of Cabano were fans. When a teacher displayed a portrait of Triquet in class, a church authority ordered her to remove it, saying there were many better models for the children to follow.[16] This reaction probably had less to do with Triquet being a military hero than with the stories that began circulating about his separation from his wife and his increasing problems with alcohol. Of course the Triquets also had many supporters in Cabano.[17] Paul's father, Florentin, shortly after the return of Duplessis's Union Nationale in August 1944, returned to his position as collector of provincial revenue for motor vehicle licences, the job he had held during Duplessis's first term. When Florentin became ill, his daughter Cécile took over this position.[18]

Lieutenant Colonel Triquet was definitely not looking for a civilian job. He remained a soldier, and the lack of respect he saw for the accomplishments of French-Canadian soldiers made it difficult for him to respect civilian society. Like so many of his comrades, he found the traumatic events he had lived through also made it difficult to adjust.[19] Claude Triquet remembered how after the war his father was known for speaking frankly to anyone, driving faster and drinking more than he should, and living by his own rules: "He seemed to feel that outside

Arrival of Brig J.V. Allard, DSO, after the war, with the officers who came to greet him: Major Yvan Dubé, Lt Col Gilles Turcot, Capt H. Roy, Brig Allard, Capt Guy Laframboise (kneeling), Capt Guy Vaugeois, Col J.H. Chaballe, MC, DSO, Lt Roger Piché, Lt Col Paul Triquet, VC. DND, DHH, Allard Collection.

the Army he could do as he pleased. He had to learn how to live with civilians."[20] As a career soldier, he did not find it easy to accept lessons from civilian authorities on how to behave; but to his military friends, particularly the commanding officers under whom he had served, he did listen and attempted to modify his behaviour.[21]

Finding him an appropriate job continued to be a problem. Dollard Ménard, the hero of Dieppe, experienced many problems similar to those of Triquet; he remembered being told by General Stuart during the war that although he had been doing a fine job, he had become "too big" a hero, and this seemed to affect his postings and chances for promotions.[22] Another consideration was language: the Canadian Army still had many years to go before becoming a bilingual institution. Brigadier J.P.E. Bernatchez and others attempted to increase the number of French-speaking officers and services for training reservists, but they were often disappointed.[23] Army authorities of course had to consider

Triquet's rank and the awards he had received overseas. In addition to his VC and Legion of Honour, he had received the Canadian Volunteer Service Medal and clasp, the 1939–45 Star, the Italy Star, the Defence Medal, and the War Medal 1939–45;[24] he was not eligible for the France-Germany star.[25]

Eventually, on 27 August 1945, he was appointed as chief instructor at an advanced training centre at Farnham, Quebec.[26] While this was his official title, he remained much involved with many aspects of Army PR. He greeted others returning home, including Jean V. Allard in September 1945; he helped with pensions for Major Ovila Garceau's mother; and in July 1945, he agreed to donate the boots he wore at Casa Berardi for a fundraising event.[27] Of the dozens of requests for appearances, some went to the adjutant general, who accepted on condition that Triquet was available.[28] Triquet received some requests directly but could not accept them; he told the mayor of Shawinigan Falls that he would be glad to attend a ceremony to honour those who had served from the city, but he had to receive permission through his chain of command at Military District No. 4.[29] His superiors at times specified that permission was granted only on condition that it not cost the department anything. Triquet's commanding officer at Farnham noted in November "that at recent occasions, when going on special duty, or going as guest of honour, Lt. Col. Triquet had been in obligation of securing his transportation at his own expense." The CO asked that arrangements be made for a vehicle to transport Triquet to distribute Christmas gifts to children at a Legion event in Montreal.[30]

Triquet now had greater freedom than during the war concerning the message he presented, and two themes dominated. The first was appreciation for those who fell and for those returning. He had great respect for the work of the Legion, and in Cabano he started the chapter that still bears his name.[31] He spoke in Moncton on 7 September 1945, encouraging veterans to join this "splendid and helpful organization" providing the invaluable service of bringing together in fellowship former comrades in arms.

He made a second speech broadcast the same day highlighting the second of his themes: francophone-anglophone cooperation: "There is the same warm hospitality [in New Brunswick] that greets me in my native Quebec. We have learned during the past six years, that whether we be French or English speaking, we are all Canadians, and as such we fought for Canada. We have worked together during wartime, and there is no reason why we cannot continue to work together, French and English alike, in the generations to come."

Listeners heard in Triquet's messages what they wanted to hear. Some may have heard that French-Canadians should do more to support the military, others that English-Canadians should recognize the contribution. At least one person heard an offer of a free truck: "On a radio broadcast by Paul Triquet, I heard that the father of a soldier who has died on the battle-field was entitled to a vehicle free of charge. I hereby apply for one and would prefer a light truck." The Public Affairs officer asked Triquet to clarify what he said, and he forwarded the speeches he had delivered, showing that no offers of free vehicles had been made.[32]

The Canadian VCs of the Second World War

As the VC had defined Triquet's life in war, it was now defining his life in peace. His case was exceptional but not unique.[33] At least one other Canadian VC, Smokey Smith, received a warning similar to Triquet's, that he was "expected to show the same sterling qualities in civilian life" as he had shown in battle, now that he had been "marked among men as a leader."[34]

The VCs attended several events as a group. On 8 November 1946 a VC Dinner was organized, and earlier in the year Triquet had spoken with John Foote at a Legion rally.[35] An interesting invitation came from the Toronto Maple Leafs' owner Conn Smythe, inviting Triquet and other Canadian VCs for a ceremony to open the season of the Maple Leafs on 27 October. National Hockey League teams had been criticized for not helping finance the war effort with a concerted plan, and their relationship with veterans was being closely watched.[36] Smythe wrote that "the Directors of Maple Leaf Gardens are doing all that is possible to have all Canadian VC winners of this war at the opening of our NHL season ... Please understand this is not a publicity scheme as the place will be sold out but it would give us an opportunity in some small way to show the respect with which you are held in this part of the country." Triquet was given permission and arrangements were made. Now experienced in the art of public relations, Triquet even wished the Leafs success for their season, but was probably not too upset when Montreal won the Stanley Cup.[37]

It was a very select club to which Triquet belonged. Of the 1,351 VCs that had been awarded since 1856, a surprisingly small number, 182, were awarded during the Second World War.[38] Standards had become increasingly strict.[39] The percentage that were posthumous increased from 30 per cent in the First World War to 48 per cent in the Second World War.[40] Of the sixteen Second World War VCs with a Canadian connection, eight were posthumous: J. Osborn, F. Peters, C. Hoey, A. Mynarski, D. Hornell, I. Bazalgette, A. Cosens, and R. Gray. After the war, five of the eight survivors returned to civilian life, with only Triquet, Mahony, and Smith remaining in the Army.[41]

Among the 1,351 VCs awarded, Canadian authors usually refer to 94 Victoria Crosses as Canadian VCs. The first was awarded during the Crimean War, two during the Indian Mutiny, one at Little Andaman Island, four in the South Africa War, seventy during the First World War, and sixteen during the Second World War.[42] Nine were awarded to Quebecers, including three francophones.[43] One historian compares the 181 VCs awarded during the Indian Mutiny of 1857–59 with the 182 awarded during the Second World War and concludes, "a soldier in the Indian Mutiny had roughly a one in 1,593 chance of earning a VC, while in the Second World War the odds were one in 21,668."[44]

Three of the sixteen usually identified as Canadian VC recipients had not been serving in Canadian uniform. Some Canadian authors consider those born in Canada, as well as those serving in Canadian uniform (even if born elsewhere) as "Canadian VCs."[45] At least one British author, perhaps applying the same criteria of considering individuals born in Britain (Osborn) and serving in the British forces (Peters, Hoey, and Bazalgette) as British VCs, refers to twelve Canadian VCs.[46] Some British authorities refer to "Canadian VCs" as those serving in Canadian uniforms, and thus to thirteen.[47] This seems more appropriate for, as the case of Triquet shows so well, a VC – particularly an Army VC – is awarded to an individual but is intended to honour the contribution of many, in the company, regiment, and supporting services.

Triquet's VC was different in several ways. First, he was the only francophone and only Quebecer of the thirteen. Five were from Ontario,

VC Recipients Wearing Canadian Uniform during the Second World War[45]

Name	Rank/ Service	Age	Province of birth	Date of act (P=posthumous)	Date of announcement
Osborn, John Robert	WO II, Army	42	(Born in the UK)	19 Dec. 1941 (P)	2 April 1946
Merritt, Charles C.I.	Lt Col, Army	33	BC	19 Aug. 1942	2 October 1942
Foote, John Weir	Rev (Capt) Army	38	ON	19 Aug. 1942	14 February 1946
Triquet, Paul	Capt, Army	33	QC	14 Dec. 1944	6 March 1944
Mahony, John Keefer	Major, Army	32	BC	24 May 1944	13 July 1944
Mynarski, Andrew C.	PO, RCAF	27	MB	12 June 1944 (P)	11 October 1946
Hornell, David Ernest	Flt Lt, RCAF	34	ON	24 June 1944 (P)	28 July 1944
Currie, David V.	Major, Army	32	SK	18 Aug. 1944	27 Nov. 1944
Smith, Ernest Alva	Pte, Army	30	BC	21/2 October 1944	20 Dec. 1944
Cosens, Aubrey	Sgt, Army	23	ON	25/6 Feb. 1945 (P)	22 May 1945
Tilston, Frederick A.	Major, Army	29	ON	1 March 1945	22 May 1945
Topham, George F.	Cpl, Army	27	ON	24 March 1945	3 August 1945
Gray, Robert Hampton	Lt (N) RCN	27	BC	9 Aug. 1945 (P)	13 Nov. 1945

four were from BC, and there was one each from Manitoba and Saskatchewan. As mentioned, Osborn was born in Britain.[48] Looking at their pre-war experiences, Triquet is the only one to have emerged from the Regular Force, while five others had served with the Non-Permanent Active Militia.[49] Triquet, at thirty-three, was slightly older than

Canadian-Born VC Recipients Wearing British Uniform during the Second World War

Name	Rank/ Service	Age	Province of birth	Date of act (P=posthumous)	Date of announcement
Peters, Frederick T.	Capt (N), Royal Navy	53	PEI	8 Nov. 1942 (killed 1943)	18 May 1943
Hoey, Charles F.	Major, Br. Army	29	BC	16 Feb. 1944 (P)	18 May 1944
Bazalgette, Ian W.	Sqdn Leader, RAF	25	AB	4 August 1944 (P)	17 August 1945

the average: four were older (Osborn the oldest at forty-two) and eight younger (Cosens the youngest at twenty-three).[50]

Each citation was of course unique. The first two Canadian VC citations, those for Merritt and Triquet, begin with a sentence summarizing the qualities of the recipient. Merritt's was "For matchless gallantry and inspiring leadership," and Triquet's was "For determined leadership and example." None of the other citations followed this form, until the final citation of Gray: "For great bravery in leading an attack." In Triquet's case this phrase was added at the last minute on 2 March by Montague. Another change suggested by Montague was to reduce the number of superlatives that had been generously applied. He asked Letson to remove twelve; only six were removed. Concerning the length of the citations, there were large variations, with Triquet's being relatively long (483 words). It is interesting that the two shortest were written for Canadians serving with British units (Hoey's citation was 157 words and Peters's was 163 words); the two longest were those for Currie (768 words) and Mahony (755 words). All citations repeated certain words: "cheerful disregard for danger," "self-sacrifice," "encouraged others by example," and "determined, inspiring leadership."[51]

Considering the numbers who served and the nature of combat, it is not surprising that ten of thirteen Canadian VCs were in the Army;[52] two served in the Air Force and one the Navy. Triquet's rank at the time was captain (acting major), he thought; however, as he was informed on 16 December, his promotion to major had been confirmed in November.

These two ranks were the most common among the thirteen. There were two other captains and a naval lieutenant, three other majors, and one lieutenant colonel as well as two Air Force officers, Flt Lt Hornell and PO Mynarski. Just over half of the ninety-four Canadian VC recipients usually recognized were officers; they were more likely to be awarded the VC than other ranks due to greater freedom of movement and control over their own destinies.[53] The percentage of officers was even higher in the Second World War. Apart from the award to Merritt and the later ones to Foote and Osborn for costly lost battles early in the war, all subsequent awards were, like Triquet's, for successful actions.

A large number of the 1,351 successful recommendations were for those rallying a small group to accomplish a great feat, and Triquet fits this mould well. He fits even more aptly the personality trait that some see as most immediately obvious: "They are a stubborn lot."[54] Some emphasize the variety of recipients, noting that some had military backgrounds or were superb athletes while others were not; most conclude that they were just regular soldiers at the right place at the right time.[55] The last surviving member of the Canadian VCs, Smokey Smith, just before his death in August 2005 offered his view of what he saw in the recipients that made them different from other men in uniform: "You get in that position where you've got to fight. Somebody's got to fight, you can't all sit around. They've got a job to do." The interviewer insisted that many did their jobs in the war – there had to be something different. Smith replied, laughing, "Crazy. They were all crazy."[56]

Camp Borden

With the other Canadian VC recipients, Triquet could be one of the guys, an "ordinary" VC among fellow peers.[57] However, he continued to have serious problems fitting into the Regular Force and adjusting to his life in Canada, particularly the never-ending requests for public speaking engagements. At the beginning of 1946 newspapers reported that he would be named to command Camp Farnham, but this report was quickly denied. Shortly after, in February 1946, a position was created and Triquet appointed to fill it, as associate commandant, Canadian School of Infantry, Camp Borden. The chief of the General Staff

(CGS) was personally involved in the appointment, authorizing the new position and ordering that he was to approve the press announcement before it was released.[58]

During eighteen unhappy months at Camp Borden, Triquet attempted unsuccessfully to fit into the regular life of a professional soldier of the Canadian Army. His job was not an easy one: he was responsible for establishing a francophone program for the French-speaking recruits. He asked for reinforcements from his friend who had led B Company in Italy, Lieutenant Colonel Gilles Turcot at Valcartier, informing him that there were not enough francophones to provide the course. Specifically, he requested a corporal, two privates, two instructors to teach arms, and two sergeant-instructors for battle drill. Turcot replied that it would be difficult to spare so many men from Valcartier at the moment, where courses were still ongoing. As usual, Triquet did not give up easily, informing Turcot that he knew it would not be easy, which is why he had asked for "and received" authorization to go himself to Military Districts No. 4 and 5 to find the staff he needed.[59]

Triquet added a personal note on how alien he found his anglophone environment: "Gilles, I am very happy to have this occasion to briefly visit the Battalion because I feel a little lost here. Borden is a real place of exile for a Quebecer, but if all this helps our people, I'll do my best to be of use for them."[60] Already uncomfortable in an anglophone community, he found the pressures of his personal life increasing as he attempted a reconciliation with his wife, Alberte Chenier.[61] She arrived in late 1946 with their two children, who attended English-language school on the base and also experienced some culture shock.[62]

In addition to these stresses, there remained the many public relations events.[63] Triquet continued encouraging cadet training.[64] In September he met General Montgomery during his visit to Canada.[65] He was also involved with the writing of a regimental history and contributed to the creation of a regimental newsletter.[66] He wrote in this new forum that he was hopeful that it would reduce the distance he and others (but mostly himself) felt between Camp Borden and the Citadelle: "Be assured that those of us far away from the unit will be very happy with this resource that will allow us to keep in contact with our comrades at the Friends of the Regiment."[67] The R22eR began celebrating the anni-

"Major Paul Triquet, The Victoria Cross," painting by Adam Sherriff Scott, ca. 1944–46. Beaverbrook Collection of Military Art. CWM 19710261-5841.

versary of Casa Berardi on 14 December 1946 with a ceremony at the Citadelle that included the presentation of a painting by Adam Sherriff Scott illustrating the events.[68]

Triquet's health started to deteriorate. His drinking did not help.[69] A friend later described his difficulties as compounded by "marital problems, drinking habits and a tendency to say the wrong thing at the wrong time in public ... he was known as a rather heavy drinker and somewhat of a playboy."[70] He told a doctor that he had been "very nervous" since April 1944 and that his throat was sore. At another examination a doctor recorded that Triquet was anxious, sleeping poorly, and feeling "tense all the time."[71] Triquet's son remembers that his qualities of great energy and determination became faults in this period as he refused to rest and attempted to do too much; excessive work led to excessive drinking and brought out the worst side of his character. His family and military friends supported him, but in June 1947 his drinking and violent outbursts became too much for Alberte, whose departure in the middle of the night by taxi to Cabano revealed how bad the situation had become. His unacceptable behaviour had also become too much for the Army.[72]

Forcing a VC recipient into retirement was not an easy decision. Chief of the General Staff Charles Foulkes accepted the recommendation of Chris Vokes, the GOC Central Command, to ask Triquet to retire under the relatively favourable terms of paragraph 267 (c) of the King's Regulations.[73] This specified that the officer's removal was to be in the interests of economy or efficiency and "shall not imply any dishonourable or improper conduct on his part."[74] Army Headquarters through the adjutant general asked Vokes to serve a "Notice of Intention" on Triquet using the following terms:

> Pursuant to the interview you recently had with the General Officer Commanding Central Command and the Officer Commanding the Royal Canadian School of Infantry, and in accordance with the views then expressed it is proposed to recommend your retirement from the Canadian Army Active Force under the provisions of KR (Can) 267 (c) in accordance with the procedure prescribed by Appendix XII thereto.
>
> You may, within a period of 14 days from the date of this letter, furnish a statement setting forth any reasons which you may wish to submit against this intended recommendation. If no such statement is received within the stated period of 14 days, I will forward my recommendation through the usual channels for necessary action.

> If you do not wish to make a statement against the foregoing recommendation, you are requested to submit a statement in the following form:
>
> 'I do not wish to make any statement against the recommendation that I be retired from the Cdn Army pursuant to KR(Can) 267 (c)'.

Vokes served the notice, Triquet quickly accepted, and Vokes forwarded Triquet's reply to the adjutant general on 18 June.[75]

As Triquet was close to completing the twenty years service required for pension, Brigadier Macklin authorized Vokes to grant him "special leave," in addition to the leave he had accumulated, to make his official retirement date 12 November 1947. He was also allowed to retain his rank.[76] It was not the ideal way to end a great career with the Permanent Force, but Triquet was perhaps relieved, in more ways than one.[77]

For many, particularly for the R22eR, Triquet remained the popular hero he had been.[78] For others he was a good man requiring support during a difficult period. As he attempted to get his life in order after being thrown out onto civvy street, he relied heavily on his military friends. His army comrades helped soften the blow; they too had seen death and suffering on the battlefields and had felt uncomfortable receiving praise for their heroism while knowing that the sacrifice of so many others could never be fully recognized. Only men who had lived through similar traumas could fully understand Triquet's case and try in some ways to help. Triquet made several visits to Valcartier in the following months.[79] He was also greatly assisted by his friend Bert Hoffmeister from the 1st Canadian Division in Italy. Hoffmeister helped to arrange a sales position for Triquet representing the Vancouver-based lumber company H.R. MacMillan Export in Quebec. Triquet told a reporter that he had selected this new career as he was attracted to the lumber business. Having been raised in Cabano, he had worked in several mills, so "it's in the blood, but perhaps more to the point, I should say that it was through the fact of having met in Sicily one of the directors of the Company, Major General Hoffmeister."[80]

Triquet was very comfortable with the position at H.R. MacMillan Export, known after the merger of 1952 as MacMillan-Bloedel. Under the influence of Hoffmeister, the company had many characteristics in its corporate structure that borrowed from the military model, and it had also developed programs for returning vets.[81] Triquet was anxious to start and glad to hear from the Army in August that he did not have to wait for his leave to end in November to begin his new job.[82] He left for six months of training in Vancouver on 19 October 1947.[83]

He made a brief statement to say goodbye to the men of the Royal Canadian School of Infantry. He wished them, "as well as the members of your family ... happiness and success ... My twenty years of service in the Army were the happiest years of my life and if I had to choose again, I would choose a military career." He added with pride what he had accomplished: "I have endeavored to stress the importance of having bilingual instructors to impart military training and knowledge to our French-speaking Canadians whereby they could obtain the same qualifications as our English speaking compatriots. The results obtained have been excellent."[84]

The author of a farewell letter to Triquet on his retirement from the Royal Canadian School of Infantry commented that it "was sad news to us and sad yet welcome news to Lt. Col. Triquet, since he had applied for it in order to have the very necessary time to adjust himself to life in a civilian occupation, having completed pension time service." He also thanked Triquet for his excellent contribution during twenty years of service, rising from "Private soldier to Lieutenant-Colonel ... [he] has earned and been awarded the Empire's highest award for Valour, surely a soldier's ultimate aim."[85] Triquet would have agreed before he won the VC, but fighting a war with the award had not been easy, and finding peace was also proving difficult.

7

A Hero's Return to the Ordinary World, 1947–1980

It is inconsistent that a serviceman should be a hero
in wartime and a curiosity in peacetime.
– Suttie Committee, 1964[1]

Hitting Civvy Street, 1947–1960

Returning soldiers had a huge impact immediately after the war as they reintegrated into society in Quebec and the rest of Canada. They would also significantly contribute to fundamental changes in the decades following the war. As Vanier had suggested, former soldiers were to play important roles. This was not always straightforward, as the vision of those who had served or continued to serve did not always correspond with that of the majority. Triquet continued to be conscious of his role as "hero"; although he now felt less pressure, he knew that many were still watching his life. He controlled his drinking, improved his behaviour, and attempted to provide, along with many others, a less public contribution towards the development of his vision of Canadian society. Joseph Campbell wrote in 1949: "It is not society that is to guide and save the creative hero, but precisely the reverse. And so every one of us shares the supreme ordeal – carries the cross of the redeemer – not in the bright moments of his tribe's great victories, but in the silences of his personal despair."[2]

As postwar societies throughout the Western world experienced significant changes from 1945 to 1980, heroic role models became less popular, while variations of individualism seemed to increase.[3] Some observers praised the greater freedom and liberties; others expressed concerns about less identifiable purposes and the "loss of a heroic dimension to life." The individualism that focused on the self led to a form of relativism that philosopher Charles Taylor describes: "Everyone has a right to develop their own form of life, grounded on their own sense of what is really important or of value. People are called upon to be true to themselves and to seek their own self-fulfillment. What this consists of, each must, in the last instance, determine for him- or herself. No one else can or should try to dictate its content."[4]

Quebec society was experiencing particularly significant changes during this period. French-Canadian nationalism since the mid-nineteeth century, through historical novels and references to national heroes glorifying the past, had focused on the *survival* of their different identity, with Catholicism being the central element of this identity and English-speaking Canada among the biggest threats.[5] This image, exaggerated in both French-speaking and English-speaking Canada, was replaced in the period from 1945 to 1980. The Quiet Revolution, usually identified with the political changes of the 1960s, had been preceded by social and ideological transformations that had been accelerating since the 1940s – most notably, urbanization and a greater openness to the outside world – largely as a result of the war. Quebecers now saw the world differently. They gave greater emphasis to elements they had in common with North Americans and during a short period built a modern, interventionist state. Thus as Quebecers changed, they tended to reject much of their previous (largely Catholic) heritage that they had used to define themselves. Many equated liberty with "*refus global*" (a rejection of everything), and this included previous role models, and even the idea of role models.[6]

Largely due to the conscription debate, French-Canadian role models associated with the war effort were not popular with the growing number of Quebec nationalists who relied on the idea of victimization to promote their cause. Conscription had been imposed on them, and that image dominated examples of remarkable sacrifices for the war effort or successful contributions to the federal political system.[7] Questions of conscription had not completely ended with the war. The chiefs of staff considered the issue in 1951; General Simonds recommended compulsory military service in public. And at certain points, right up to 1980, there were calls for it.[8] There was even surprising support in Quebec for some forms of it.[9] Triquet now made his views on conscription known much more openly than he had during the war, repeating his opposition. He insisted that soldiers had to be there because they wanted to be, and that volunteering remained "*la meilleure formule*."[10]

Triquet's postwar contribution to Canadian society did not include many political activities, as the gulf separating anglophone and francophone views of the nation remained wide even among veterans. The attachment that many English-speaking Canadians felt towards Great Britain remained strong into the 1960s.[11] The only attempt by veterans as a group to intervene significantly in political issues occurred during the debate over whether Canada should have its own flag. According to one historian, "The [English-speaking] veterans were wrong in 1964–65, and they discredited themselves – not least because they seemed to have interpreted a distinctive Canadian flag as pandering to Quebec, and Quebec, in veterans' eyes, had not carried its share of the war's burdens."[12]

Triquet had some success fitting into a new role in the world of business. During the final three decades of his life, without the awkward weight of living under heroic expectations, he was less separated from his peers, who were also adjusting to new lives. After six months of training in British Columbia with MacMillan, he returned to Quebec.[13] He continued to appear occasionally in the media and used one radio interview to explain the advantages of West Coast lumber and also his desire to contribute: "Since I returned from overseas after the war I have had the opportunity of travelling all over Canada under the direction of the Government and I have had the good fortune of meeting executives in all the Provinces ... I became inspired and enthused by the boundless potentialities of this great country, and, well, I just felt that I must play some part, some place in the picture, therefore I chose for the balance of my life, the business world."[14] While administration had not been his strength in the army when he had other things on his mind, once he adapted to the role, he appears to have excelled and become quite fond of it. He introduced a sales organization in Quebec and in 1950 opened a distribution centre for MacMillan products in Quebec City. He was district manager during the 1950s, and in 1960 he established another distribution centre in Rimouski which he managed from Quebec City.[15]

Although he enjoyed his new life in business, he remained very much attached to the military. He kept in touch regularly with his former regiment and continued to communicate his messages. Their newspaper recorded in February 1949 that the "lumber man" had dropped by and seemed to like saying "us civilians." The article concluded with what was obvious to all seeing Triquet wearing civilian clothes – that he remained "more than a little military."[16]

When the Korean War broke out, Triquet surprised no one by immediately volunteering in early August for service with the Canadian Army Special Force being organized. Three months later he was told that there "was no vacancy for an officer of his rank and qualifications at present," but that his offer was appreciated and if he were needed later, he would be advised.[17] The delay and eventual refusal were due in some measure to his having received the VC, but due much more to his postwar misconduct.[18] His disappointment at not being allowed to go to Korea was softened shortly after when he was accepted back into the army with the Reserve Force. His application of October 1950 was accepted, and he was attached for training with Le Régiment de Lévis, effective 1 February 1951.[19]

Given the task of training officer cadets, Triquet carried this out "with competence and enthusiasm." He wanted to contribute to society and found educating young recruits in the military family a comfortable position. He had put his life in order since 1948, according to an officer from Eastern Quebec who supported his admission to the Reserves: "Lt. Col. Triquet has been known as a thoroughly reformed character. He has a good position in civilian life and works hard. He went 'on the wagon' completely, has rehabilitated himself thoroughly and is now highly regarded by all those with whom he comes into contact. Many local people, service and civilian, have furthermore remarked on the great change which has occurred in Triquet during recent years. One and all, they now speak of this gentleman in the highest terms."[20]

Shortly after, the question of command arose at Le Régiment de Lévis, and of course Triquet was considered and strongly recommended by the outgoing CO.[21] But the request was denied by the chief of the General Staff (CGS), General Foulkes, whose decision was explained by the director of army personnel: "Bearing in mind the circumstances under which Triquet left the Active Force two years ago [it had in fact been four years], I do not recommend consideration of his appointment to command a Reserve Force Regiment. If Triquet were to be given this job, it would only be a matter of three of four years before he would be in line for command of a brigade in Quebec and I do not consider that Triquet is fit to command a Reserve Brigade."[22] As the CGS changed in 1951 and General Simonds replaced Foulkes, this may have encouraged Eastern Quebec Command to try again.

The commander of the Eastern Quebec Area, Brigadier Fleury, provided Army HQ with a list of advantages and disadvantages of appointing Triquet:

> This Officer has something of a nation-wide reputation. It is no secret that he was "fired" from the Active Force. His rehabilitation in recent years may not be so well known outside the Quebec Area ... There is always some danger in appointing a former [Permanent Force] officer to command a RF Unit. This may give rise to dissatisfaction, not only within the Unit itself but in RF circles generally. Obviously this blocks promotion and can be considered a reflection on the quality of the Unit's Officers ... Triquet's compulsory retirement, with consequent pension, was based on his unsatisfactory performance at the time and this is a matter of record. His re-appointment to the RF at this time might give rise to queries from the Treasury Board ... [Finally, Triquet] may subsequently re-apply for the [Permanent Force]. AHQ would have to consider this possibility and decide what action to take in this eventuality.

But Fleury considered there were more advantages than disadvantages and recommended Triquet:

> [He] is without doubt the best qualified Officer available ... his interest in all things military and his love for the Army are apparent at every turn. He would undoubtedly be very happy to get back "in the swim" and this would of course make him all the more valuable as OC ... military authorities might well gain in stature and prestige by demonstrating their willingness to recognize that this Officer is not really the same man who was com-

Triquet meets Field Marshal B.L. Montgomery at Quebec, 1952. DND-DHH photo.

> pulsorily retired several years ago. His rehabilitation is a fact ... In these times when qualified, energetic Officers are in short supply ... [he] is not only willing but anxious to serve. There was some question about this Officer's relationship with Church authorities who, it was understood, had taken a rather low view of his performance in 1945–46. Following an informal enquiry ... I am able to advise that there would be no objection from this quarter.[23]

Soon after, Major General Bernatchez announced to Le Régiment de Lévis that Triquet would be their new commander.[24]

Throughout 1952 and 1953 Triquet continued to work with MacMillan-Bloedel and to carry out his duties as commander of a Reserve Force unit. He attended Valcartier summer camp and other duties such as church parades, exercises, and Remembrance Day parades. He also continued with several PR activities, but only the ones he wished to accept, and these rarely involved public speaking to crowds. By all accounts he was very happy to make the rounds with young soldiers and speak with them individually. He was on special duty in England with the Canadian coronation contingent from 26 April to 12 June 1953.[25] He socialized with both younger and older comrades at various messes, and in speeches to youth he emphasized the importance of keeping the military family together.[26]

A revealing aspect of Triquet's life during the 1950s was his relationship with some authorities of the Catholic Church. Quebec society was going through significant changes, but the church's influence remained strong with some of its members actively involved in social reforms.[27] Although not a religious man, Triquet realized how important Catholicism was for the men of his regiment. According to his son, Claude, "He was very respectful but was not a believer. He would often use the padres in the Army. When he had problems with his men, he used the padres to help with various psychological problems, for example ... He saw that the Church had a strong influence on people. He was a great friend of Mgr Maurice Roy, archbishop of Quebec, whom he knew from the Army. There was also Mgr Jobidon, another priest who had been in the Army."[28] Although not deferential to authorities of the church who had opposed the war – in 1945 in reply to words of congratulations from a priest who had earlier penalized him for his involvement in the Army, Triquet responded, "Monsignor, you didn't think that in 1938!" – he was more respectful with those who had served.[29] One of his most visible activities in 1952 was helping to organize a campaign to provide each soldier in combat in Korea with a copy of the New Testament. Mgr Roy prepared an introduction and Abbé Gérard Fortin helped with the distribution. Triquet helped raise close to $2,000 for two thousand copies.[30]

The year 1954 would be the last for Le Régiment de Lévis. A committee chaired by Major General H.F.G. Letson to evaluate the role of the reserve units in the country's defence plans recommended its amalgamation with Le Régiment de la Chaudière. The amalgamation was announced 9 July 1954 and effective 1 September; the Drill Hall would be in Lévis. Historians of Le Régiment de la Chaudière have noted that the "integration of one unit with another is difficult to accept for those involved, no matter how excellent the formations ... Nevertheless, the good will of some and the understanding of others helped smooth over any difficulties." Lieutenant Colonel W.A. Atkinson of Le Régiment de la Chaudière maintained command and met with officers of both regiments to plan the way ahead together.[31]

Triquet's reaction was mixed. The newspaper of the R22eR reported: "Le Régiment de Lévis had existed for 90 years and naturally their Lieutenant Colonel Triquet was shocked to hear the unfortunate news, but he recovered quickly, commenting that there was certainly not a place for two infantry regiments on the south shore of the district of Quebec."[32] Triquet was also pleased that he would be promoted to command the newly created 8th Militia Group. He would become acting colonel and, if all went well, brigadier two years later.

This good news for Triquet was not received so well by Colonel J.F. L'Espérance, who had been commanding the 12th Infantry Brigade since 1952 and was counting on being promoted to brigadier but was instead forced to retire.[33] He recruited his father-in-law to write to Prime Minister St-Laurent, who replied that the Department of National Defence considered it would be fair that the commander of Le Régiment de Lévis took command of the militia group to "compensate for the disappearance of Le Régiment de Lévis."[34] Not satisfied, L'Espérance himself wrote to the prime minister. He also sent a long letter of grievance to the headquarters of the Eastern Quebec Area. Brigadier Fleury, commander of Eastern Quebec Area, defended his decision to appoint Triquet, noting that the decision had also been approved by the CGS and the minister. He reminded L'Espérance, "Triquet's war record and military background do not compare unfavourably by any means with your own ... you will not have overlooked the fact that he has also a Victoria Cross and a reputation which extends far beyond the boundaries of Eastern Quebec Area."[35]

Things did go well, according to Brigadier Fleury, who strongly recommended Triquet's promotion two years later: "Col. Triquet's performance as Commander No 8 Militia Group has been more than satisfactory. I know of no other Officer in the Militia who has spent more time or shown more devotion to the Militia than Col. Triquet." Fleury hoped that the announcement could be made by the end of August, when he was relinquishing command, but the final decision was delayed.[36] By October 1956 Major General Paul Bernatchez was general officer commanding (GOC) at HQ Quebec Command, and Brigadier Jean Allard had replaced Fleury as commander of HQ Eastern Quebec Area. Triquet had strong supporters in these three friends, but Army Headquarters remained hesitant.[37] Eventually, effective 1 September 1956, Triquet was promoted acting brigadier general. He was confirmed in the rank two years later, on 30 April 1958. Brigadier Dollard Ménard, CO HQ Quebec Command, confirmed the substantive rank of brigadier. Triquet continued to attend summer camp in 1954 and 1955 but from 1956 to 1959 was more involved with administration.[38]

Brigadier Triquet relinquished his command in 1959. More responsibilities with his lumber business meant he no longer had the time he felt necessary for his position with the militia. He wrote to inform HQ that the end of his three-year term as brigadier, on 1 September 1959, would be his last. He asked to be kept on the Supplementary List: "I am still within the age limit for my rank and quite prepared to serve on active duty if any emergencies arise in our country."[39] He was also named in September 1959, with twenty-two other officers, honorary aide-de-camp to Governor General Georges Vanier.[40] On his retirement the GOC of Army HQ in Quebec, Dollard Ménard, wrote to thank him for the excellent work with the 8th Militia Group. Knowing as well as anyone what Triquet had gone through, Ménard closed his letter by telling Triquet that he could retire saying, as St Paul had said: "I have fought a good fight, I have finished my course, I have kept the faith."[41]

Retirement, 1960–1980

When he retired, Triquet added that he still intended to remain involved, that he would always be "close to the Army."[42] The mid-1960s were years of change in the Canadian Armed Forces, with a major review in the White Paper of 1964 and the unification of the Forces in 1968. Triquet sat on an important commission looking into the reorganization of the Canadian Army (Militia).[43] Chaired by Brigadier E.R. Suttie, the report of June 1964 made several recommendations, with the first of twenty-six areas looked at being public relations.[44] The commission recommended "that a positive public relations program in support of the activities of the Militia be implemented immediately."[45] The report stated that this was needed as "the public has either a false image or no image at all of the Militia soldier. Generally speaking the public sees the Militia as 'through a glass, darkly.' Any distortion must be corrected and the best way to accomplish this is by means of a properly planned program which utilizes the facilities of the various news media. It is inconsistent that a serviceman should be a hero in wartime and a curiosity in peacetime."[46]

The Suttie Commission also referred to the growing problem of attracting young people to the Armed Forces: "The youth of the country, properly motivated, will accept the obligation of serving in the Militia. Social distractions which did not exist a generation ago are largely responsible for the difficulty in attracting and holding young men in Militia units. This condition can only be offset by vigorous and continuing public relations efforts."[47] Although he had experienced more than he would have preferred of public relations, Triquet was well aware that his VC still made him a model that young people looked up to. He continued to devote his time to encouraging young people to try the military. He considered the discipline, responsibility, and skills learned to be a great preparation for civilian life; during a television interview in 1970 he announced that the main reason he had joined the military was for the teamwork, the satisfaction of building a society together.[48]

Informal conversations fit more naturally with his character than formal speeches to large crowds.[49] He helped to organize and promote a long march in his native Témiscouata, involving sixty young soldiers from A Company of the Fusiliers du St-Laurent. "La Marche du Grand-Portage" was, he announced, a wonderful exercise for training the youth of the country.[50] Later, in 1977, he received an honorary degree from the Royal Military College in Kingston, where he took the time to speak with many students.[51] He replied to letters from young admirers and told one boy of fourteen that he had just returned from a trip to Toronto to the National Exhibition with twelve other Canadian VCs and that the boy, if he chose, might one day follow in the footsteps of the old VCs as they faded away.[52]

While he was glad to encourage those attracted to the military, he did not attempt to convert anyone. He was undoubtedly pleased when his son, Claude, joined the reserves and later commanded a squadron of Royal Canadian Air Cadets at Thetford Mines.[53] However, Claude appreciated that his father never tried to recruit him (or his sister) for the Army or for any of the many promotional activities – they each respected what the other decided to do. During the 1950s, father and son had been able to get to know each other better, living together while Claude was studying engineering at l'Université Laval. Claude remembers that Triquet controlled his drinking and enjoyed his work with the Militia as well as his civilian job with MacMillan-Bloedel, and the two got along well.[54] Triquet's daughter, Yolande, also joined the Army, working as a nurse in Quebec City from 1953 to 1957 before going to Kingston where she met her husband. Like her brother, she never felt any direct pressure from her father: "The army was in our heads. My father, I guess, was glad. But my main goal was to improve my English."[55]

Triquet's continuing PR activities made it preferable, perhaps to him but more likely to others, that he finalize his divorce from Alberte Chenier in order to marry his companion, Raymonde Trahan, in the summer of 1969. Divorce in Quebec had by this time become much easier. The court was told that, due to special circumstances, it would be "in the public interest" that the usual delay of three months before the divorce was irrevocable be reduced. It was specified that with his work as a retired brigadier general helping veterans of the Royal 22e Régiment, Triquet was in constant contact with the public. As he had lived for several years with Raymonde, "if his marital status is not regularized without delay there is a risk of public indignation, especially due to his past military service, which puts him in contact with a large number of Army veterans."[56]

During the final years of his life, despite increasingly fragile health, Triquet remained active at Remembrance Day ceremonies and with many veterans' associations.[57] One veteran remembers him as most comfortable when he found someone with whom he could talk about the war.[58] After his retirement from MacMillan-Bloedel, Triquet moved to California for a time, but he found the distance too great and instead spent winters in Florida to help his arthritis.[59] He kept in contact with some of the families of those who had fallen at Casa Berardi, letting them know that the cemetery was well maintained. When in Quebec City, he continued to visit the mess (he was particularly fond of dominoes) and to work with the R22eR museum. In September 1974 he helped the museum obtain the medals of Lieutenant Jean Brillant, whom he had always looked up to as "an example of superhuman courage." He had donated his own medals to the museum, occasionally borrowing them for events.[60] He was named president of the Royal 22e Régiment Association in October 1964. Jean Allard, who commanded the 4th Division of the British Army of the Rhine from 1961 to 1963 before

Triquet (back row, middle) on board the SS *Homeric*, which brought him and 34 other Canadian VC recipients to London in June 1956. DND, DHH, Allard Collection.

being appointed chief of defence staff in 1966, was also involved with the association during this busy period for Triquet and thanked him for his commitment to the regiment. Another old friend, Paul Bernatchez, had become colonel of the regiment and thanked Triquet for help in organizing events such as those associated with the regiment's fiftieth anniversary in 1964.[61]

In addition to the many ceremonies where he continued receiving honours and awards, Triquet chaired a committee aimed at helping reintegrate members of the military back into civilian life.[62] The committee was particularly interested in those who had served ten years or more

Some of the Canadian VCs in London, 1 July 1956. DND, DHH-00.8-D73.

and who, "due to their long period of service ... have lost contact, to a certain degree, with the customs of the business world, industry and the public service."[63]

More comfortable with his military comrades than civilians, Triquet particularly enjoyed meeting with VC recipients from around the world. The group first met in June 1956 for the centenary of the VC when all of the approximately four hundred living VCs were invited to London.[64] The Canadian delegation of 130 included thirty-six VC recipients and their families. When Richard Turner and Triquet, the two VC recipients residing in Quebec City, boarded ship on 13 June 1956, they were accompanied by a guard of honour of seventy soldiers of the 2nd and 3rd Battalions of the R22eR.

In total, three hundred VCs attended, included twenty-two in wheelchairs.[65] Lieutenant General Turner, at eighty-five the senior Canadian VC, led the Canadian VCs, including Major General Pearkes, two brigadiers, and a few colonels, in a "vigorous" march to be reviewed by the queen. According to one account, "as his gallant band neared the royal dais, Sir Richard rapped out briskly, 'Canadian Contingent, Eyes Right.' His voice was as vigorous as his step and the audience seemed to have

Canadian VC holders passing HM Queen Elizabeth II, Hyde Park, 26 June 1956. DND, DHH-000.8-D73.

'extra warmth' in their applause and smiles."[66] The event led to the creation of a VC association, later including George Cross recipients in a VC and GC association. Triquet became an active member, rarely if ever missing a meeting. One meeting of VC and GC recipients in Canada from 16 to 18 June 1967 included eighteen Canadian recipients, with six absent from the event.[67]

Triquet was accompanied in 1956 by his daughter, Yolande, who enjoyed the trip and meeting the queen. She remembers her father showing more emotion on this trip than she was accustomed to, particularly when they stopped by Casa Berardi, Triquet's first return to the site. She recalled that after the war the Italian campaign did not receive as much attention as the northwest European theatre, and she had been glad to learn more about it.[68] There was an increasing interest, more amongst veterans than the general population, to commemorate events of the Second World War. In 1953, on the tenth anniversary of Casa Berardi, a small notice had appeared in the regimental newspaper, but no significant ceremonies had taken place. For the twentieth anniversary, however, seven years after his visit of 1956, Triquet returned with other vets.

He also participated in a ceremony at the officers' mess of Valcartier on 14 December 1963.[69]

Another more formal return trip to Casa Berardi was organized for the summer of 1964. Triquet and Allard made arrangements for about twenty-five Canadians, mostly from the R22eR but also including Snuffy Smith of the Ontario Regiment (all paying their own way) and about ten officers serving in Cyprus, to attend a ceremony. Allard unveiled a plaque and made a speech that inevitably noted that Triquet's "valour and courage made it possible to capture the town of Ortona from the enemy." But Allard's focus was on rebuilding and the sacrifice of the fallen: "Over twenty years ago, we came to this lovely country to help you get rid of an invader. But in so doing, we destroyed some of your homes and cities and even this little chapel. Fortunately, our regimental chaplain, now the Archbishop of Quebec, was able to contribute to its restoration. We also lost in this vicinity some fifteen hundred Canadian soldiers now resting in this well kept cemetery – all too many of these are from my own Royal 22e Régiment."[70]

On the twenty-fifth anniversary of the battle a group including Triquet, Allard, and Cardinal Roy went to the site in September 1968 for a ceremony. Snuffy Smith also attended. He had by now become almost a member of the regiment – soon after, Triquet sent him three regimental ties. The tour began in Rome with a visit to the Vatican where Pope Paul VI spoke of his admiration for the Canadian soldiers in Italy during the war and their sacrifices to safeguard common values.[71]

Triquet made a fifth and final trip back to Casa Berardi for a ceremony in the summer of 1974. Signora Maria Teresa Berardi was there to greet the delegation and show the plaque on the side of the house that read: "Casa Berardi, Medaglia d'Oro, Capt. Paul Triquet, Royal 22nd Regiment, Canadian, Ortona 1943." Although Triquet's health was poor, his determination to accomplish his mission still showed. A journalist reported, "He's lost one eye, has almost lost the sight of the other. He has arthritis, gout, diabetes and has had three heart attacks. But called upon to place a wreath, he puts aside his cane, takes a bearing and moves straight ahead like a drill sergeant."

"I always wanted to be a soldier," Triquet told the reporter, who added that although Triquet might have retired from the army, "the army never retired from him."[72]

Paul Triquet died on 4 August 1980. The Canadian Forces notice announced that he had died of kidney disease following a short hospital stay at St-Ambroise Hospital in Loretteville, Quebec. Among the eight Canadian VC survivors of the Second World War, he was the second to die, after Topham in 1974. The press focused naturally on Triquet's VC but also on his lifetime career as a soldier.[73]

There was little doubt that it would be a military funeral: Triquet had even arranged a military funeral for his father when he had died in 1962.[74] In August 1973 he had expressed the desire to have a military and religious ceremony himself – something that was far from automatic for a divorced man at the time. Lieutenant Colonel Georges Bernier accompanied Triquet and his second wife, Raymonde, to visit Cardinal Roy, who accepted the request, noting that the church had become more flexible.[75]

The service was held at La Basilique Notre-Dame de Québec, 7 August 1980 at 10:00, after a funeral parade from 09:30 from the Manège militaire de la Grande Allee. During the ceremony Cardinal Roy stressed that the military was vital in war and peace and that Triquet had showed valour through courage. Ottawa sent the minister of national defence, Gilles Lamontagne, a bomber pilot with the RCAF during the war, who was a good friend of Triquet.[76] CDS General Ramsey Withers was also there, while MNA J.J. Bertrand represented the provincial government. Honorary pallbearers included General Allard, Lieutenant General G. Turcot, Lieutenant General H. Tellier, Lieutenant General J. Chouinard, Major General P. Bernatchez, Major General R. Reid, Brigadier General M. Richard, Brigadier General R. Trudeau, Colonel G. Poulin, and Lieutenant Colonel M.A. (Snuffy) Smith. After an eleven-gun salute and Last Post, Major General Bernatchez presented Triquet's wife, Raymonde, with the flag.[77]

A journalist noted that the entire regiment, or rather an entire nation, was deeply moved. It was moving to lay to rest a man "who during the Second World War had brought such honour to his unit the Royal 22ième Régiment and to his people while remaining good, simple and always helpful. He was a real soldier and a great one."[78] Among the tributes, one of the soldiers from Casa Berardi commented that he had never known a braver man.[79] Another soldier wounded at Casa Berardi admired Triquet for having conducted himself as a hero: "It's in these moments that the force of character is revealed, the commitment to discipline and the sense of duty to our superiors. I am very proud to have served under him."[80]

Triquet's ashes were buried inside the Citadelle;[81] in 1973 Triquet had also asked that his ashes be interred there, where Major General Georges Vanier had been buried in March 1967 (and where Pauline Vanier would be buried beside her husband in 1991). Bernatchez wrote to Triquet to notify him that this request was accepted but added that he should follow closely the advice of his doctors. The regiment reconfirmed the arrangements in the summer of 1979, specifying that there would be a military and religious ceremony and that his ashes (but not those of his family) would be placed in the memorial.[82] Triquet had once said, "I have loved [the Citadelle] from the start. It is my second home."[83] His daughter, Yolande, remembers that at lunches at the Citadelle, her father was "very much at home, it was his place."[84] His son, Claude, recalls his father often saying that the regiment was his family. Knowing he meant it, Claude was not surprised by his father's wish to be buried inside the Citadelle – it would have been surprising for him to be buried anywhere else.[85]

With Triquet immortalized in the chapel of the Citadelle, the importance of his story and how it would be told to future generations grew. As the Casa Berardi battle became one of the most celebrated in regimental history, others had expressed concern about how it would be remembered.[86] The focus on Triquet and his C Company created some tension, perhaps envy, and legitimate questions about appropriate representation. Even more disturbing to some in D Company, the release in 1956 of the official history of the campaign had widely publicized the war diary account that C Company had been alone throughout the day because D Company was lost and did not provide the planned support until much later that evening. A soldier of D Company, who had followed Triquet's C Company on the south side of the gully, felt their contribution was neglected during the ceremony in 1963:

> The speeches of the "VIPs" during this memorable evening were very good, except that people seemed to have forgotten the famous and brave Major Ovila Garceau who was killed and between us

> was the only one responsible, with his Coy, for the advance and success of the capture of Casa Berardi by the now Brigadier P. Triquet, V.C. From where we were (Coy of Garceau and at the time I was his "CSM"), we were the only ones to have seen, followed, and supported (with our arms) visually each step of the advance of Triquet's Coy from morning to night.[87]

Claude Châtillon, one of the platoon commanders in D Company during the battle, published an account from their perspective in 1987, suggesting that Triquet had received too much attention.[88]

Triquet had also been concerned with how the battle and his role were being remembered. When in 1968 he attended a ceremony in Cabano to honour the twenty-fifth anniversary of Casa Berardi,[89] local papers carried an account that corresponded more with the public perception of what a heroic action should look like: Triquet had been "wounded," in the "defence of a strategic point" at Casa Berardi on 9 March 1944.[90] Yet the war diary of the regiment established him as one of the few not wounded during this offensive operation in December 1943.[91] He encouraged efforts in Cabano to establish a military museum, offering artifacts and advice and insisting repeatedly that the focus be on the contribution of all those serving from the region rather than himself.[92]

Just before his death in 1980 he told his friend Charles Chaveau that he hoped to write a more complete story of Casa Berardi "in order to give proper credit to those who deserve it."[93] He still remembered telling reporters in 1944 to focus on others, notably one young soldier who had been "alone there and utterly exhausted but he whispered 'don't worry sir. I'm all right. They won't pass.' He died later that day. They're the heroes you want to write about, not me."[94] Instead, reporters wrote about Triquet and credited him with the words. Yet he continued to emphasize the role of his men, the artillery, and the armour. He was particularly eager to praise the roles of Bernatchez and Allard and to demonstrate that "the victory was possible particularly thanks to the effort of the Coy Commanders Garceau et Yvan Dubé." He had written a six-thousand word article in 1962 on the battle for the regimental newsletter, making all these points, but it was not widely distributed. He ended that article by saying that he would be entering the hospital "for a fairly serious operation" and would return to Canada from the United States at the end of May to finish his story of Casa Berardi to "prevent that it be told by someone else, because it is fairly difficult to present events as they occurred without having lived through them."[95]

Many people still had messages they sought to deliver through their accounts of the war, and Triquet had his.[96] Throughout his career in the Regular Force and the Reserves, he attempted to make the army more accommodating to francophones. He encouraged anglophones to be more welcoming by understanding French-Canadian linguistic obstacles, recognizing their participation and not insisting on conscription. He told one reporter in 1970 that he had been trained in English but, once the firing began, it was automatic for him to speak French: "Which is why it is absolutely necessary that the troops be trained in their own language."[97] Describing the important work of the Canadian Forces, he encouraged his people to join voluntarily. When he was given the chance to express himself, his speeches consistently referred to the benefits of anglophone-francophone cooperation.

He did not participate in the debate leading to the referendum on sovereignty association of 20 May 1980. The military discouraged interventions from serving members, and he had always avoided commenting in public on contemporary political issues. That spring he was ill and probably did not vote.[98] Perhaps his most direct attempt to influence Canadian politics was at the end of his regimental newsletter article of 1962:

> United in the same effort, directed towards the same objective, nothing was able to stop us [anglophones and francophones], and it is only logical to presume that, no matter what obstacle that bars our route, if we remain united, nothing will stop us. That's the lesson that comes from this episode, and I hope that this lesson may be of some use at this time when a certain movement, going against history, is attempting to isolate us, to "separate" us from our Canadian brothers. That is why I have written "Casa-Berardi."[99]

But heroes do not write their own myths. Whether others would draw the same lessons from the episode would depend on the subsequent evolution of Canadian society.[100]

EPILOGUE

Remembering Triquet

> I remember when Major Paul Triquet ... won the first Victoria Cross among Canadians fighting in the Italian campaign and I remember the pride we all felt in that great achievement and how symbolic it was that Triquet was a Francophone, his regiment 90 percent French speaking.
>
> – John Bassett , 1990[1]

How Triquet has been remembered and forgotten since his death in 1980 reveals two significant differences between the Canadian societies of 1944 and today. First, references to Triquet often reveal an evolution of ways in which francophones and anglophones see each other. In the 1940s more than today, French-Canadians sought the recognition of English-speaking Canada; they wanted to be accepted as good soldiers, in some ways as the "same," participating in the struggle, voluntarily – but also as different, Catholic and francophone.[2] Triquet referred to this dual aspiration in a message to young recruits on the thirty-fifth anniversary of the R22eR in 1949:

> The 22e battalion was formed in 1914 in order to group the French-speaking Canadians in the same unit, to train them and send them into combat under the orders of a commander who spoke their language and knew how to understand them. This experience *proved to other Canadians* the qualities and courage of our people ... [in the war of 1939–45] ... they proved once again the warrior qualities and the courage of our people when they can go into the battle *under the orders of Canadians who speak the same language.*[3]

Maria Teresa Berardi assisting Gen Allard during an unveiling ceremony on the fiftieth anniversary of the battle at Casa Berardi in 1993. DND, DHH, Allard Collection.

Many French-Canadians in 1944 had been proud of their hero and particularly proud that his feats had been widely recognized by the English-Canadian press.

Recognition was an important objective for French-Canadians in 1944 because many English-speaking Canadians saw French-Canadians, Aboriginals, and Canadians of immigrant origins as "not quite on a par with Canadians of British origin."[4] Anglophone public relations efforts, illustrated by the Wartime Information Board, reflected this vision of Canadian nationalism. While some messages from the government and anglophone press emphasized that Triquet's VC showed that francophones were in the war and doing a good job, others used the story to argue that more could be done, some journalists even falsely claiming that Triquet supported conscription. The imposition of conscription for service overseas in November 1944 a few months after Triquet's publicity tour became a clear symbol to French-Canadians of recognition denied,

Maria Teresa Berardi, fiftieth anniversary of the battle at Casa Berardi, 1993. DND, DHH, Allard Collection.

remembered decades later by Quebec nationalists much more clearly than any recognition of Triquet's feat or the French-Canadian contribution to the war effort.[5]

Today English-speaking Canadians' identification with Great Britain has almost disappeared, and most have a greater appreciation for the contributions of French-Canadian language and culture to the current vision of a more multicultural Canada.[6] Since the First World War, military events have played an important part in the English-Canadian construction of a national identity, with most histories of the wars presenting Canadian participation in a context of nation building.[7] This trend has been particularly apparent since the 1990s.[8] Military myths such as the battle of Vimy Ridge are used to highlight francophone-anglophone unity and recognition of the Canadian nation in Washington and London.[9]

Consequently, Triquet's story is increasingly used by anglophones to reinforce their vision of the Canadian identity. His story is used to show that Quebec was in the war, that anglophones and francophones made sacrifices and worked together. Traces of his story are well displayed in a prominent exhibit in the Canadian War Museum including his portrait, a radio, and photos.[10] In June 1990, a difficult time for national unity in Canada when the Meech Lake Accord failed to receive sufficient support in English-speaking Canada, John Bassett, chairman of Baton Broadcasting Inc, remembered Triquet:

> I started to think about my many companions who had answered the challenge in 1939–1940 and particularly those from whom fate had demanded the ultimate sacrifice. I could not help but wonder where today in this bountiful land was that spirit of self-sacrifice, that willingness to subjugate personal and regional selfish interest for the common good, where was that tolerance and understanding that under the crucible of war had brought men and women of all backgrounds, of all colours and races united in the common cause. I remember when Major Paul Triquet, of the Royal 22nd Regiment – The Vandoos, won the first Victoria Cross among Canadians fighting in the Italian campaign and I remember the pride we all felt in that great achievement and how symbolic it was that Triquet was a Francophone, his regiment 90 percent French speaking.[11]

In November 2006 the fourteen statutes in the Valiants Memorial erected in downtown Ottawa to honour individual Canadian war heroes included one of Triquet. The description of the project on the memorial website specifies how the project seeks to contribute to a Canadian national identity:

> The men and women memorialized here stand as symbols for a nation shaped by conflict and strengthened through sacrifice. It is war, as much as peace, that unites us; for valour knows no bounds. They belong to us all, these remarkable figures from our past … these are the heroes who have helped give us shape and purpose throughout four centuries. We have been called a cool people, the product of a frosty environment, and it is true that we do not indulge in the hot-blooded emotion that distinguishes

Triquet's sculpture included as one of the fourteen valiant Canadian military heroes in Ottawa. Photo, Marie Rose, November 2008.

those from warmer climes. Overblown celebration is not our style, but we know, deep in our hearts, that without the hard example provided by the kind of Canadian remembered here, this country would not dare call itself a nation.[12]

When some questioned the choices of heroes, feeling some groups were under-represented, and others considered it to be "too militaristic," one veteran defended the project using the example of Triquet. He argued that a statue of the "ultra-brave" Paul Triquet would help national unity by illustrating to young Quebecers visiting the site in the future that their contribution is recognized and appreciated.[13] Demonstrating that Quebec participated in the war has now become a more important message in English Canada than in French Canada.

Today French-speaking Quebecers identify much more with a Québécois nationalism than they did in 1944. Charles Taylor has pointed out that "exactly in the decades during which 'English Canada' has begun to awaken to Quebec," francophones have become much less interested in the other solitude; there is not the same fear for survival that existed during the Second World War. They do not see the armed conflicts of the past century as contributing to their identity; as support for participation in the Second World War was divided, that event cannot easily be used in the formation of their identity.[14] The objectives of Québécois sovereignists are not advanced with references to the French-Canadian nation that existed before or to stories of previous anglophone-francophone cooperation. "*Je me souviens*" is the motto for both Quebec and the Royal 22e Régiment, but what each has remembered is very different.

Despite an increase in military studies in some Quebec universities during the past decade, veterans and some historians lament that interest in the Second World War (referred to in the title of one book as "the forgotten war") remains low.[15] In a study appearing in *Actualité* at the end of the century, featuring the magazine's selection of the hundred most influential Québécois of the twentieth century, military personnel and events were absent.[16] That Triquet was not remembered among that one hundred is somewhat surprising; even more surprising is that in dictionaries published in the 1990s containing thousands of famous Quebecers, he is not mentioned.[17]

Triquet's sculpture (far left), included as one of the fourteen valiant Canadian military heroes beside the war memorial in Ottawa. Photo, Marie Rose, November 2008.

When his name does appear in Quebec, it is not usually associated with his military feat nor his message of unity. In 1999, Jean Charest, then Opposition leader, referred to Triquet as a figure known in Quebec City due to the long-term health care centre for veterans named in his honour.[18] La Maison Paul Triquet, announced in May 1987, was an appropriate tribute to a man who spent so much of his time helping veterans; he is remembered there by some veterans and through a small display. But Triquet could be known in Quebec City for more.[19] In Cabano, street signs and the Legion Hall still bear his name, but fewer and fewer members of the community know his story. The Legion Hall has an excellent display of his uniforms, reproductions of his medals, photos, and memorabilia protected by a glass cover (and most of the time, a thick curtain), but few ever see it.[20] In 1993 Cabano celebrated the fiftieth anniversary of Triquet's VC with an exhibit at Fort Ingall and a speech on the theme "A strategy for doing better in our daily lives and making every day a heroic one."[21] The ceremonies did not hide Triquet's military achievement but seemed to focus more on his role as an ordinary man doing his best in whatever he did.[22] Speakers emphasized the importance of honouring all ordinary soldiers.[23] Moreover, messages of Canadian unity disappeared. While Triquet's six-thousand word account of events at Casa Berardi, originally written in 1962, was reprinted in a booklet almost in entirety, the final lines carrying his message of what he considered "the lesson" of the episode – "if we remain united, nothing will stop us" – were gone.[24]

Another way in which Triquet (along with the other Canadian VCs) is remembered reveals a second difference between the societies of 1944 and the present. We no longer expect (or believe) heroes to be demigods with "superhuman qualities" and have greater admiration for "ordinary" lives. The definition of "hero" has changed.[25] Canadians today seem even more sceptical of heroic role models presented as perfect examples to follow.[26] Canadian soldiers fighting in Afghanistan are rarely singled out by the media for individual attention, even when they are honoured with prestigious awards.[27]

This does not mean that admiration for exceptional individuals has disappeared, but to it has been added a much greater admiration for ordinary lives than in previous eras. On 12 September 2001 a group near Ground Zero held a banner reading "WE NEED HEROES NOW"; but during the US war against Iraq, when commanders created heroic myths around the stories of soldiers Jessica Lynch and Pat Tillman, Lynch told a congressional investigation (on what families are told about how soldiers die) that such myths are inappropriate because "the truth is always more heroic than the hype."[28] Charles Taylor has referred to what he considers an extremely important fact about modern moral consciousness: a tension between the affirmation of ordinary life, "to which we moderns are strongly drawn," and moral distinctions. "Indeed, it is too simple to speak of a tension. We are in conflict, even confusion, about what it means to affirm ordinary life ... We are as ambivalent about heroism as we are about the value of the workaday goals it sacrifices. We struggle to hold on to a vision of the incomparably higher, while being true to the central modern insights about the value of ordinary life. We sympathize with both the hero and the anti-hero; and dream of a world in which one could be in the same act both."[29]

This tension was revealed in March 2007 when rumours emerged that the Department of National Defence would be creating and awarding the first Canadian VC to the unknown soldier. Some opposed the move. The Legion president argued that the unknown soldier should be commemorated as an ordinary soldier: "To award honours would sever the bond he shares with all those who gave their lives without thought of reward or recognition. As requested by the veterans, the Legion urges politicians to allow our Soldier to rest with dignity and honour simply as 'one of us.'"[30] The higher the honour, the less the soldier could be "one of us." Yet others embraced the idea, Christopher McCreery replying that "the bestowal of the medal would serve as an acknowledgement of all those who fought for King/Queen and Country and never received formal recognition ... [and] official recognition of the great respect in which all Canadians hold this fallen warrior."[31]

Triquet as one of the fourteen "valiants" and neighbour to the unknown soldier – all under the Canadian war memorial[32] – has become part of this debate about what we should be honouring during military commemorations. He is one individual selected to represent the sacrifices of many in the Canadian Army during the Second World War. But views differ on how ordinary the fourteen valiants, and the unknown soldier, are allowed to be.

There is no doubt that Triquet was uncomfortable with the pressure of being a hero to Canadian society in 1944. Those in the Canadian government, army, and media who sought a hero did not want an ordinary man. Even today, as the story of Billy Bishop shows, some refuse to consider that the military heroes, presented as semi-gods during the wars, could have had faults.[33] Triquet was an ordinary man with strengths and weaknesses, but he could not show ordinary weakness. It was a burdensome role to play and had important consequences for his life.

Sometimes flowers are appreciated by the receiver; sometimes they are necessary for the presenter and accepted by the receiver. Paul Triquet would have preferred to avoid many of the ceremonies he sat through. He had suffered an emotional shock but found it difficult to accept counselling or admit that he had been affected.[34] The award separated him from many in the army and society: he was no longer an ordinary soldier, "one of us," to many of his peers. He was separated from their support. He knew that recognition for French-Canadians and for his regiment was important, so he accepted the weight of individual recognition. Accepting the role of hero, in which the individual is imagined standing alone, was particularly difficult for a man who had so strongly identified as a member of his group.[35] He knew the award represented the acts of many ordinary soldiers whose actions would otherwise have gone unrecognized, and so he participated in ceremonies that continually brought back horrific memories. In a similar way, fighter pilot Buzz Beurling was honoured in the spring of 1943: "To the accompaniment of ballet music, twenty-eight Girl Guides and a Brownie each presented the hero with a blood red rose – one for each of his kills. It was intended, of course, that the girls with their roses would honour Beurling. Actually, this display was in dubious taste. Sadly, the blood-coloured flowers could not help but bring to the pilot's consciousness a nightmare that had been haunting him since leaving Malta."[36]

When Triquet died in 1980, the media announced his wish that, instead of flowers, people send donations to help the veterans association of the regiment.[37]

NOTES

Introduction

1 Joseph Campbell in *The Hero with a Thousand Faces*, first published in 1949, writes that there is "always the one, shape-shifting yet marvelously constant story." He notes that individuals selected by societies as heroic role models share five steps: "a call to adventure" followed by "a road of trials," "achieving the goal," "a return to the ordinary world," and finally "application" of what the hero has gained to improve the world (3). Works of Carl Jung and Sigmund Freud reveal how myths emerge spontaneously from the human psyche as all seek some form of the heroic myth. Jung suggested in the 1930s that individuals share a collective unconscious with all of humanity that has produced mythical figures, through all times and cultures, that share many common characteristics (*Dialectique du moi et de l'inconscient*, 46). See also Karen Armstrong, *A Short History of Myth*, 7; Lucy Hughes-Hallett, *Heroes*, 6.

2 Pierre Grimal, "Man and Myth," in *Larousse World Mythology*, argues that by studying myths "it will become possible to discern – underlying the particular mythical form – extremely ancient schemes of thought, the instinctive moulds, as it were, into which the thought of a society flows" (15). Joseph Campbell writes in *Hero*, "It would not be too much to say that myth is the secret opening through which the inexhaustible energies of the cosmos pour into human cultural manifestation" (3).

3 Approximately twelve other Canadians received VCs while fighting with British units, including three during the Second World War.

4 In addition to Merritt, two other men in Canadian uniform would be awarded the VC in 1946 for their actions that had occurred before 1944: John Osborn,

posthumously for actions at Hong Kong in December 1941, and John Foote for actions at Dieppe in August 1942. Frederick Peters, born in Prince Edward Island, wore the uniform of the Royal Navy when he was awarded his VC for action in November 1942.

5 G.W.L. Nicholson, *The Canadians in Italy, 1943–1945*; Bill McAndrew, *Canadians and the Italian Campaign, 1943–1945*; Douglas E. Delaney, *The Soldiers' General: Bert Hoffmeister at War*; Mark Zuehlke, *Ortona*; Charles-Marie Boissonnault, *Histoire du Royal 22e Régiment*; Serge Bernier, *The Royal 22e Régiment, 1914–1999*, 111; Jean-François Pouliotte, "Le Royal 22e Régiment pendant la Deuxième Guerre mondiale."

6 Arthur Bishop, *Our Bravest and Our Best*; George C. Machum, *Canada's V.C.'s*; Douglas A. Melville, *Canadians and the Victoria Cross*; John Swettenham, *Valiant Men.*

7 Adam Nicholson in *Seize the Fire* focuses on why Nelson became a hero at that time: "In England there was a need for a hero like him who was a saviour, a man not from the established ruling class but outside it" (xix). See also David Lowenthal, *The Heritage Crusader and the Spoils of History*; Jay Winter, *Sites of Memory, Sites of Mourning.*

8 Richard Corliss in "On Duty, Honour and Celebrity: Clint Eastwood Takes an Intimate Look at the Public Face of War," *Time* (23 October 2006), notes that the director's "compassionate, cautionary tale speaks eloquently about a time when America needed heroes, and does so when we are no longer sure what they look like." See also John Gillis, *Commemorations*; James Mayo, *War Memorials as Political Landscape.*

9 Hugh Halliday, *Valour Reconsidered.*

10 Brereton Greenhous, *The Making of Billy Bishop*; Brian Nolan, *Hero: The Buzz Beurling Story*; Pierre Vennat, *Général Dollard Ménard.*

11 Ronald Rudin, *Founding Fathers*; Cecilia Morgan, *Heroines and History*; Lionel Groulx, *Dollard: Est-il un mythe?*; Alan McNairn, *Behold the Hero.*

12 Particularly useful were Tim Cook, *Clio's Warriors*; H.V. Nelles, *The Art of Nation-Building*; Jonathon Vance, *Death So Noble.* See also Serge Bernier, Robert Comeau, et al., *Dix ans d'histoire militaire en français au Québec*; Laura Brandon, *Art or Memorial?*; Suzanne Evans, *Mothers of Heroes, Mothers of Martyrs*; Alan Gordon, *Making Public Pasts*; Jacques Mathieu and Jacques Lacoursière, *Les mémoires québécoises*; John Pierce, "Constructing Memory: The Vimy Memorial," 5–8; Allan Young, "'We Throw the Torch': Canadian Memorials of the Great War and the Mythology of Heroic Sacrifice," 5–28.

13 F. Scott Fitzgerald, "Note-Book E," in Edmund Wilson, ed., *The Crack-Up*, 1945.

Chapter One

1 Florentin Triquet, quoted in Florence Triquet, *La petite histoire de la famille Triquet, 1840–1995*, 53: "Le Dimanche, 12 septembre: L'embouchure de la Gironde est dangereuse à cause des sous-marins ennemis: trois vapeurs ont été coulés deux jours auparavant. Nous devons coucher tout habillés pour parer à toute éventualité. Il y a des femmes qui pleurent, des hommes qui se découragent. Quant à moi, j'ai toujours le moral bon; je sais que la peur n'évite pas le danger. Advienne que pourra, telle est ma devise."

2 Florence Triquet in *La famille Triquet,* 49–50, remembers Hélène Triquet's reply to Florentin, "Oui, peut-être. Ça te permettrait de voir ce qui se passe au lieu de te ronger d'inquiétude. En même temps, tu aurais l'occasion de revoir ta famille que tu n'as pas vue depuis plus de onze ans." See also *Casa-Berardi*, 25; *Le St. Laurent*, "Paul Triquet VC est un gars de chez-nous," 16 March 1944.

3 Canadian Postal Museum, Triquet collection, G15-25.11, vol. 2, Florentin Triquet to wife, 9 March 1915, "Prions Dieu que cette vilaine guerre finesse au plus vite."

4 Unknown author, "The Biography of Paul Triquet, VC Chevalier de la Légion d'honneur," ca. 1946, 2, in R22eR archives, Paul Triquet Collection, FPA-43. This twenty-five-page biography was based on interviews with Paul Triquet. See also Florence Triquet, *La famille Triquet,* 58: "Mon père a été affecté par les gaz toxiques ... À son retour, sa vision ayant baissé, il doit demeurer dans une chambre noire durant plusieurs semaines. Au bout de quelques temps, il recouvre la vue, mais jamais comme auparavant. Le lumbago contacté dans les tranchées le fait souffrir."

5 Florentin Triquet, quoted in Florence Triquet, *La famille Triquet,* 53: "Le vendredi, 24 septembre [1916] ... À 9 heures trente, le train entre en gare de Cabano. Une cinquantaine de mes camarades sont là qui m'attendent sur le quai. Je suis si ému que j'ai peine à les reconnaître. Tout le monde me traite en héros ... Je reprends la vie ordinaire, heureux au milieu des miens et je remercie Dieu d'être revenu sain et sauf."

6 Ville de Cabano brochures. See also www.ville.cabano.qc.ca.

7 Florence Triquet, *La famille Triquet,* 12–29, 42: "Le Français est à l'eau!" Florentin Georges Triquet (he would use Georges in later years) was born in 1882 to Louis-Désiré Triquet and Florentine Boulanger (30–2). Hélène Pelletier was born in 1880. Her parents, Démérise Belzile and Hilaire Pelletier, moved from Trois Pistoles to Notre-Dame-du-Lac in 1889. See "Biography of Paul Triquet," 1.

8 Claude Triquet, interview, 31 January 2006. Paul Triquet's daughter, Yolande McArthur, in an interview of 31 January 2006 adds that her grandfather "was

different from others in that town. He wore a beret and a flower in his lapel, and walked with a cane. He was quite a character. He was very well respected." Also Lucie Latulippe, interview, 31 December 2005; Georges Fraser, interview, 31 December 2005; Raymond Pelletier, interview, 31 December 2005.

9 The three sons were Louis, 1906–71, Paul, 1910–80, and Bernard, 1920–88, and seven daughters, Marie-Louise, 1907–84, Cécile, 1909–73, Florence, 1911–2005, Gabrielle, 1912–95, Thérèse, 1914–90, Yvette, 1916–95 and Marie-Marthe, 1921–24 (Florence Triquet, *La famille Triquet,* 115).

10 Ibid., 58–9: Florentin returned to the sawmill in 1916 and during the 1920s held several jobs involving accounting and insurance.

11 "Biography of Paul Triquet," 4–6.

12 Janice Dickin, "Influenza," *Canadian Encyclopedia*, 1164.

13 "Biography of Paul Triquet," 4–7.

14 Georges Fraser (interview, 31 December 2005) recalls comments in Cabano about how central the military was to young Triquet's life. Thomas Green in the *Winnipeg Tribune* article of 11 March 1944, "We Could Depend on Him," refers to the many military mementoes that filled his family home.

15 Yolande McArthur, interview, 31 January 2006: "My grandfather was a military man at heart." Florence Triquet in *La famille Triquet,* 62, remembers the local school board complaining, "Ce maudit Français va tuer nos enfants."

16 "Biography of Paul Triquet," 2, 5–6.

17 Claude Triquet, interview, 31 January 2006: "D'après ce que j'ai su, c'était un enfant assez aventureux ... pendant les cours de violon qu'il suivait il a joué au poker avec son professeur." Cf. "Biography of Paul Triquet," 6–8: he did not like being at home with six sisters (with different interests from his) and in September 1924 asked to go to a boarding school with male teachers instead of the Cabano College with all female teachers; however, his parents did not have enough money. See also Florence Triquet, *La famille Triquet,* 62, 66.

18 "Biography of Paul Triquet," 8–10. Years later the Fusiliers du St-Laurent and Paul Triquet would both underline their brief relationship with pride. See François Dornier and Marie-Claude Joubert, *Soldats de la côte*, 83–6. Lt Col J. Pineau and Capt Casgrain in March 1960 confirmed (to support Triquet's affirmation to the department) that Triquet "had done local training with our 'A' coy" (LAC, RG 24, Triquet Personnel File, 6th folder).

19 LAC, RG 24, Triquet Personnel File, 2nd folder, attestation paper: his date of birth is recorded as 2 April 1908, his height 5'8", weight 136 lbs and his trade "labourer."

20 The 22nd Battalion, on 1 April 1920, became the 22nd Regiment of the Canadian Regular Militia (General Order No. 37). On 1 June 1921, it became the

Royal 22nd Regiment (General Order No. 149). For the inter-war activities of the unit and the reorganization of the forces, see Bernier, *Royal 22e*, 79–82. For the ten battle honours (the maximum permitted) on the regimental colours, see Bernier, 86; also G.W.L. Nicholson, *Canadian Expeditionary Force, 1914–1919.*

21 Georges Vanier, *Paroles de guerre*, 23–4; Bernier, *Royal 22e*, 75. On the daily life of soldiers, see Jean-Pierre Gagnon, *Le 22e Bataillon (canadien-français), 1914–1919*; Desmond Morton, *When Your Number's Up.*

22 Vanier in Robert Speaight, *Vanier: Soldier, Diplomat and Governor General*, 129.

23 "Biography of Paul Triquet," 10–11.

24 Bernier, *Royal 22e*, 80: "discipline and tradition, which may lead to a third, solidarity – that invisible but tangible bond that unites the members even when they are apart."

25 "Biography of Paul Triquet," 11–12.

26 Bernier, *Royal 22e*, 80, 11. For a list of commanding officers from 1920 to 1945 see Boissonnault, *Royal 22e*, 70. For the register of officers, 1920–46, see LAC, RG 24, vols. 1598, 1601, and 201.

27 W.L.M. King Diary, 27 August, 1928, 240: "A truly memorable day." The treaty was named for French Foreign Minister Aristide Briand and US Secretary of State Frank Kellogg. On military cuts during the 1920s, see Desmond Morton, *A Military History of Canada*, 170–3.

28 Jean Allard (with Serge Bernier, *The Memoirs of General Jean V. Allard*, 25) remembers that English-Canadians were encouraged to join, but in French Canada in 1939 "a man in uniform was often seen as an opportunist or worse."

29 Bernier, *Royal 22e*, 81–5: General Order No. 98.

30 LAC, RG 24, Triquet Personnel File, 2nd folder, "List of Promotions, etc."; "Biography of Paul Triquet," 12–17.

31 Claude Triquet (interview, 31 January 2006) remembers that his father liked to lead others and that he was determined but would move quickly and skip steps.

32 LAC, RG 24, Triquet Personnel File, 2nd folder, "Physical Training, Canadian Permanent Active Militia, Report on Student," 31 October 1930; same folder, "List of Promotions, etc."; see also "Biography of Paul Triquet," 17–19.

33 The member for Quebec Centre was Joseph Samson, mayor of Quebec City from 1920 to 1926 and Liberal MPP from 1927 to 1935.

34 "Biography of Paul Triquet," 19–20. Claude Triquet (interview, 31 January 2006): "Comme tout le monde militaire [mon père] se méfiait un peu des civils puis les politiciens en particulier. Il n'avait pas de haine contre les politiciens. Il avait affaire avec eux dans le domaine de ses affaires et dans l'armée. Mais il m'a jamais parlé d'une alliance politique, ou d'un intérêt politique marqué."

35 LAC, RG 24, Triquet Personnel File, 4th folder, Capt J.L. Mignault, Adjutant, R22eR, to Florentin Triquet, 28 December 1931: "Le Caporal Triquet a quitté le régiment de son propre gré pour s'engager dans la Police Provinciale. Cependant comme il n'a pu obtenir cette situation il est revenu au régiment, et, heureusement, nous avons pu le reprendre."

36 "Biography of Paul Triquet," 20–1.

37 LAC, RG 24, Triquet Personnel File, 2nd folder, "List of Promotions, etc."; see also "Biography of Paul Triquet," 21–3. Courses included were at Beauceville, 2–14 May 1932, and at the Connaught Rifle Range, September 1932.

38 Morton, *A Military History*, 174–5; John MacFarlane, *Ernest Lapointe and Quebec's Influence on Canadian Foreign Policy*, 75–122.

39 "Biography of Paul Triquet," 16.

40 LAC, RG 24, Triquet Personnel File, 2nd folder, "Physical Training, Canadian Permanent Active Militia, Report on Student," 29 June 1935. Triquet became Permanent Force Instructor 1st class, 18 November 1935 (and fully qualified 10 June 1936); the same folder has "List of Promotions, etc."; see also "Biography of Paul Triquet," 24–5

41 "Biography of Paul Triquet," 22–3; LAC, RG 24, Triquet Personnel File, 2nd folder, "List of Promotions, etc." He also went to Kingston for courses in 1935 (and passed French and math with first class honours). He re-engaged for three years on 21 December 1934.

42 Jean Pariseau and Serge Bernier, *French-Canadians and Bilingualism in the Canadian Armed Forces,* 97. See also Allard, *Memoirs,* 43.

43 "Biography of Paul Triquet," 23–4.

44 LAC, RG 24, Triquet Personnel File, 7th folder, DOC, MD No. 5 to the Secretary, DND, 17 December 1937.

45 LAC, RG 24, Triquet Personnel File, 7th folder, Major General C.F. Constantine to DOC, MD No. 5, 23 March 1938.

46 LAC, RG 24, Triquet Personnel File, 2nd folder, "Employment Sheets." Typical comments were: "intelligent, reliable, good worker." See also André Courtemanche, interview, 8 August, 2007; Armand Gagnon, interview, 8 August, 2007: Triquet was "dur mais juste ... quelqu'un militaire."

47 Bernier, *Royal 22e*, 99: "In the 1930s the regiment grew more and more like a family. This spirit was fostered by summer festivals, sports competitions for all ages and an annual Christmas party during which gifts were distributed to the children of members of the regiment. The first Midnight Mass was celebrated in the Citadel chapel on 24 December 1935. A New Year's Day levee likewise became a tradition."

48 *Canadian Senate Debates*, 29 May 1939, 521, "Divorce Statistics"; Alleyn Taschereau (avocat) to Paul Triquet, 14 June 1938, seeking $242, LAC, RG 24,

Triquet Personnel File, 3rd folder, and Georges Roy (avocat) to Lt Col Flynn, Citadelle, 19 December 1938, seeking help to recover $294 from Paul Triquet for legal expenses of Mme Alberte Chenier Triquet. Also Lt Col Percy Flynn, Commanding R22eR, to Headquarters, MD No. 5, 13 April 1938.

49 Morton, *A Military History*, 175–9.

50 John MacFarlane, "Double Vision," 93–111.

51 On 24 August, shortly after Hitler's pact with Stalin, Ottawa ordered all leaves for personnel at the Citadelle to be cancelled.

52 MacFarlane, *Ernest Lapointe*, 138–58.

53 On mobilization, see Bernier, *Royal 22e*, 99–101

54 Pariseau and Bernier, *Bilingualism*, 95; Charles Chauveau, *Soixante-cinq ans*, 291 (for a nominal roll, see 250–9).

55 George Fraser, interview, 31 December, 2005; "Biography of Paul Triquet," 15.

56 Florence Triquet, *La famille Triquet*, 75.

57 Ibid.

58 C.P. Stacey, *Six Years of War*, 35–6, and chapter 2 on mobilization, 38–71.

59 Ottawa spent, for all three services in 1939–40, $112,352,437, and in 1944–5, $2,938,309,630. See C.P. Stacey, *Arms, Men and Governments*, 534, also 6–16; Stacey, *Six Years of War*, 35, 40–1, 527.

60 The 24,089 number is a "snapshot figure" of the militia as the total available was higher.

61 The Canadian Army's peak strength on 22 March 1945 was 495,804 (Stacey, *Six Years of War*, 522–3). On the importance of the Permanent Force, see 50–2.

62 LAC, RG 24, Triquet Personnel File, 2nd folder, "Record of Service," 1939–47, on *HMT Aquitania*.

63 Ibid. Triquet had been promoted QMSI on 5 Oct 1939, and RSM (WOI) on 15 November 1939. Other copies of his record of service are available in folders 6 and 8 of his personnel file.

64 LAC, War Diary of 3rd Canadian Infantry Brigade, reel T-11078, 20 December 1939 (for routine), 26 January 1940 (for night training), 2 January 1940 (for letter from Brigadier C.B. Price to orderly sergeants on the need for improved discipline).

65 Jean-François Pouliotte, "Le Royal 22e Régiment pendant la Deuxième Guerre mondiale," 92. Yves Tremblay in *Volontaires*, 86, also notes that many francophones had little military experience and had to learn quickly.

66 Boissonnault, *Royal 22e*, 77–8; Bernier, *Royal 22e*, 100–3; Stacey, *Six Years of War*, 34.

67 For a complete list of units in the division see Nicholson, *The Canadians in Italy*, 687–9; also Allard, *Memoirs*, 38, 53.

68 LAC, RG 24, Triquet Personnel File, 2nd folder, "Record of Service," 1939–47; Boissonnault, *Royal 22e*, 83.

69 LAC, War Diary of 3rd Canadian Infantry Brigade, reel T-11078, 22 January 1940 (visit of king on 24th), 27 January 1940, progress report by Brig C.B. Price: "Only fair progress has been made this week, owing to the loss of time occasioned by the visit of His Majesty."

70 Department of National Defence, *The Canadians in Britain, 1939–1944*, 24; C.P. Stacey and Barbara M. Wilson, *The Half-Million*, 3–10. By February 1940 there were 23,000 Canadian soldiers in Britain, most near Aldershot, 50 kms southwest of London. On 23 June most moved to near Oxford.

71 Allard, *Memoirs*, 34. Tremblay, in *Volontaires*, 28, adds that the view of volunteers for the war effort became more favourable after the fall of France in 1940. On movements and activities of the R22eR during 1940, see Bernier, *Royal 22e*, 105; Boissonnault, *Royal 22e*, 91–4.

72 LAC, RG 24, Triquet Personnel File, 2nd folder, "Record of Service," 1939–47. He went on leave in July 1940 and in October was transferred to a Canadian Infantry Holding Unit (CIHU) pending his return from Canada. LAC, Regimental War Diary, C-3, vol. 15235 (1939/09–1940/08): "9 octobre, visite du lieutenant Triquet, notre ancient RSM. Il revient du Canada." Many thanks to Yves Tremblay for his help with these references; see also his book *Instruire une armée*.

73 Stacey, *Six Years of War*, 387–8, 437–9: in December 1941, during the disastrous Canadian mission to Hong Kong, 1,975 men were lost or spent the war in Japan's prison camps. During the infamous Canadian raid on Dieppe in August 1942, of roughly five thousand men sent, one thousand were killed and two thousand became prisoners.

74 Morton, *A Military History*, 188–91.

75 John MacFarlane, "Quebec and Conscription," *The Beaver* 75, no. 2 (April–May 1995), 26–31.

76 J.L. Granatstein and J.M. Hitsman, *Broken Promises*; Claude Châtillon, *Carnets de guerre*, 12–14. Earlier attempts to recruit francophones had been criticized for being insensitive, as most francophones were not moved by calls to defend the British Empire.

77 Morton, *A Military History*, 91; Allard, *Memoirs*, 43.

78 LAC, video, VI-8708-0004, Triquet, interviewed by France Fortin and André Jean on the show *Camera Verité*, 1970; Florence Triquet, *La famille Triquet*, 84.

79 LAC, War Diary of 3rd Canadian Infantry Brigade, reel T-11136: EX Beaver 2 in February 1942, EX Mouse in March, and EX Tiger with the 1st Division in

May. Stacey and Wilson in *The Half-Million,* 50–3, describe the movements of the regiment and relations with the population.

80 LAC, RG 24, Triquet Personnel File, 2nd folder, "Canadian Training School Report," November 1942. Also LAC, Regimental War Diary, C-3, vol. 15235, Battle Drill Course (12 August–3 November 1943) and combined operations training in February 1943; "Report on Injuries," 23 November 1942, with witness testimony by Lt M. Pariseault.

81 John English in *The Canadian Army and the Normandy Campaign* describes some ways that the training could have been better.

82 DHH, Report 92, CMHQ: "General Activities, Canadian Army Overseas, June 1942–April 1943," 27 April 1943, A-2.

83 Bernier, *Royal 22e*, 117: "Its full war complement was 850, but its actual combat strength was slightly less than 800, distributed among four infantry companies, each with some 120 men (at a maximum when on the front lines), a support company (tracked vehicles, mortars, antitank, pioneers), a B echelon (signals, transport, supplies, pay, etc), a command post and LOBs (men left out of battle for a variety of reasons)."

84 *L'Amicale du 22e, Album-souvenir* (1941).

85 R22eR archives, J.P.E. Bernatchez Collection, biography: born 1 March 1911, died 13 November 1983, enrolled 14 June 1934 to 16 March 1965. See also biography in *L'Amicale du 22e* 18, no. 3 (July 1964).

86 Bernier, *Royal 22e*, 111: He graduated from RMC after five years in the program that normally took four, and joined the regiment in June of 1934. On the challenges for francophones at RMC, see also Charly Forbes, *Fantassin*, 95–111.

Chapter Two

1 Boissonnault, *Royal 22e*, 158, quoting Bernatchez's reply to those who thought he was too close to the action with his daily tours of the regiment.

2 Nicholson, *The Canadians in Italy,* 5–6, 20–2. Americans had preferred to focus on northwest Europe, but British leaders successfully argued the importance of following victories in Northern Africa with the securing of the Mediterranean to provide naval and air support to strike at the "underbelly" of German-occupied Europe. In addition, by the Allies attacking Italy, the Germans would be forced to commit divisions from other theatres.

3 Field Censors (Home) Report, 21 April–5 May 1943, First Canadian Division, in Nicholson, *The Canadians in Italy,* 23. On public opinion and appeals from Ralston and King, see 20–6. Many troops had been disappointed when American troops and not Canadians landed in North Africa in November 1942.

4 DHH, Report No. 182, CMHQ: "The Strategic Role of First Canadian Army, 1942–1944," 23 May 1949, 65–6. On plans for a francophone brigade, see Stacey, *Six Years of War*, 45.

5 Boissonnault, *Royal 22e*, 109–17. General Simonds replaced General Salmon, who died in an accident in late April (Nicholson, *The Canadians in Italy*, 30, 39).

6 DHH, Report No. 135, CMHQ: "Canadian Operations in Sicily, July–August, 1943."

7 Nicholson, *The Canadians in Italy*, 62–74. McAndrew in *Italian Campaign*, 42, notes that the Allies landed nearly 160,000 men, 600 tanks, 1,800 guns, and 14,000 vehicles. One advantage of keeping the Canadian divisions together soon appeared when General Montgomery refused permission to General McNaughton, responsible for the Canadian Army, to visit his troops. Ensuring that public announcements of the landings mentioned Canadian forces proved difficult and met surprising resistance.

8 R22eR War Diary, quoted in Boissonnault, *Royal 22e*, 133; see also 126–8.

9 There were about 40,000 Germans in Sicily on 10 July, rising to 70,000, in addition to the 230,000 Italian troops, who fought with less conviction (Nicholson, *The Canadians in Italy*, 55, 116–42, 195; Boissonnault, *Royal 22e*, 149).

10 LAC, RG 24, Triquet Personnel File, 2nd folder, "Record of Service," 1939–47, RO 4452 and RO 4067. See also Nicholson, *The Canadians in Italy*, 141.

11 G. Simonds, interview by Stursberg, August 1943, in DHH, Report No. 135, CMHQ: "Canadian Operations in Sicily, July–August, 1943," app. C: "The R22eR also deserves special mention for it was their active patrolling and initiative that gained us the first crossing of the Simeto River"; Ross Munro, "Sicily" report to Canada, reprinted in *L'Amicale du 22ième* 5, no. 6 (October 1951): "Les compagnies des capitaines Bernard Guimond, de Québec, et Paul Triquet de Cabano, ont franchi le Simeto, suivies des [autres compagnies]. "

12 DHH, Report No. 135, CMHQ: "Canadian Operations in Sicily, July–August, 1943," 1–3. Montgomery and McNaughton are quoted in Boissonnault, *Royal 22e*, 152–3; Leese is quoted in Nicholson, *The Canadians in Italy*, 179.

13 Michael Boire interview with Willy Fretz, 19 February 1999, Michael Boire collection: Fretz "joined the German 3 Regiment as a reinforcement ... He claims this never made a difference in the way he was accepted in the German airborne. However, the difference in status is made by those who were among the originals."

14 Châtillon, *Carnets de guerre*, 46: "Tous les officiers ont les yeux sur nous, les derniers venus. Certains d'entre eux ont ce demi-sourire condescendant, genre: 'attends mon vieux, tu n'as encore rien vu'; d'autres nous serrent la main, et quelques-uns nous accueillent chaleureusement."

15 Lt Gen Gilles Turcot (ret.), interview, 3 August 2007.

16 Allard, *Memoirs,* 51–3.

17 Nicholson, *The Canadians in Italy,* 86, 181–8. At the Trident Conference in May 1943, Britain continued to focus on Italy, with the United States preferring to prepare for operations in northwest Europe; American acceptance of the focus on Italy was thus conditional on it not harming preparations for what they considered the main objective. Canadians were informed of the plans, and agreed to participate in them, in mid-August (McAndrew, *Italian Campaign,* 60).

18 DHH, Report No. 144, CMHQ: "Canadian Operations in Italy, September 1943"; Nicholson, *The Canadians in Italy,* 165, 196–8, 202, 212, 233, 265–6.

19 DHH, Report No. 161, CMHQ: "Canadian Operations in Italy, October–November 1943." A table lists the Canadian casualties for September (233, including 50 killed), October (683, including 168 killed), and November (279, including 87 killed). See also Nicholson, *The Canadians in Italy,* 241–7.

20 Paul Triquet, "Activités de la Compagnie 'C' du 5 au 15 octobre 1943," 20 October 1943, reproduced in *L'Amicale du 22ième* 3, no. 11 (March 1950).

21 Canadian Postal Museum, Triquet collection, G15-25.11, vol. 2, Paul Triquet to Cécile, 31 October 1943: "La santé est bonne et la moral excellent. Depuis quelques jours nous sommes au repos. Un repos qui est bien mérité car nous avons fait beaucoup de chemin depuis que nous sommes débarqués en ce pays."

22 Nicholson, *The Canadians in Italy,* 267–87. On page 272 he notes that at the end of October 11 the Allies had divisions in Italy and Germany. See also Boissonnault, *Royal 22e,* 175–84; Paul Triquet, "Activités de la Compagnie 'C' du 5 au 15 octobre 1943": "Digne des meilleurs restaurants: un macaroni au fromage, suivi d'un plat de volaille et comme digestif un verre de vin du pays."

23 Boissonnault, *Royal 22e,* 164–73. A German veteran of the Italian campaign remembered, "All my battles were dangerous. But if you survived the first three months, you had good chances of survival because you had learned the skills you needed to smell danger ... and avoid it" (Michael Boire interview with Willy Fretz, 19 February 1999, Michael Boire collection). At the end of October, the Allies had eleven divisions in Italy to the Germans' twenty-one.

24 Delaney, *Hoffmeister,* 87–8.

25 McAndrew, *Italian Campaign,* 42, 83. Craig Cameron, in *Born Lucky,* 76, writes that "Ortona scarred men, both physically and mentally."

26 LAC, War Diary of 1st Canadian Division, reel T-1876, November 1943, appendix. He started by noting the important progress of the Allies, taking about one-third of Italy, but added that the Germans still had Rome. See also Nicholson, *The Canadians in Italy,* 270–4.

27 Delaney, *Hoffmeister*, 77, 89–90. On page 83 he quotes a 1942 War Office pamphlet on tactics, used by Canadians, emphasizing the importance of fire power. See also Nicholson, *The Canadians in Italy*, 290.

28 DHH, Report No. 165, CMHQ: "Operations of 1 Cdn Inf Div and 1 Cdn Armd Bde in Italy, 25 Nov 43–4 Jan 44," 1–5; Nicholson, *The Canadians in Italy*, 288.

29 Quoted in Nicholson, *The Canadians in Italy*, 291. See also Delaney, *Hoffmeister*, 91.

30 Major General C. Vokes, War Diary, January 1944, in DHH, Report No. 129, CMHQ: "Canadian Operations in Italy, September–December, 1943," 40. On German views, see Michael Boire interview with Fritz Illi, 20 February 1999, Michael Boire collection: "Ortona was the battle that marked a new phase of the Fallschirmjaeger's war. We weren't withdrawn to Germany after that fight. We could no longer be allowed to leave because we were so short of soldiers."

31 War Diary, HQ, Eighth Army, 7 December 1943, in DHH, Report No. 165, CMHQ: "Operations of 1 Cdn Inf Div and 1 Cdn Armd Bde in Italy, 25 Nov 43–4 Jan 44," 25–33; Nicholson, *The Canadians in Italy*, 292–4.

32 War Diary, 1st Cdn. Div., 9 December 1943, in Nicholson, *The Canadians in Italy*, 303.

33 Zuehlke, *Ortona*, 188: On 12 December Montgomery sent an officer to ask why Vokes was moving so slowly. Vokes was still relying on intelligence reports that the Germans would retreat. "The entire enterprise at the Gully was a departure from the Eighth Army manner of doing business – mostly due to haste. Montgomery harried Allfrey; Allfrey harried Vokes" (Delaney, *Hoffmeister*, 98–102). However, Allfrey does seem to have been concerned with the haste and advised Vokes to take a pause for better planning in mid-December. See Nicholson, *The Canadians in Italy*, 306–7; McAndrew, *Italian Campaign*, 76.

34 LAC, War Diary of 1st Canadian Division, reel T-1876, December 1943; Charles Comfort, *Artist at War*, 82.

35 5 Corps Summary of 13 December 1943 in DHH, Report No. 165, CMHQ: "Operations of 1 Cdn Inf Div and 1 Cdn Armd Bde in Italy, 25 Nov 43–4 Jan 44," 65; Nicholson, *The Canadians in Italy*, 290, 310.

36 Zuehlke, *Ortona*, 197–201; McAndrew, *Italian Campaign*, 75.

37 Châtillon, *Carnets de guerre*, 100: On 12 December, "le padre Gratton obtient la permission de réunir le régiment dans un grand champ. Il monte sur une boîte de bois … 'par l'autorisation qui m'a été conférée, je vous donne sans confession l'absolution de tous vos péchés. Agenouillez-vous et faites l'acte de contrition.'"

38 Bernatchez, quoted in Allard, *Memoirs*, 25, 59. See also Boissonnault, *Royal 22e*, 194.

39 *Casa-Berardi*, 4: "Au cours de ses ordres, le commandant avait mentionné qu'il avait choisi 'Triquet' pour attaquer avec l'appui des chars vu mon expérience à travailler avec ceux-ci. Je n'ai pas protesté mais je savais dans mon for intérieur, que mon expérience était surtout théorique pour avoir enseigné les tactiques infanterie-chars à de nombreux officiers et sous-officiers à l'occasion de cours d'entraînement en Angleterre. J'acceptai la tâche; j'aurais enfin l'occasion de prouver que ce que j'avais enseigné en théorie s'appliquait en pratique – de là ma volonté infrangible de réussir." This account was written in 1962 and also published in *L'Amicale du 22ième* 16, no. 10 (April 1962); *La revue de la Citadelle* 1, no. 6, December 1965; and in Chauveau, *Royal 22e*, 47–61.

40 LAC, RG 24, vol. 15238, War Diary of the Royal 22e Régiment, 1–31 December 1943, "Coy Attack on the Ortona Lateral Rd." This is appendix B in the diary. The full strength would have been roughly forty more men, according to "Infantry Instructions," reprinted in Tremblay, *Volontaires* (illustration, 64–5).

41 Triquet in *Casa-Berardi*, 4–5. This account was written in 1962.

42 Major G.D. Mitchell, with Brian Reid and W. Simcock, *RCHA – Right of the Line*, 112; Zuehlke, *Ortona*, 204.

43 Triquet in *Casa-Berardi*, 5–6; See also R22eR archives, Paul Triquet Collection, FPA-43, registration certificate, 30 June 1944 for "trophée de guerre (Casa Berardi)."

44 LAC, RG 24, vol. 15238, War Diary of the Royal 22e Régiment, 1–31 December 1943, "Coy Attack on the Ortona Lateral Rd."

45 Allard, *Memoirs*, 59–60.

46 LAC, RG 24, vol. 15238, War Diary of the Royal 22e Régiment, 1–31 December 1943, "Coy Attack on the Ortona Lateral Rd."

47 DHH, Report No. 165, CMHQ: "Operations of 1 Cdn Inf Div and 1 Cdn Armd Bde in Italy, 25 Nov 43–4 Jan 44," 68–9.

48 *Casa-Berardi*, 6–7: "Je suis heureux de me rappeler que les Allemands et les Canadiens, par humanité, cessèrent leurs tirs meurtriers pour permettre à cette pauvre femme et à ses gosses de sortir vivants de cet enfer ... Nous sommes encerclés, l'ennemi est en avant, en arrière et sur nos flancs – l'endroit encore le plus sûr, c'est l'objectif." On events, see LAC, RG 24, vol. 15238, War Diary of the Royal 22e Régiment, 1–31 December 1943, "Coy Attack on the Ortona Lateral Rd."; Nicholson, *The Canadians in Italy*, 311.

49 Corporal E. Bluteau, "Parmi mes souvenirs," *L'Amicale du 22e* 3, no. 7 (November 1964): 20: "Notre artillerie martèle sans arrêt les positions allemandes; l'ennemi n'a pas l'air d'aimer ça. Si nous sortons de cette impasse nous le devrons en grande partie à notre artillerie." See also *Casa-Berardi*, 6–7. On 11 December the war diary of the 3rd Field Regiment recorded that with the amazing total

of 2,880 rounds landing on a target, "thank God I'm not working for Adolph!" (G.W.L. Nicholson, *The Gunners of Canada*, 168).

50 Mitchell, *RCHA – Right of the Line*, 112. See also CWM archives, Oral History Project, Interview 31D1 with George (Duff) Mitchell, by Quiller Graham, 28 November 2000, 12–15.

51 Zuehlke, *Ortona*, 374.

52 LAC, RG 24, vol. 15238, War Diary of the Royal 22e Régiment, 1–31 December 1943, "Coy Attack on the Ortona Lateral Rd."

53 *Casa-Berardi*, 7; Lex Schragg, *History of the Ontario Regiment, 1866–1951*, 165.

54 Châtillon, *Carnets de guerre*, 107: "Je prends mes jumelles et observe. Quel spectacle! Côté gauche de la Casa des Allemands se replient, se cachent derrière des arbres, d'autres tirent en reculant. Coups de carabines, de mitrailleuses. Des Allemands tombent, d'autres culbutent et se cachent derrière une meule de foin, plusieurs fuient vers la cour arrière du bâtiment. Puis je vois de nos soldats qui avancent protégés par deux tanks." He adds, "Quelques-uns de nos soldats filent dans la cour arrière pour encercler la maison. On cesse de tirer. C'est la prise de la Casa Berardi par le 22e!"

55 LAC, RG 24, vol. 15238, War Diary of the Royal 22e Régiment, 1–31 December 1943, "Coy Attack on the Ortona Lateral Rd."

56 DHH, Report No. 165, CMHQ: "Operations of 1 Cdn Inf Div and 1 Cdn Armd Bde in Italy, 25 Nov 43–4 Jan 44," 70–1.

57 *Casa-Berardi*, 8. There were five Bren guns and five Thompsons. Lt Gen Henri Tellier suggests that of those not arriving at the house, in addition to those killed, wounded, or captured, some men may have been stragglers, soldiers who "having gone to ground (quite properly and usually as a result of enemy fire) did not get up and go forward when the time came to do so" (quoted in J.L. Granatstein, *Canada's Army*, 237).

58 DHH, Report No. 165, CMHQ: "Operations of 1 Cdn Inf Div and 1 Cdn Armd Bde in Italy, 25 Nov 43–4 Jan 44," 69–70. For Smith quote, see Mitchell, *RCHA – Right of the Line*, 113; on the orderly, see *Casa-Berardi*, 11.

59 Nicholson, *The Canadians in Italy*, 312; Châtillon, *Carnets de guerre*, 103–10.

60 *Casa-Berardi*, 8–10, quotes Triquet: "Il me fallait, pour rester debout, m'appuyer sur un char sinon je risquais de tomber endormi ... La réponse du groupe fut la bonne voix du Major Ovila Garceau qui me dit 'Ne t'en fais pas Paul, on vient t'aider.' Je ne crois pas que jamais dans la vie je ne ressentirai une émotion aussi vive que celle que j'ai éprouvée en entendant dans la nuit la voix de mon meilleur ami qui, avec sa compagnie, apportait du renfort à notre petit groupe épuisé."

61 DHH, Report No. 165, CMHQ: "Operations of 1 Cdn Inf Div and 1 Cdn Armd Bde in Italy, 25 Nov 43–4 Jan 44," 70–5; Nicholson, *The Canadians in Italy*, 313.

62 DHH, Report No. 165, 70–5; Châtillon, *Carnets de guerre*, 110–15; Mitchell, *RCHA – Right of the Line*, 114.

63 DHH, Report No. 165, 70–5: "Strengths were reported: 'D' Coy, 27; 'B' Coy, 28; 'A' and 'C' Coys [24]." On Gibson and Vokes, see Nicholson, *The Canadians in Italy*, 315.

64 Triquet in *Casa-Berardi*, 9–11: "Toute la journée du 15, les Allemands ne cessèrent de nous bombarder ... La tension et la fatique étaient grandes et afin de maintenir le moral, après chaque bombardement intensif, je faisais l'appel des noms des hommes qui étaient encore avec la Compagnie C ... [plus tard il ne me restait] plus un homme de mon quartier général de compagnie et je passai le reste de la journée à sauter d'un trou à l'autre en me déplaçant par bonds. Mon départ d'un trou était toujours suivi d'une rafale de mitrailleuses ennemies mais comme j'avais toujours atteint l'autre tranchée, je disais, pour distraire mes hommes: 'ils ne savent pas tirer.' Ce mouvement continuel de ma part était très important pour les hommes et encore plus pour moi; dans l'état d'âme où je me trouvais, voyant tous ces morts qui jonchaient mon secteur et que nous ne pouvions inhumer, j'avais besoin, pour tenir le coup, de pouvoir parler aux quelques survivants qui restaient."

65 "Their Springtime of Life: The Italian Campaign," CBC documentary with Triquet and Allard interviews, 5 September 1972, video clip at CBC archives at www.archives. cbc.ca.

66 Allard, *Memoirs,* 72.

67 DHH, Report No. 165, CMHQ: "Operations of 1 Cdn Inf Div and 1 Cdn Armd Bde in Italy, 25 Nov 43–4 Jan 44," 72–4; Allard, *Memoirs,* 53, 60; Nicholson, *The Canadians in Italy,* 315.

68 Triquet in *Casa-Berardi*, 12–13: "L'arrivée de ces renforts eut un effet salutaire sur le moral du régiment; la confiance de tous grandit en même temps que la conviction qu'il serait possible de contenir l'ennemi jusqu'à l'entrée en action d'autres unités de la division. Tous ceux qui ont vécu cette nuit ne pourront jamais l'oublier; les liens de camaraderie, l'esprit d'entraide et de solidarité étaient ressentis par tous et chacun de nous."

69 Latour quoted in Maurice Desjardins, "Un médecin militaire intrépide," *L'Amicale du 22e* 5, no. 14 (March 1952): 20–2: "Il avait la barbe longue, l'air fatigué mais le sourire aux lèvres ... ses yeux pétillaient, 'ils n'auront pas la peau d'un vieux soldat,' dit il, avalant d'un seul trait son verre de rhum." When starting out, Triquet told Allard: "On va les avoir les Boches" (Allard, *Memoirs,* 59–60).

70 DHH, Report No. 165, CMHQ: "Operations of 1 Cdn Inf Div and 1 Cdn Armd Bde in Italy, 25 Nov 43–4 Jan 44," 73–4: "Un grand sang froid demeura dans la

22ième; Tenir ou Mourir. Tel était le mot d'ordre. Le vieil esprit de Vimy et de Courcelette avait soufflé sur le 22ième."

71 Triquet in *Casa-Berardi*, 11–12: "Il me dit d'un air résolu: 'Ne vous inquiétez pas, mon Capitaine, ils ne passeront pas ici.'"

72 Ibid., 14: "Chaque officier et soldat du Royal 22e Régiment était peiné de voir partir ce commandant qui avait tant fait pour notre bataillon; c'est lui qui nous avait entraînés, en Écosse, qui nous avait dirigés lors de l'invasion de la Sicile et qui nous avait commandés sans arrêt depuis ce jour-là jusqu'à Casa Berardi. Le major Allard, son successeur, était déjà très estimé au régiment et dès son arrivée, on réalisa que, encore une fois, nous serions entre de très bonnes mains." See also Allard, *Memoirs,* 60–1; Châtillon, *Carnets de guerre*, 116.

73 Allard, *Memoirs,* 63. On page 61 Allard describes where he positioned each company. Triquet in *Casa-Berardi*, 15, recalls: "Par maladresse, un coup partit et je faillis blesser mon bon ami le Capitaine Bernard Guimond qui se trouvait à mes côtés ... le Major Allard, sur un ton paternel, me dit que j'étais trop fatigué et que je devais dormir un peu."

74 5 Corps Intelligence Summary, 17 December 1943, in DHH, Report No. 165, CMHQ: "Operations of 1 Cdn Inf Div and 1 Cdn Armd Bde in Italy, 25 Nov 43–4 Jan 44," 75. On artillery, see Nicholson, *Gunners of Canada*, 167–8; Mitchell, *RCHA,* 110.

75 Nicholson, *The Canadians in Italy,* 315, 318.

76 Triquet, *Casa-Berardi*, 16: "Le 20 décembre, les morts du RCR furent également enterrés non loin des soldats du 22e; canadiens-français et anglais dorment là, côte à côte, témoins des combats furieux et héroïques qui se sont livrés en ces lieux." On events, see Nicholson, *The Canadians in Italy,* 320; Zuehlke, *Ortona*, 224–47.

77 Hoffmeister quoted in Delaney, *Hoffmeister*, 104. On the debate about bypassing, see 100–2. See also McAndrew, *Italian Campaign,* 84.

78 Allfrey Diary, quoted in McAndrew, *Italian Campaign,* 83. See also Delaney, *Hoffmeister*, 105.

79 LAC, RG 24, reel T-11136, War Diary, 3 CI Bde, January 1944, Brigadier Gibson, "Report on Bde Training, 5 Jan–8 Feb 1944," appendix 1.

80 DHH, Report No. 129, CMHQ: "Canadian Operations in Italy, September–December 1943: Preliminary Report," appendix A: The highest number of casualties of the nine was 253 among the West Novas. The lowest was 129 of the 48th Highlanders. The total for all ten battalions, including the MG Bn, was 1,829.

81 Châtillon, *Carnets de guerre,* 123.

82 LAC, RG 24, vol. 15238, War Diary of the Royal 22e Régiment, 1–31 December 1943, "Coy Attack on the Ortona Lateral Rd."

83 Quotes, with other similar remarks, in Nicholson, *The Canadians in Italy,* 313; also Boissonnault, *Royal 22e,* 213–14; Zuehlke, *Ortona,* 211–12.

84 Michael Boire, interview with Fritz Illi, 20 February 1999. Also from collection of Michael Boire, diary of Carl Bayerlein, First German Airborne Division, 26 December 1943: "We could delay the enemy advance but we were not able to stop him."

85 Nicholson, *The Canadians in Italy,* 314. A total of 20 VCs were awarded during the Italian campaign (C.E. Lucas Phillips, *Victoria Cross Battles of the Second World War,* 9).

86 Major C. Simard, "Le R22eR en Sicile et en Italie," *L'Amicale du 22e* 1, no. 2 (June 1947): 15: It was at Casa Berardi "que la tenue et vaillance de la compagnie C valurent la Croix Victoria à son commandant, le Capt. Triquet." See also Boissonnault, *Royal 22e,* 211–13; DHH, Report No. 165, CMHQ, "Operations of 1 Cdn Inf Div and 1 Cdn Armd Bde in Italy, 25 Nov 43–4 Jan 44," 70–1. The reference to Smith is in McAndrew, *Italian Campaign,* 75.

87 "Their Springtime of Life: The Italian Campaign," CBC documentary with Triquet and Allard interviews, 5 September 1972, video clip at CBC archives at www.archives.cbc.ca. Also Fort Ingall Archives, Fonds Paul Triquet, File "Letters," Adjt Fernand Trépanier to A. Imbault (of the Historical Society), 3 September 1993, notes that he served in Triquet's company that day and his leader inspired all.

88 Major B. Guimond, "Casa Berardi," *L'Amicale du 22e* 1, no. 8 (December 1947): "Un courage à toute épreuve ... il est l'exemple parfait du chef et du soldat accompli."

89 Armand Gagnon, interview, 8 August 2007; André Courtemanche, interview, 8 August 2007; "Canadians in Italy Proud of Victoria Cross Winner," *Hamilton Spectator,* 7 March 1944, 1.

90 Gregory Clark, *Toronto Daily Star,* "'I'm Proud to Don Battledress,' King tells V.C.," 27 March 1944.

Chapter Three

1 Campbell, *The Hero,* 30, 109: "The standard path of the mythological adventure of the hero [monomyth] is a magnification of the formula represented in the rites of passage" (separation, initiation, return).

2 Simonds, commander of 1st Canadian Division, in his guidelines for awards issued to commanding officers, 25 October 1943.

3 On politics in strategy, see Nicholson *The Canadians in Italy,* 20: "The considerations which brought about this substitution [adding Canadians in Italy] were not exclusively military. In Canada towards the end of 1942 public opin-

ion … was becoming increasingly vocal through the press and on the rostrum in exerting pressure upon the Government to get its forces into action as soon as possible."

4 John D. Clarke, *Gallantry Medals and Decorations of the World*, 11.

5 M.J. Crook, *The Evolution of the Victoria Cross*, 5–9; C.E. Lucas Phillips, *Victoria Cross Battles of the Second World War*, 6.

6 Phillips, *Victoria Cross Battles,* 2: The queen "was not animated by any concept of boosting morale or stimulating her sailors and soldiers to higher endeavor. A professional admiral or general might have thought in such terms, but not the Queen. As sovereign of a vast empire, she felt a deep sense of personal gratitude to those who were brave in her cause."

7 Crook, *The Evolution,* 16–18; Phillips, *Victoria Cross Battles,* 3.

8 Crook, *The Evolution.* The RAF awards committee in April 1941, considering a case, noted that "the grant of a high award would enhance the morale of those engaged in anti-submarine warfare" (Halliday, *Valour Reconsidered,* 32).

9 Lord Roberts quoted in Halliday, *Valour Reconsidered,* 32.

10 Brereton Greenhous, *The Making of Billy Bishop*, 12. Halliday, *Valour Reconsidered,* 47, adds that both Robinson and fellow Zepplin killer Reginald Warneford were "timely heroes whose Victoria Crosses were awarded in record time from deed to gazetting – five and three days respectively."

11 Greenhous, *Billy Bishop,* 13, 205; Halliday, *Valour Reconsidered,* 150.

12 Field Marshal B.L. Montgomery, quoted in Phillips, *Victoria Cross Battles,* 6.

13 DND, *Canadian Honours and Awards Bestowed upon Members of the Canadian Forces*, 1: "Gradually Canada began to create its own awards and the turning point was the Order of Canada in 1967. The system started to expand in 1972." See also Christopher McCreery, *The Canadian Honours System*; F.J. Blatherwick, *Canadian Orders, Decorations and Medals.*

14 LAC, MG 27 III B11, Ralston Papers, vol. 49, "Honours and Awards," 8 December 1940, King to Ralston, replying to Ralston letter of 6 December.

15 DHH, Report No. 112, CMHQ: "Policy with Respect to Honours and Awards, Canadian Army Overseas, 1939–44," paras. 8 and 30.

16 Ibid., para. 28.

17 LAC, RG 24, 20,152, "Honours and Awards – General," news clippings, 1940s and 1950s; DHH, Report No. 112, CMHQ, paras. 40–1.

18 DHH, Report No. 112, CMHQ, para. 52: "French-speaking recipients appear to be as follows: Of 3 CB's nil, of 3 CBE's nil, of 12 OBE's 1, of 28 NBE's 3, of 23 BEM's 4, of 6 RRC's nil."

19 Serge Bernier, "Participation des Canadiens français aux combats, 15–24; Stacey, *Arms, Men and Governments,* 422, quotes a report of 1 March 1944 that

estimates that in 1944 19.5 per cent of the army and 14 per cent of its officers were French-Canadian.

20 DHH, Report No. 112, CMHQ, para. 58.

21 DHH, 96/47, file 25: Canada Medal. PC 8160 of 22 October 1943, noted that Prime Minister King had submitted the proposal to King George VI on 18 August 1943 for a "Canadian Volunteer Service Medal," and details were provided in appendix A.

22 General C. Allfrey quoted in Strome Galloway, *The General Who Never Was*, 192.

23 Halliday, *Valour Reconsidered*, 42. He notes that anti-submarine actions, and survivors, did not receive many naval VCs during this period (45).

24 DHH, Report No. 112, CMHQ, paras. 89–92. Awards were announced in the *London Gazette* of 2 October 1942; those to the Canadian Army appeared in a separate list under the heading "Department of National Defence, Ottawa."

25 Halliday, *Valour Reconsidered*, 79–80, writes that "one can guess that another consideration would be that matters would appear unseemly if a VC went to one of 800 British Commandos with no comparable award to any of the nearly 5,000 Canadian soldiers involved."

26 Ibid., 16.

27 In World War II 351 DSOs were awarded to Canadians – seventeen bars and two double bars (to Triquet's friends J.V. Allard and Bert Hoffmeister; see John Blatherwick, *Canadian Army: Honours, Decorations, Medals, 1902–1968*, 24–30). David Riddle and D. Mitchell in *The Distinguished Service Order to the Canadian Expeditionary Force*, 126, write that 841 DSOs were given to Canadians from 1915 to 1920, as compared to seventy VCs.

28 R22eR archives, Jean Allard Collection, 172/17/1/67, Army Public Relations bulletin, 11 April 1944, for actions on 30 December 1943 when he "personally directed an attack by his unit which secured a dominating spur vital to any further advance."

29 Halliday, *Valour Reconsidered*, 62: "Lance Corporal Gagnon's case is striking, given that no recognition whatsoever was accorded him."

30 CP, "Quebec Officer Wins V.C. at Moro River," *Globe and Mail*, 7 March 1944; CP, "Canadians in Italy Proud of Victoria Cross Winner," *Hamilton Spectator*, 7 March 1944.

31 The recommendation for an award to David Currie was increased to a VC at the divisional level by Major General H.W. Foster in August 1944 (Donald E. Graves, *Century of Service*, 291). Halliday in *Valour Reconsidered*, 9, notes that upgrading (and downgrading) was constant during World War I, at times to maintain morale.

32 Guidelines of Major General Guy Simonds to all commanders and commanding officers of 1st Canadian Division on 25 October 1943, in LAC, RG 24, vol. 10917, "Honours and Awards"; also Halliday, *Valour Reconsidered,* appendix C.

33 LAC, RG 24, vol. 12738, file 21, H.H. Smith to Officer Commanding R22eR, 22 December 1943.

34 Ibid., "Statement by Lance Corporal Comeau," 20 January 1944, doc. 59.

35 Ibid., doc. 60

36 Ibid., recommendations/Triquet, folio, 53–100, Gibson report, doc. 62.

37 DHH, 713.065 (D2), "Honours and Awards, 1939–45."

38 LAC, RG 24, vol. 12738, file 21/recommendations/Triquet, folio 53–100: army form W.3121 recommending Triquet for a VC and describing his action.

39 Ibid., Major A.G. Robertson for C-in-C, to the Under-Secretary of State, War Office, 11 February 1944.

40 Ibid., doc. 65, Montague to Letson, 23 February 1944.

41 Ibid., doc. 70, Letson to Montague, 24 February 1944. See also doc. 72, Frederic Hudd of Canada House to Sir Eric Machtig in the Dominions Office; he added that "the ordinary channel for such recommendations would be through CMHQ in London to the Dept of National Defence in Ottawa for consideration and thence for submission to His Majesty through Governor-General, whereas in this case submission has been made through the War Office." See also doc. 68, Lt Col Fleury, CMHQ, to Ritchie, Canada House London, 28 February 1944.

42 Halliday, *Valour Reconsidered,* 34. He suggests that the chances of death for VC recipients after 1940 was 85 per cent or greater (1).

43 LAC, RG 24, vol. 12737, file 21/policy 2, Montague to Letson, 27 March 1944, discussed George Cross standards with Sir Robert Knox, a British authority. The George Cross was instituted in 1940 by King George and recognized very brave acts not in the face of the enemy and by civilians; it became the second highest Commonwealth award for bravery and was awarded to nine Canadians during the war (Swettenham, *Valiant Men,* xii). Halliday in *Valour Reconsidered,* 26, notes that previous precedents had discouraged VCs for saving others, unless such actions helped the success of the operation.

44 Halliday, *Valour Reconsidered,* 24–5.

45 Phillips, *Victoria Cross Battles,* 6.

46 Halliday, *Valour Reconsidered,* 36.

47 Air Chief Marshal Sholto Douglas, Air Officer Commanding, Coastal Command to the Air Ministry, 4 July 1944, quoted in Halliday, *Valour Reconsidered,* 92–3. Halliday also notes (162) that Smokey Smith "was chosen" to represent the contribution of his regiment. That individuals were often selected to honour

their units is also suggested by the Canadian policy on foreign awards, which refused in several cases that other countries honour regiments, but did allow individuals to receive such honours; see LAC, RG 24, vol. 12732, file "Foreign Awards Policy," Lister to Murchie, November 1945. The French government offered to honour the Régiment de la Chaudière with the Croix de Guerre, but the Canadian foreign awards policy did not allow distinguishing units so General Simonds informed that the request, like previous French requests, should be declined.

48 For examples of some inquiries and the procedure involved, see Phillips, *Victoria Cross Battles,* 204–41.

49 Nicholson *The Canadians in Italy,* 310, 314. DHH, Report No. 112, CMHQ: "Policy with Respect to Honours and Awards, Canadian Army Overseas, 1939–44," paras. 96–101, lists honours and awards for the Italian campaign.

50 LAC, RG 24, vol. 12737, file 21, Policy/2, E.L.M. Burns (Lt Gen–Cmd 1 Cdn Corps) to Minister of National Defence, 28 September 1944. E.L.M. Burns, Lt Gen commanding 1 Cdn Corps, told Ralston that the system of granting awards in the Italian theatre was unsatisfactory. The number of allotted immediate and periodic awards was limited to one per 250 over four months, meaning that thirty-four good ones were not considered. He recommended greater flexibility.

51 LAC, RG 24, vol. 12737, file 21/policy 2, General Wemyss to Montague, 14 October 1944.

52 Gregory Clark, *Toronto Daily Star,* "'I'm Proud to Don Battledress,' King tells V.C.," 27 March 1944. See also G. Vanier in Speaight, *Vanier,* 283.

53 *Canada Gazette* no. 8, vol. 78, 6 March; *London Gazette* no. 36408 of 6 March.

54 *London Gazette,* 6 March 1944; *Canada Gazette,* 11 March 1944.

55 LAC, RG 24, vol. 12738, file 21/recommendations/Triquet, folio 53–100: doc. 69, 26 February 1944.

56 LAC, RG 24, vol. 12737, file 21/policy 2, Lt Gen H.D.G. Crerar, GOC 1 Cdn Corps, to OIC, Canadian Section GHQ, 15 February 1944.

57 LAC, RG 24, vol. 12734, file 21/Gen/6, Defensor to Canmilit, 2 March 1944. LAC, RG 24, vol. 12738, file 21/recommendations/Triquet, folio 53-100: doc. 75, War Office to GOC, First Cdn Army, 2 March 1944.

58 LAC, C-10106-1967-0032/143680, Triquet recording of 27 March 1944 with Marcel Ouimet.

59 George Powell, "Funny How the Word Arrived," *Legion Magazine,* March/April 1998, 34–5. Powell, the reporter for the army newspaper the *Maple Leaf,* arrived to interview Triquet and began, "May I extend congratulations on your

prestigious award, sir? All of Canada basks in reflected pride" (CP, *Hamilton Spectator*, "Canadians in Italy Proud of Victoria Cross Winner," 7 March 1944).

60 Ralph Allen, *Globe and Mail*, "Seems VC Hero on First Day's Leave Can Do Anything but Buy New Shirt," 28 March 1944.

61 LAC, RG 24, vol. 12738, file 21/recommendations/Triquet, folio 53-100: doc. 74, War Office to Senior Military Officer, CMHQ, 1 March 1944; doc. 71, Montague to Letson, 1 March 1944; doc. 83, CMHQ to Flambo, 4 March 1944.

62 LAC, RG 24, vol. 20204, file "PR-Press Censorship," Minister of National War Services, "Statements by Minister on Military Matters," 9 September 1942. Also included in file are letters between Malcolm MacDonald and N.A. Robertson in November 1942.

63 LAC, RG 24, vol. 12738, file 21/recommendations/Triquet, folio 53-100: doc. 89, Defensor to Canmilitary, 7 March 1944; doc. 95, Montague at Canmilitary to Defensor, 10 March 1944.

Chapter Four

1 R22eR archives, Paul Triquet Collection, FPA-43, Allard to Triquet, 28 March 1944: "Paul tu as offert généreusement ta vie en service de ta patrie et cette même patrie l'a prise, elle ne t'appartient plus."

2 H. Blair Neatby, *William Lyon Mackenzie King*, vol. 3, 14. William Robert Young in his Ph.D. thesis, "Making the Truth Graphic," 7, writes that "getting out war news to Canadians agitated the Prime Minister."

3 MacFarlane, *Ernest Lapointe*. Some of the issues included the question of when and how to confront the nationalists in Quebec between 1937 and 1941 over issues involving treatment of suspected communists, participation in the war, relations with Vichy France, and above all, conscription. According to journalist Grant Dexter in February 1942, "King felt absolutely sure that the plebiscite would carry" (190).

4 MacFarlane, "Quebec and Conscription," 26–31. In cabinet, Minister of Defence Ralston sought more men for the Army, while Minister of Munitions and Supply C.D. Howe preferred more men for industry.

5 LAC, RG 24, vol. 20204, file "PR-RCN-information," report "Naval Information, 1940–1964," 1–2: "Naval Information had its beginnings in mid-1940, when it became evident there was a requirement for specialized personnel to deal with requests and inquiries from the press, and to gather, produce and disseminate informational material for the press." Lt John Farrow headed this group. William H. Dumsday, director of Public Relations, described in January

1963 three functions of public relations: to provide quick and accurate information to the press and public; to gather, produce, and disseminate interesting info; and to provide community relations programs (LAC, RG 24, vol. 20204, file "PR Press interviews – 1963").

6 LAC, RG 24, vol. 20203, file "PR Background," speech by Squadron Leader J.D. Harvey, "An Appreciation of RCAF Public Relations," 1958: "The RCAF entered the public relations field in the hectic days of the Second World War ... It should be understood by everyone that the RCAF must have public support to exist. It must have full public support if it wishes to succeed in its mission. Only public relations can muster that support." A/C L.E. Wray affirmed, "as public relations goes so goes recruiting" (LAC, RG 24, vol. 20204, file "PR Conference, 1952"). In the same file, W.M. Lee on 16 October 1958 described public support as vital to provide funding, attract recruits, and assure civilians they were efficiently protected.

7 LAC, RG 24, vol. 20203, file "Glassco Commission on Public Relations, 1962," Extract from Report on Public Information Services, 24 May 1962. The total numbers involved in public relations work (190) were: RCN, 25, including 14 officers and 11 civilians; RCAF, 76, including 31 officers, 36 other ranks, and 9 civilians; Army, 89, including 22 officers, 31 other ranks, and 36 civilians. James Ferrabec in "Information Services Growing," *North Bay Nugget*, 7 August 1974, suggested that these numbers grew in the following decade as the number of information services groups in the federal government doubled between 1968 and 1974 (LAC, RG 24, vol. 20203, file "PR Background").

8 Keshen, *Saints, Sinners, and Soldiers*, 14–16; Robert Bernier, *Un siècle de propagande*; Jeffrey Keshen, *Propaganda and Censorship during Canada's Great War*; Claude Beauregard, *Guerre et censure au Canada, 1939–1945*; Florent Lefebvre, Elizabeth Armstrong, and R.B. Oglesby, *La Presse canadienne et la Deuxième Guerre mondiale.*

9 Young, "Information Structure and Programs," 8, 12, 17, 36. Walter Thompson was director of Public Information until February 1940 when G.H. Lash replaced him, with Claude Melançon as associate director (Keshen, *Saints, Sinners, and Soldiers*, 14). Keshen adds that by 1942 the BPI had produced 18 million booklets and flyers presenting an optimistic tone with factual information (17).

10 Young, "Information Structure and Programs," 39.

11 Stacey, *Arms, Men and Governments*, 124. The first chair of the WIB was Vining, with vice-chair Phillippe Brais (government leader in Quebec's Legislative Council). It issued King with monthly reports on public opinion and suggested policy recommendations. On the growing budget of the WIB from $787,575

in 1941–42 to $1,473,747 in 1942–43, see the appendix in Young, "Information Structure and Programs," 443–5. See also Owram, *The Government Generation*.

12 DHH, 96/47, file 95, Crerar's citations recommending the MBE (civil) for Maurice Desjardins, Mathew Halton, Lionel Shapiro, Frederick Griffin, Bert Wemp, and Ross Munro, all dated 26 June 1945. See Brennan, *Reporting the Nation's Business*; Young, "Information Structure and Programs," 59, 82.

13 The Associated Press had blown up the importance of capturing Ortona and turned "a limited tactical operation into a long and costly 'prestige' battle" (Nicholson *The Canadians in Italy,* 329). Soon after, Headquarters Allied Armies in Italy instructed public relations officers and censors to ensure "a truer presentation of what has actually taken place ... than has been the case in previous battles" and warned, with Ortona in mind: "DON'T before Rome is captured claim it as a great military objective" (Vokes, quoted in Chris Vokes with J. MacLean, *Vokes: My Story*, 143). Vokes confessed after that he did not like the press being around and did not cooperate with them: "I was leery of the press at all times, I confess now. I wanted to keep them in the picture but out of the frame."

14 Keshen, *Saints, Sinners, and Soldiers*, 17–19.

15 Chapnick, *The Middle Power Project,* 38–9, describes American views. One member of the previous program complained that Ottawa "could not have done worse if it had tried to hide from Quebec that this is our war and tried to conceal from the US that we were doing anything about it" (Young, "Information Structure and Programs," 40). Vining's report of 10 July 1942 was absorbed with Canadian-US relations.

16 Young, "Information Structure and Programs," 51. King appointed Norman A.M. Mackenzie as chairman responsible for policy and John Grierson of the NFB for operational aspects (who was then replaced by Davidson Dunton).

17 Chapnick, *The Middle Power Project,* 41: "The WIB submitted a detailed, confidential report advising the government to promote past and present Canadian achievements more actively at home."

18 Queen's University Archives, Chubby Powers papers, Box 67, file D-1109, report HQS-8841: "French-Canadian Representation in the Army, Progress Report as of 1 December 1943" (others were prepared on 1 April 1943 and 1 December 1943, and the last report was 1 March 1944). Representation included "one associate director, one news editor, five additional French-speaking officers and civilians in Canada and overseas. This personnel prepares press announcements on behalf of the Army in French." See also Stacey, *Arms, Men and Governments,* 420–2; Lefebvre, Armstrong, and Oglesby, *La Presse canadienne.* On

fact sheets, see Keshen, *Saints, Sinners, and Soldiers*, 18; Young, "Information Structure and Programs," 208–9.

19 Young, "Information Structure and Programs," 203: "The BPI's sporadic and ineffective efforts to defuse anti-Quebec sentiments" included one intervention by Director of Public Information G.H. Lash refuting allegations that Quebec had not done its share.

20 "Rowe Attacks $500,000 Outlay for Recruits," *Globe and Mail*, 28 July 1944. Conservative MP Earl Rowe argued that Quebec would accept conscription as Triquet and Father Sabourin, chaplain of Les Fusiliers Mont-Royal at Dieppe, "show what the French-Canadians would have done if given proper leadership in the past 25 years." A *Globe and Mail* editorial, "Heroes to Be Proud Of," 18 December 1944, repeated later that Triquet and Dollard Ménard proved that "if the French-Canadian people had not been for more than 20 years subjected to persistent doses of political miseducation for partisan ends, their contribution to the national war effort would have been as complete as that of any other elements in the population." See also Tremblay, *Volontaires*, 17–18.

21 Stacey, *Arms, Men and Governments*, 424, 590; Tremblay, *Volontaires*, 17–18. The quote on moving French Canada only slightly is in Stacey, *Canada and the Age of Conflict*, vol. 2, 372.

22 Stephen Clarkson and Christina McCall, *Trudeau and Our Times*, 42. See also Max and Monique Nemni, *Young Trudeau*.

23 Serge Durflinger, *Fighting from Home*, 29–34; Béatrice Richard, *La mémoire de Dieppe, radioscopie d'un mythe* and "La mémoire collective de la guerre au Québec: Un espace de résistance politique?," 17–20.

24 Young, "Information Structure and Programs," 33, 198–207. These calls were led by Ernest Lapointe and Claude Melançon. A poll in July 1942 indicated that only 33 per cent of Quebecers believed that Canada would be in the war if the country were not part of the British Empire (Keshen, *Saints, Sinners, and Soldiers*, 18–20).

25 Young, "Information Structure and Programs," 62, 73. Young describes the resignation of Claude Melançon (46) and how Vice-Chair Brais "did not develop into an important voice in decisions" (61). LAC, MG 27 III B11, Ralston Papers, vol. 81, "Public Relations, Directorate of," details pay for each military district including $3,072 for Montreal and Quebec, only one-eighth of a total budget of $24,401.

26 Young, "Information Structure and Programs," 200–14. The poll is in Keshen, *Saints, Sinners, and Soldiers*, 18.

27 Some considerations were discussed during a postwar incident when an officer and two other ranks of the RCN had been recommended for the Queen's Commendation for brave conduct. The three had extinguished a fire in May 1959,

but officials were concerned about "unfavourable publicity on the grounds that the search and rescue organization had failed to make an adequate and expeditious response when the M/S 'Ferngulf' took fire." Thus the awards "might not be treated by the press and public as a recognition of praiseworthy actions of persons but as an endorsement of the actions of the department." They recommended delay. See LAC, RG 24, vol. 20700, file "CSC minutes," Defence Council Minutes of 95th meeting held 31 August 1959 on "Public Relations implications of the award of the Queen's Commendation."

28 "Into Battle," a radio play fifteen minutes in length: "Way back around 1914, just before the First World War, Father Triquet, and his family, left their native Normandy and took ship for Canada" (LAC, C-9352-acc.1984-0164, "Into Battle," broadcast 27 April 1944; text also at LAC, RG 24, vol. 20155, file Honours and Awards /Triquet, written by Gordon Boshell, produced by Brigid Maas). The Témiscouata paper, *Le St. Laurent*, was eager to correct this (Archives, Société d'histoire et de généalogie de Rivière-du-Loup, *Le St. Laurent*: "Paul Triquet V.C. est un gars de chez nous," 16 March 1944, 1). Some papers also identified him as a Montrealer: "VC Is Awarded to Major Paul Triquet, Montreal," *Hamilton Spectator*, 6 March 1944, 1; "Five Minute Summary" prepared for radio broadcasts: LAC, RG 24, vol. 20155, file "Honours and Awards," 6PN 82, 6 March 1944. Triquet's age also caused confusion, as he was still officially on army records as being born in 1908, but he clarified that he was born in 1910.

29 DND Public Affairs, Press Releases PN 143-44, in R22eR archives, Paul Triquet Collection, FPA-43.

30 Claude Triquet, interview, 31 January 2006; Florence Triquet, *La famille Triquet,* 87–91: "J'ai peine à le reconnaître tant son attitude me déconcentre. J'étais accoutumée à le voir plein d'entrain et d'humour et voilà que son regard est indifférent et ses mouvements lents. À mes questions il ne répond que par monosyllabes ou ne répond pas du tout."

31 Florence Triquet, *La famille Triquet,* 80–1: "Une nuée de journalistes s'abattent sur nous. Ils sont partout où ils peuvent trouver des Triquet! Mon père, en vieux militaire, est ravi de la nouvelle; mais ma pauvre mère reste tourmentée au sujet de Bernard ... Ils forcent mes parents à se faire photographier avec un beau sourire. Tous les autres membres de la famille y passent aussi. Ils viennent même à Sainte-Anne-de-Bellevue ... on m'ordonne de me rendre à l'hôpital où se trouve Bernard pour une photographie ensemble. Ce n'est que devant l'appareil que je réalise combien ces gens sont cyniques."

32 Gregory Clark, "Canadians' Artillery Just Blew Nazi Back," *Toronto Daily Star,* 17 January 1944; Archives, Société d'histoire et de généalogie de Rivière-du-Loup, *Le St. Laurent,* "Le Capitaine Paul Triquet se signale en Italie," 27

January 1944, 1, based largely on account by Maurice Desjardins. Gilles Turcot in an interview on 3 August 2007 remembered little focus on Triquet before March 1944. On the regulations for reporting news from the front during the war, see Timothy Balzer, "In Case the Raid Is Unsuccessful."

33 Cpl Yvan Piuze and Lt Cpl Romeo Ducharme, quoted in Foster Barclay, CP, "Gallant Quebec Major Inspired Men at Ortona," *Globe and Mail*, 8 February 1944.

34 *Montreal Daily Star*, 30 March 1944, "Feathers in His Cap," 30 March 1944; *Belleville Intelligencer*, 1 April 1944.

35 Foster Barclay, CP, "Gallant Quebec Major Inspired Men at Ortona," *Globe and Mail*, 8 February 1944. The information was repeated later in Foster Barclay, CP, "VC Winner Almost Lost as Award List Shuffled," *Hamilton Spectator*, 6 March 1944.

36 Ralph Allen, *Globe and Mail*, "Seems VC Hero on First Day's Leave Can Do Anything but Buy New Shirt," 28 March 1944.

37 J.L. Ralston, *CHCD*, 6 March 1944, 1158–9; CP, "Quebec Officer Wins V.C. at Moro River," *Globe and Mail*, 7 March 1944, 1.

38 Gordon Graydon, *CHCD*, 6 March 1944, 1162–3. He claimed that a soldier named William Manley of Brampton had joined the British Army and was awarded the VC in 1941. A William Manley was awarded the VC, but in 1864, and he was born in Dublin in 1831.

39 Jean-François Pouliot, *CHCD*, 9 March 1944, 1305.

40 "It Is in the Hands of Our Young Men," *Vancouver Sun*, 27 April 1944: "There is something satisfactory in the thought that this highest honor the King can bestow upon his Canadian fighting men should have been merited first in this war by an Easterner and a Westerner – one of them a French-speaking Canadian, the other an English-speaking Canadian – each of them typifying one of the two great racial cultures that come together in the making of Canada." Also "The Tanks and the Van Doos," *Toronto Daily Star*, 31 January 1944: Smith asked Triquet four times "'if he was prepared to continue.' Triquet always said 'Yes'." This was one of many stories of cooperation of "gallant men of British and of French descent, and indeed of many other origins."

41 DND Public Affairs, Press Releases PN139-44, 142-44, 143-44, in R22eR archives, Paul Triquet Collection, FPA-43. On the song, see PN 320-44, in LAC, RG 24, Triquet Personnel File, 7th folder: The author was a lady from England whose sources of "inspiration were the words quoted above, shouted by the slim fighting Canadian above the din of battle in the Italian campaign."

42 Lt J.L. McKenna, "Canadian Wins VC," *Maple Leaf* 1, no. 25 (7 March 1944): 1–4. The subtitle was "Others were marvelous: VC winner ready to talk about everyone who took part in the 'show' but himself." On the *Maple Leaf*, see K.

Rose, "Frontlines and Headlines: The 'Maple Leaf' Newspaper and Army Culture during the Second World War," *Canadian Army Journal* 9, no. 3 (winter 2006); "When Heroes Meet," *Maple Leaf* 1, no. 32 (15 March 1944): 1. The US sergeant was Charles Kelly. Copies are available in R22eR archives, Paul Triquet Collection, FPA-43.

43 R22eR archives, Paul Triquet Collection, FPA-43, brochure by Jean-P. Guérin, "Mission à Casa Berardi," Montreal, 10 April 1944, 1.

44 R22eR archives, Paul Triquet Collection, FPA-43: "Comrades in Arms," script for broadcast no. 76, 7 March 1944, by Public Relations Officer Major Dispecker. On the last page the author concludes: "To major Paul Triquet, the Victoria Cross is not a reward in the material sense of the word. It is a symbol. The symbol of a people's gratitude to him for the inspiration that will fire the spirits of other men" (31).

45 Archives, Société d'histoire et de généalogie de Rivière-du-Loup, Maurice Desjardins, in *Le St. Laurent*, "Paul Triquet VC chez le Roi Georges," 30 March 1944.

46 *Ottawa Citizen*, 29 March 1944, excerpt in LAC, RG 24, vol. 20155. See also H.R. Armstrong, "VC Won by Capt. Paul Triquet Is Third for 22nd Regiment," *Toronto Daily Star*, 6 March 1944: "It fought with distinction through the last war."

47 Thomas Green, "We Could Depend on Him," *Winnipeg Tribune*, 11 March 1944: "The VC was awarded to Major Paul Triquet, company commander of the famous French-Canadian regiment, the Royal 22nd Regiment, of Quebec."

48 Aimé-Jules Bizimana, "Les correspondants de guerre Canadiens-Français de 1939 à 1945," 168.

49 Jacques Gouin, *Lettres de guerre d'un Québécois (1942–1945)*, 161. He wrote to his wife on 9 March 1944 about Triquet's VC: "J'espère que nos petits freluquets d'embusqués ne tendront pas dans leurs feuilles de chou, à diminuer (à leur propre valeur) ce geste d'héroïsme. Je les connais ces cerveaux empoisonnés et ignorants pour avoir lu et écouté leurs propos abracadabrants." I thank Yves Tremblay for this reference.

50 Archives, Société d'histoire et de généalogie de Rivière-du-Loup, *Le St. Laurent*, "Héroes du 22e," 17 February 1944, 1: "Cette participation des Canadiens Français dans l'un des plus retentissants succès militaires des Forces canadiennes et britanniques outre-mer a été fort heureusement reconnu de toute la presse au Canada." Two weeks earlier, the newspaper (published weekly) included the account of Gregory Clark, anglophone correspondent, noting it arrived a week after that of Maurice Desjardins published on 27 January. The week before, on 10 February, they published a biography of Triquet highlighting his modesty,

by another correspondent, Foster Barclay: "Un grand major canadien: Paul Triquet, Cabano."

51 Michael Valpy, "The Making of a Myth," *Globe and Mail*, 7 April 2007, F4, refers to the importance of the 1917 battle of Vimy Ridge being "recognized as a Canadian victory in places that mattered to Canadians then, as now – the American and British press."

52 DHH, Allard Fonds, 84/126-oversize book, "Le résultat de la vie au grand air," often full of imagination and initiative: "Ils n'ont pas leurs pareils pour improviser et se tirer des impasses mêmes les plus critiques"; "A son retour à Londres, M. Desjardins fait l'éloge des Canadiens-français" (no source but sent on 10 March by CP wire and probably in *La Presse,* and other papers on 11 March 1944): On being Catholic, it was added that all "puisent dans l'exercice de leurs devoirs religieux le courage et l'inspiration qui leur aident à supporter les dures épreuves de la vie au front ... Dans leurs rangs se trouvent des centaines de héros en puissance n'attendant que l'occasion de prouver leur valeur."

53 Archives, Société d'histoire et de généalogie de Rivière-du-Loup, *Le St. Laurent*, "La famille Triquet," 16 March 1944, 1, reprinted from *La Presse*. The same story, that his wife was "amazed and thrilled" and his father saw a great honour for the Triquets and Cabano, provided by Army PR, was present but less so in the anglophone press. See CP, "Canadians in Italy Proud of Victoria Cross Winner," *Hamilton Spectator*, 7 March 1944, 1.

54 LAC, RG 24, vol. 20155, file "Honours and Awards," copies passed by press censor for UK press, 7 March 1944.

55 Ibid., copy passed by press censor for UK *Daily Herald*, 7 March 1944. Triquet had said in an interview, "I'm not the type that wins medals."

56 Marcel Ouimet, "Le héros Paul Triquet," *La Revue Moderne*, April 1944, 7; Foster Barclay, CP, "Gallant Quebec Major Inspired Men at Ortona," *Globe and Mail,* 8 February 1944; *Le St. Laurent*, "Ils ne passeront pas!," 9 March 1944, 1: "Le mot immortel du maréchal Pétain à Verdun au cours de la dernière Grande Guerre a de nouveau été gravé dans l'airain par un officier canadien-français."

57 LAC, RG 24, Triquet Personnel File, 1st folder, Col W.G. Abel, DDPR, CMHQ, to ADPR, Canadian Section, GHQ, Allied Armies in Italy, 11 April 1944: "I do not consider that we are justified in undertaking all of the program outlined in your letter because of the expense involved and because Major Triquet has been invested and is now in Canada ... Consequently there is no news value in this picture at the present time."

58 LAC, RG 24, Triquet Personnel File, 1st folder, Murchie to Stuart, 15 March 1944, Montague (for Stuart) to Burns, 16 March 1944.

59 Vennat, *Général Dollard Ménard,* 126–36, describes how Ménard spoke out against injustices in the army and anglophone media. In the CWM Archives, the online database "Democracy at War: Canadian Newspapers and the Second World War" contains many samples of how speeches of Ménard and Joseph Armand Sabourin were presented. The *Globe and Mail,* 9 January 1943, reported how Sabourin's praise of British policy was reported in the *London Times*: "Lauds Speech of Sabourin." The *Hamilton Spectator,* 29 October 1942, highlighted Sabourin's calls for recruits: "French Canada Asked to Fight."

60 R22eR archives, Paul Triquet Collection, FPA-43, Paul Trahan to Triquet, 31 March 1944: "Soyez méfiant ... L'on se servira de vous pour faire de la propagande ... Ne faites pas comme le major (Abbé) Sabourin, lors du 5ième emprunt: RIRE DES CANADIENS-FRANÇAIS, pour se donner du poids auprès des autorités militaires." Emphasis in original text.

61 Gregory Clark, "'I'm Proud to Don Battledress,' King tells V.C.," *Toronto Daily Star,* 27 March 1944; Ralph Allen, *Globe and Mail,* "Seems VC Hero on First Day's Leave Can Do Anything but Buy New Shirt," 28 March 1944: Triquet had stood guard over the palace as the regimental sergeant-major of the detachment chosen from the Van Doos in May 1940, and he had been the right-hand marker of the Royal 22nd guard of honour when the king and queen visited Quebec. See also "Triquet Meets the King to Receive VC (March 1944)," audio clip 0:59, CBC archives at www.archives.cbc.ca (also at LAC, C-02609-1968-33). Interview with Triquet after meeting king, with Marcel Ouimet (27 March 1944), audio clip 4:24, CBC archives at www.archives.cbc.ca (also at LAC, C-10106-1967-0032-143680): "I was very sorry to leave Italy without going back to the unit ... I am happy [to be in Canada] but I would like to [return] to Italy ... rejoin the unit."

62 Phillips, *Victoria Cross Battles,* 6.

63 Léonide Ouellette, interview, 4 January 2006; "Biography of Paul Triquet, VC" (1 April 1944), audio clip 14:40, CBC archives at www.archives.cbc.ca (also at LAC, 132875 C-09315).

64 LAC, C-10106-1967-0032/143680, Triquet recording of 27 March 1944 with Marcel Ouimet; also Archives, Société d'histoire et de généalogie de Rivière-du-Loup, Maurice Desjardins, in *Le St. Laurent,* "Paul Triquet VC chez le Roi Georges," 30 March 1944: "En me décernant cette décoration j'ai l'impression que le roi a voulu reconnaître le mérite des Canadiens en général et non pas celui d'un seul individu."

65 "Capt. Triquet Is the 12th Catholic to Win VC," *Universe* (UK), 10 March 1944; also, "Latest VC Won by a Catholic," *Catholic Times* (UK), 10 March 1944; "VC Had a Happy Time in Scotland," *Glasgow Evening Citizen,* 7 March 1944; R22eR archives, Paul Triquet Collection, FPA-43. Triquet's former student

Ernest Côté wrote on 9 March "Il n'y a personne que je connais dont le tempérament était mieux forgé à la bataille et préparé au VC que toi-même." Major General Price wrote on the 14 March that "it was a great delight but not in the least surprising" to hear the news; DHH, Allard Fonds, 84/126-oversize book, "Le Major Triquet, CV revoit ici son premier instructeur [Ovila Gilbert] du 22e" (no source but perhaps *Le Nouvelliste,* 31 March 1944). A BC paper compared Triquet to their VC recipient, Merritt: "Second Canadian V.C.," *Victoria Colonist*, 7 March 1944; Manitoba papers highlighted the role of Smith: "Much of the honour and credit must go to Major H.A. Smith, of Dauphin, and his tank squadron. Thanks to his understanding of how he was to co-operate with the infantry, we were able to take our objective," Triquet said, in "Quebec VC Pays Tribute to Dauphin's 'Snuffy' Smith," *Winnipeg Tribune*, 6 April 1944. See also "Trois héros du Bas St. Laurent, détenteurs de la Croix Victoria," in *Le St. Laurent*, 27 December 1962: in an article featuring the Fusiliers du St-Laurent, it is noted that Triquet spent some time with them.

66 Minutes of Proceedings of the Legislative Council of the Province of Quebec no. 16, for Tuesday, 11 April 1944, quoted in LAC, RG 24, Triquet Personnel File, 7th folder, letter from Major General H.F.G. Letson, Adjutant General, to CMHQ, 18 April 1944; also Ralston to W. Bovey (of Legislative Council), 17 April 1944.

67 Ralph Allen, *Globe and Mail*, "Seems VC Hero," 28 March 1944. That day Triquet managed time to meet Bernatchez for lunch.

68 R22eR archives, Paul Triquet Collection, FPA-43, Leese to Triquet, 8 March 1944. The letter was reproduced in *L'Amicale du 22ième* 3, no. 8 (December 1949), and also in Chauveau, *Royal 22e,* 62. He added, "I want to tell you how very pleased we all are in the 8th Army; and how proud we are that you are serving us. Your magnificent action won the day at a critical time in the battle; when it was essential for the Army plan that your battalion should achieve its objective."

69 DHH, Allard Fonds, 84/126-oversize book, Allfrey to Allard, 7 March 1944. He added "it is always such a joy when VCs are not posthumous. It is a great honour for the Regiment and you must be immensely proud to be commanding."

70 CP, "Canadians in Italy Proud of Victoria Cross Winner," *Hamilton Spectator*, 7 March 1944, 1.

71 LAC, reel T-1877, War Diary, 1st Canadian Division, 6 March 1944.

72 LAC, War Diary, 3CIBde, March 1944, appendix 2.

73 Allard, *Memoirs*, 71. A member of A Company remembers the pride that his company felt when a member of the regiment was awarded the VC (Auguste Côté, interview, 4 January 2006).

74 Vanier to Tremblay, quoted in Speaight, *Vanier,* 283.

75 R22eR archives, Paul Triquet Collection, FPA-43, Bernatchez to Triquet, 7 March 1944: "Je suis naturellement extrêmement heureux de voir que ton dévouement et ta grande bravoure soient ainsi reconnus par le roi ... [J'étais encore commandant et] je sais parfaitement alors comment tu as bien mérité cette haute marque de distinction. Il y a déjà longtemps que tu travailles pour le plus grand bien du régiment et que tu nous fait honneur. Aujourd'hui tu deviens une source de fierté pour le régiment et pour tous les Canadiens français. Demain et toujours tes exploits demeurent un point de mire pour ceux qui te suivront au 22ième ... Paulo, si tu me permets, comme ton ami (et comme petit père que j'étais pour tous mes gars) j'aimerais souligner qu'il serait peut être sage, que tu te ferais grande justice si tu pouvais tout arranger avec ta femme – Il me semble que tu y gagnerais beaucoup, que tu n'en serais que plus heureux – surtout maintenant que tu es devenu une *figure Canadienne française.*"

76 R22eR archives, Paul Triquet Collection, FPA-43, Allard to Triquet, 28 March 1944: "Paul tu as offert généreusement ta vie en service de ta patrie et cette même patrie l'a prise, elle ne t'appartient plus."

77 DHH, Triquet file, "Case History Sheet," Pte Bernard Triquet. On 29 March it was reported that "patient greeted his brother after a normal fashion but had little to say during the visit." See also "Major Triquet, VC, Ortona Hero, Arrives Here after Bumpy Flight," *Montreal Gazette*, 30 March 1944.

78 "Triquet Goes to Valcartier," *Montreal Daily Star*, 31 March 1944: On 30 March he was at Valcartier, 31 March at Spencerwood for lunch with Lt Gov Eugene Fiset, then to the Garnison Club for dinner on 1 April and on 2 April at the Citadelle Chapel mass before going on 3 April to Cabano for ten days.

79 R22eR archives, Paul Triquet Collection, FPA-43, Allard to Triquet, 28 March 1944; Roger Champoux, *La Presse*, "Ovation à Trois-Rivières," 30 March 1944; "Canuck VC Winner Cheered in Quebec," *Toronto Evening Telegram*, 1 April 1944. At a later reception Triquet met with "hundreds of family members of Trois-Rivières' sons overseas": DHH, Allard Fonds, 84/126, file 74, ca. April 1944.

80 R22eR archives, Paul Triquet Collection, FPA-43, Mme V.C. Garceau to Triquet, 3 April 1944, and Triquet to Mme Garceau, 7 April 1944. He added, "Vous pouvez être fière de votre fils car en action il est le meilleur exemple de courage qu'un soldat peut donner. Nous avons souvent travaillé en coopération."

81 R22eR archives, Paul Triquet Collection, FPA-43, Mrs A.D. Smith to Triquet, 31 March 1944, and Triquet to Mrs A.D. Smith, 7 April 1944. He added, "This

award was granted to me due to the close co-operation between 'Snuffy' and his boys and the men of my coy."

82 *Montreal Gazette*, "Maj. Triquet, V.C. Is Feted at Quebec," 31 March 1944.

83 Vennat, *Général Dollard Ménard*; Serge Durflinger, *Fighting from Home*, 43–6.

84 Archives, Société d'histoire et de généalogie de Rivière-du-Loup, *Le St. Laurent*, "Un autre gloire de chez nous," 9 March 1944, 1: "Avec enthousiasme dans toute la province de Québec, et plus particulièrement dans sa place natale à Cabano comme dans toute la région ... [cet honneur pour Triquet] le classe désormais au rang des plus beaux héros de notre histoire." CP, "Home Town Warmly Greets Major Triquet," *Globe and Mail*, 4 April 1944, quotes Cabano's mayor praising Triquet as a "'national hero' whose award had 'honoured Cabano,' the French-Canadians and the whole of Canada."

85 Ralph Allen, *Globe and Mail*, "Seems VC Hero," 28 March 1944.

86 Archives, Société d'histoire et de généalogie de Rivière-du-Loup, *Le St. Laurent*: "Cabano acclame Triquet," 6 April 1944. The paper described Triquet's return to Cabano as having a "joie profonde et d'autant plus sincère qu'elle s'accompagnait d'un sentiment de respect profond et de vénération affectueuses pour son enfant le plus glorieux," adding that the region of Témiscouata was a bit jealous of Cabano but not in a bad humour as "sa renommée rejaillit sur son terroir témiscouatain."

87 Raymond Pelletier, interview, 31 December 2005; Paul Dumont, interview, 31 December 2005; Archives, Société d'histoire et de généalogie de Rivière-du-Loup, *Le St. Laurent*, "Cabano acclame Triquet," 6 April 1944; *Le St. Laurent*, "Rivière-du-Loup a acclamé Triquet," 20 April 1944, describes the reception at Rivière-du-Loup on 14 April: "Malgré un froid presque sibérien ... plus de deux milles personnes ont tenu à se rendre à l'arrivée du train qui ramenait dans notre ville le major Paul Triquet, CV."

88 Claude Triquet, interview, 31 January 2006. Réjean Gagnon (interview, 6 August 2007) was eight in 1944 and joined later. See also Georges Fraser, interview, 31 December 2005; Paul Edgar Dumont, interview, 31 December 2005.

89 DHH, Triquet file, Army Deputy Minister to Mrs Hélène Triquet, 23 March 1944. The letter notes that Hélène Triquet had been informed on 4 January 1944 that her son was "mentally ill" and on 19 February that he had returned from overseas and was at Ste Anne's Hospital. A file in the Canadian Postal Museum, Triquet collection, G15-25.11, vol. 2, Paul Triquet to Father and Family, 31 October 1943, describes Bernard's unusually violent behaviour and his time in military prison, and concludes "Je n'y comprend rien."

90 DHH, Triquet file, "Case History Sheet," Pte Bernard Triquet, 30 March 1944. On 31 March it was reported that "patient has shown a remarkable change in

the past two days. Today he appears mentally alert, correctly oriented and able to carry on a normal conversation ... The rather dramatic clearing of his mental state may be only temporary though it is certainly hopeful."

91 Ibid. On 6 April it was advised that patient should not be released, and on 15 April that the family insisted and had signed responsibility forms. On 17 April in a telephone call the family said all was well and permission was granted to keep him one more week, but on 22nd April his father and sister brought him back, stating "that he had become restless at home." Shock treatment was recommended to begin as soon as the official discharge from the army was completed.

92 Claude Triquet, interview, 31 January 2006.

93 LAC, C-9352-acc.1984-0164, "Into Battle," broadcast 27 April 1944, written by Gordon Boshell, produced by Brigid Maas. Text also at LAC, RG 24, vol. 20155, file Honours and Awards/Triquet.

94 Melba Lent, "Hero's Wife Has Busy Day," *Montreal Daily Star*, 30 March 1944.

95 Florence Triquet, *La famille Triquet,* 82.

Chapter Five

1 R22eR archives, Paul Triquet Collection, FPA-43, Major General T.L. Tremblay to Triquet, 4 November 1944: "Je comprends votre désappointement de ne pas servir directement au Royal 22ième quoique je vous l'avoue franchement, nous tenons à garder la seule Croix Victoria que nous possédions vivante."

2 Keshen, *Saints, Sinners, and Soldiers*, 31–4, describes the organization of ten wartime and one postwar drives that sold $12.5 billion worth of bonds ($550 per capita). Good Friday was on 7 April that year.

3 Sir John Smyth, *Great Stories of the VC*, 127, notes that a common characteristic shared by many VCs was "a loathing of personal publicity." Claude Triquet expressed in an interview on 31 January 2006: "Il n'a pas toujours trouvé ça drôle de se promener de même et de faire la vente avec son nom qui était connu au coton; il ne détestait pas ça mais il y avait des périodes où ça l'a fatiqué c'est certain ... Surtout pendant les périodes quand il se sentait moins bien. Quand quelqu'un est obligé de faire une vie publique, et ça devrait être vrai pour tous les hommes publics, ce n'est pas tout le temps drôle."

4 LAC, RG 24, Triquet Personnel File, 1st folder, medical report, 31 March 1944: "extinction partielle de la voix, fatigue et douleurs à parler."

5 R22eR archives, Paul Triquet Collection, FPA-43, Allard to Triquet, 28 March 1944: "quelques lignes pour te dire comment nous sommes fiers de toi, et comment tes actes sont devenus l'exemple de tous ceux qui sont appelés à combattre.

[Le tour est] pour le bien de tous les Canadiens-Français ... mon seul désir est que tu nous reviennes dans le plus court délai. Permets-moi de te rappeler mes paroles quand je te disais 'Paul tu as offert généreusement ta vie en service de ta patrie et cette même patrie l'a prise, elle ne t'appartient plus,' et aujourd'hui tous tes actes se reflètent sur ton Régiment et les Canadiens-français. Alors rappelle-toi de notre conversation et accepte comme tu l'as toujours fait, le sacrifice qui t'est demandé."

6 *Quebec Chronicle-Telegraph*, 29 March 1944; Vennat, *Général Dollard Ménard*, 142–3.

7 Gregory Clark, "'I'm Proud to Don Battledress,' King tells V.C.," *Toronto Daily Star*, 27 March 1944.

8 CP, "Ortona Valley Beauty Queen Reigns Despite Loud Protests," *Globe and Mail*, 5 May 1944.

9 "Response Disappointing to B.C. 'Go Active' Call," *Globe and Mail*, 24 April 1944: The campaign to raise a volunteer brigade from troops of 6th Division led to 500 draftees, or 3 per cent, going active. "The stirring plea of Major Paul Triquet, the French-Canadian VC, to men of the Le Régiment de Hull, netted exactly 40 volunteers from 700 men," or 6 per cent.

10 "Home Defence Units Urged to Help European Invasion," *Hamilton Spectator*, 22 April 1944.

11 "Response Disappointing to B.C. 'Go Active' Call," *Globe and Mail*, 24 April 1944. See also Roy, *Pearkes*, 212.

12 LAC, RG 24, vol. 2207, file HQ-54-22-84.16, Director of Army Recruiting, 11 August 1944, replying to questions of who should be paying bills associated with Triquet's tour (see letter from Colonel H.M. Wallis, 26 July 1944).

13 LAC, MG 27 III B11, Ralston Papers, vol. 79, "Speeches 1944–July," no date.

14 "Ralston Denies Coercion Used on Conscripts," *Globe and Mail*, 28 April 1944.

15 "Quebec House, 55-4, Votes against Sending Conscripts Overseas," *Globe and Mail*, 27 April 1944.

16 Minutes of Proceedings of the Legislative Council of the Province of Quebec no. 16, for Tuesday, 11 April 1944, quoted in LAC, RG 24, Triquet Personnel File, 7th folder, letter from Major General H.F.G. Letson, Adjutant-General, to CMHQ, 18 April 1944. See also Ralston to W. Bovey (of the Legislative Council), 17 April 1944. The resolution that Ralston and Letson circulated for publication read: "That this House has learned with pride of the magnificent gallantry of Major Paul Triquet and of the award to him by His Majesty of the Victoria Cross and desires to record its admiration of Major Triquet and of all the sons of the this Province now fighting by sea, land and air."

17 "Humiliating That VCs Must Appeal to Men in Uniform," *Toronto Telegram*, 4 April 1944: Minister Ralston had agreed to send troops when needed, and "that need exists now, according to Major Triquet and Major Gen. Pearkes."

18 Triquet, *La famille Triquet*, 84: "J'aurais donné n'importe quoi pour ne pas me trouver sur son chemin."

19 Canadian Postal Museum, Triquet collection, G15-25.11, vol. 2, Paul Triquet to sister Cécile, undated: "Je vois que tu t'occupes toujours de l'instruction. Tache de dégraisser nos petits canadiens. Aujourd'hui plus que jamais nous avons besoin de bons hommes."

20 "Isolationists Fight Call-up While VC Winner Looks On," *Toronto Evening Telegram*, 12 May 1944. Triquet made these comments after journalists sought his reaction to comments of J.S. Roy during a parliamentary debate he witnessed on 12 May in Ottawa.

21 "Home Defence Units Urged to Help European Invasion," *Hamilton Spectator*, 22 April 1944.

22 King Diary, 22 April 1944; "Must Support New Loan, Mr. King Warns Nation," *Globe and Mail*, 24 April 1944.

23 "Put Victory First," *Globe and Mail*, 25 April 1944.

24 "300,000 Watch Loan Parade." *Globe and Mail*, 24 April 1944.

25 Archives, Société d'histoire et de généalogie de Rivière-du-Loup, *Le St. Laurent*, "Honneur au mérite," 27 April 1944: "Tout le peuple canadien-français est fier aujourd'hui de louer hautement la bravoure du grand héros qui vient de recevoir la Croix Victoria, le major Paul Triquet, CV qui nous a si vaillamment défendus à Casa Berardi. Mais tous ceux qui sont partis librement en 1940–41–42 et 1943 pour combattre l'ennemi de nos libertés, tous ceux-là méritent aussi nos louanges ... et notre appui." See also *Le St. Laurent*, "Rivière-du-Loup-Témiscouata à l'honneur," 25 May 1944, 1, for a local message asking people to walk in the footsteps of Triquet and do their part: "Stimulé par l'héroïque exemple sur les champs de bataille d'un fils de la région."

26 "Put Victory First: Triquet and Loan Campaign" (24 April 1944) – audio clip 25:45; CBC archives at www.archives.cbc.ca.

27 Keshen, *Saints, Sinners, and Soldiers*, 31: in 1945 a poll suggested that more Ontarians bought war bonds as an investment (45%) than for patriotism (34%). In Quebec the ratio was 62% to 22%.

28 "Put Victory First," *Globe and Mail*, 25 April 1944.

29 "Power Points to Bond Sales to Services," *Globe and Mail*, 10 May 1944. He also visited Hamilton ("VC Winner Visits Hamilton Units," *Hamilton Spectator*, 9 May 1944).

30 LAC, RG 24, Triquet Personnel File, 7th folder, Manson to Murchie, 8 May 1944: Triquet finished on 11 May after trips to Toronto on 9 May, Brockville on 10 May, and Ottawa on 11 May.

31 Claude Triquet, interview, 31 January 2006: "Si j'avais eu dix cents des bons que j'ai vendus je serais millionnaire."

32 LAC, RG 24, Triquet Personnel File, 7th folder, Murchie for Director of Public Relations (Army) Major G.G. Yates, 8 May 1944.

33 LAC, RG 24, vol. 20155, file "Honours and Awards," DND Public Relations Office, MD no. 4, Press Release, 14 May 1944: "Aux yeux de tous, le major Triquet prit subitement figure de symbole: symbole de réconciliation des hommes de bonne volonté." Details on the Legion of Honour, created in 1802, are presented briefly.

34 LAC, RG 24, Triquet Personnel File, 7th folder, Vanier to Norman Robertson, 11 May 1944: "If you concur, to award the Cross of the Legion of Honour to Major Paul Triquet, V.C. ... In view of short time limit I would appreciate your informing me not later than May 12th."

35 Dumont, *La société québécoise,* 307, 324; Rudin, *Making History,* 172.

36 Jose E. Igartua, *The Other Quiet Revolution*, 13, argues that throughout the 1940s and '50s, French-Canadians, Natives, and Canadians of immigrant origins were seen by English-speaking Canadians as "not quite on a par with Canadians of British origin."

37 Archives, Société d'histoire et de généalogie de Rivière-du-Loup, *Le St. Laurent*: "Triquet décoré de la Légion d'honneur," 18 May 1944, 1: "Avec la Croix Victoria, la plus haute décoration de l'Empire britannique, que lui avait octroyée le roi d'Angleterre ... le major Paul Triquet portera désormais sur sa poitrine une autre décoration qui devra lui être particulièrement chère, puisqu'elle lui vient de son ancienne mère patrie, la France."

38 LAC, RG 24, vol. 20155, file "Honours and Awards," DND Public Relations Office, MD no. 4, Press Release, 14 May 1944: "C'est mon père qui sera content ... c'est un vrai Français lui."

39 LAC, RG 24, vol. 12733, file "French Awards," Vanier letter, 9 November 1945.

40 LAC, RG 24, Triquet Personnel File, 2nd folder, Major Chambers for Colonel R.E.A. Morton, Camp Comd, Camp Borden, to HQ MD no. 2, 23 May 1946, informing that Triquet received the award from the French ambassador to the US but this had not appeared in the CARO. Thus seek "notification of entitlement to wear the medal." The adjutant general, Major General E.G. Weeks, replied on 4 June 1946 that the award "was inadvertently omitted from Routine Orders. The award will now appear in Routine Orders of 17 June 1946. Other

recipients had received permission earlier." LAC, RG 24, Triquet Personnel File, 7th folder.

41 Allard, *Memoirs,* 76–9.

42 "VC Winner's Wife Robbed in Store," *Montreal Star,* 7 June 1944.

43 "Second héroïsme de Triquet," in *Casa-Berardi*, 22–4: There is a rumour that "Triquet est bien ennuyé de voir les organisateurs de l'Emprunt abuser de son nom et de sa personne pour en faire un instrument de propagande commerciale ... On ne saurait donner à notre peuple une leçon plus vivante de courage et de générosité qu'en multipliant les démonstrations triomphales autour de l'un de ses fils qui, à force de bravoure et de savoir-faire, a pu réaliser, avec ses compagnons du même sang, un exploit de très grande envergure. Après avoir admiré les héros de l'Antiquité, pourquoi mettre sous le boisseau la gloire des nôtres? ... une leçon de fierté nationale plus féconde que toutes les propagandes livresque ou verbales, si éloquentes et si poétiques soient-elles ... En supportant avec le même courage le poids d'honneurs sans fin et démonstrations interminables. Si les deux héroïsmes servent à la fois la cause de notre pays et du monde civilisé, pourquoi nous en attrister? ... On peut le regretter tant qu'on voudra, mais la guerre, fléau permis par Dieu, ne se gagne pas sans réels sacrifices. Et le moindre de tous les sacrifices, en temps de guerre, c'est de tolérer qu'on parle autour de soi d'un événement qui intéresse tous les civilisés."

44 John Smyth, *Great Stories of the VC*, 120–2. The two were Capt Arthur Martin Leake (1902, 1914) and Capt Noel Godfrey Chavasse (1916, 1917), whose second VC was awarded posthumously.

45 LAC, RG 24, Triquet Personnel File, 1st folder, Murchie to Stuart, 15 March 1944.

46 Ibid., Montague (for Stuart) to Burns, 16 March 1944.

47 Ralph Allen, *Globe and Mail,* "Seems VC Hero," 28 March 1944.

48 Archives, Société d'histoire et de généalogie de Rivière-du-Loup, Maurice Desjardins, in *Le St. Laurent*, "Paul Triquet VC chez le Roi Georges," 30 March 1944: "Je veux retourner à mon unité, n'importe où. Et s'ils veulent me garder au Canada, je trouverai bien le moyen de revenir."

49 Ralph Allen, *Globe and Mail,* "Seems VC Hero," 28 March 1944.

50 CP, "Home Town Warmly Greets Major Triquet," *Globe and Mail*, 4 April 1944: Triquet "is said to be slated for an important post in Canada when his leave at home is completed. There was no official indication of what the post would be."

51 LAC, RG 24, Triquet Personnel File, 7th folder, notes by Colonel M.G. Carey, 19 April 1944 and Brig R.E.G. Roome, 20 April 1944.

52 LAC, RG 24, vol. 20155, file "Honours and Awards," press release, 14 July 1944.

53 "Major Triquet Back in Italy," *Kingston-Whig Standard*, 1 August 1944.

54 Boissonnault, *Royal 22e*, 272.

55 "King Decorates Canadian Officer [Mahony] for VC Action," *Hamilton Spectator*, 2 August 1944.

56 "Canada Stowaway VC Finally Gets His Wish," *Calgary Herald*, 26 May 1951. See Mahony file, LAC, RG 24, fol. 20156: Mahony later joined 27th Brigade Group to Korea in May 1951, to command one of the infantry battalions: "He's been struggling for years against the 'penalty' that says a VC can't fight again ... [Seven years ago he won the VC ...] those were the greatest 24 hours in Jack Mahony's life. They became the cause of some of his worst frustrations."

57 LAC, RG 24, vol. 12737, file 21, Special Awards/2, Montague to War Office, 3 July 1944; Burns to HQ 21 Army Group, 18 December 1944.

58 R22eR archives, Paul Triquet Collection, FPA-43, Letter from an Italian Girl, "Your Pitou," no date: "Paul I'm talking at you with a familiar voice – the voice of love that wills all the distances, all the differences of country and of customs ... Paul don't forget that you have still something to do, don't forget it. The life is not so sad as you believe." A letter from a friend in Quebec, Ray Garneau, to Triquet, 7 November 1944, suggests that Triquet would be coming home soon to look for civilian work (R22eR archives, Paul Triquet Collection, FPA-43).

59 R22eR archives, Paul Triquet Collection, FPA-43, Triquet to Col J.H. Christie, 19 September 1944. He also sent a letter to General Leese on 5 August 1944.

60 R22eR archives, Paul Triquet Collection, FPA-43, Triquet to "Colo," a name by which Triquet seems to have called both Colonels Bernatchez and Allard but in this context appears to be the former (September 1944): "Mon cher Colo ... Je lis sur le *Maple Leaf* d'aujourd'hui que les Canadiens Français se battent bien sur l'Adriatique. Je suis un peu jaloux de vous tous. Comme j'en ai assez d'être Chef Instructeur à une école où il n'y a pas de candidats, j'envoie une demande pour retourner au bataillon. Je vous envoie ici copie de la lettre que j'ai envoyé à mon Commandant actuel. Si on ne veut pas de moi je désire que l'on me retourne au Canada où je pourrai au moins trouver quelque chose à faire. Je sais très bien que l'on m'a envoyé ici seulement que pour se débarrasser de moi. Je ne trouve pas ça très chic."

61 R22eR archives, Paul Triquet Collection, FPA-43, Major General T.L. Tremblay to Triquet, 4 November 1944; Reply to Triquet's letter of 26 October.

62 R22eR archives, Paul Triquet Collection, FPA-43, Major General T.L. Tremblay to Triquet, 4 November 1944; Reply to Triquet's letter of 26 October: "Vous vous rappelez de mon fils Jacques qui est à Debert depuis quelque temps et est très désappointé de ne pas être rendu plus loin. De plus, il a dû être hospitalisé pour un accident au genou subi à l'entraînement, et, je comprends qu'il

en a pour au-delà d'un mois. Sa principale difficulté est qu'il est loin sur la liste de priorité et vous connaissez son anxiété de rejoindre le 22ième le plus tôt possible. Si à votre bout, vous pouvez faire quelques chose dans ce sens, je sais qu'il vous en serait très reconnaissant."

63 LAC, RG 24, Triquet Personnel File, 1st folder, "Reports – Periodic and Special," for 1–31 October 1944, Colonel J. Christie, 3 November 1944: Triquet: "is doing good job." His lowest marks, CS, were for his language skills, as he was performing mostly in English. Christie recommended that he "remain in present appointment" when francophones were needed and then "be posted to a French Cdn unit or given the appointment as a Liaison Officer with the Free French." His appointment was 2 I/C I Cdn Base Rft Bn., I CBRD.

64 "Triquet to Command New Quebec Regiment," *Vancouver News Herald*, 22 November 1944; "Two Quebec Units to Reinforce Troops Overseas," *Hamilton Spectator*, 22 November 1944. The new battalions would be support battalions from which reinforcements would be drawn as necessary rather than replacing entire units.

65 LAC, MG 26, Louis St-Laurent papers, vol. 1, "Correspondence Diverse – Conscription," many letters, mostly against conscription, 1944 and 1945.

66 LAC, RG 24, vol. 20126, 21 November 1944, "Speech by Major General L.R. LaFlèche, Minister of National War Services, to 2000 French-speaking NRMA Soldiers at Petawawa."

67 LAC, RG 24, vol. 20126, July 1945, DND Public Affairs News Release (HQ-1772-45-22): 12,736 NRMA men went overseas, about two thousand saw action, and fifty-five were killed.

68 Queen's Archives, Grant Dexter papers, vol. 2142, box 3, file 26, Power memo to Dexter, 10 December 1944, 6–8.

69 "French-Canadian Zombies Ordered Back to Quebec," *Hamilton Spectator*, 29 November 1944. Lt Col Paul Garneau was appointed to command the 2nd Battalion of the R22eR.

70 "Canada's 7th VC of This War Has Been Awarded to a Saskatchewan Man," *Saskatoon Star-Phoenix*, 28 November 1944. See Currie file in LAC, RG 24, fol. 20156.

71 LAC, RG 24, vol. 9979, file "Congratulatory Messages to Canadian Formations, AAI and AEF," Smith to Triquet, 23 December 1944; Smith to King, 23 December 1944.

72 LAC, RG 24, vol. 12737, file 21, Special Awards/2, Walford (Defensor) to Montague, 2 December 1944. On 4 December 1944 Montague replied that he agreed (Graves, *Century of Service*, 332).

73 LAC, RG 24, Triquet Personnel File, 1st folder, Brigadier W.G.H. Roaf, Commanding Officer Canadian Sec GHQ 1 Ech to Major General Weeks, CMHQ, 22 December 1944.

74 LAC, RG 24, Triquet Personnel File, 1st folder, Lailey and Booth notes added to Roaf letter of 22 December on 2 January; views of chief of staff also added on same letter.

75 Ibid., Major General E.G. Weeks, I/C Administration, CMHQ to Brigadier W.G.H. Roaf, Commanding Officer Canadian Sec GHQ 1 Ech, 15 Army Gp, CMF, 3 January 1945.

76 Ibid., Colonel F.J. Fleury, CMHQ to Candex, 18 January 1945: "Triquet not selected for reasons outlined" but because he and two others were unacceptable at rank of lieutenant colonel and a "heavy influx of reinfs requires immediate handling as offrs appointed to comd trg bns must be of high caliber." Also, Triquet was the only French-speaking nominee so far.

77 Ibid., CANDEX to CMHQ, 22 January 1945: comments on paper by Col. F.J. Fleury accepts. Approved by Maj Gen E.G. Weeks, CMHQ.

78 Ibid., CANDEX to CMHQ, 22 January 1945.

79 Ibid., Major R. Montrose for Brigadier W.G.H. Roaf, Commanding Officer Cdn Sec GHQ 1 Ech to CMHQ, 9 February 1945.

80 Henri Tellier, interview, 6 September 2006. Gilles Turcot (interview, 3 August 2007) remembers some at headquarters insisting on the importance of keeping Canadian VCs alive.

81 LAC, RG 24, Triquet Personnel File, 1st folder, Major General J.H. Roberts to CMHQ, 27 January 1945. Haldenby to HQ, March 1945, approved the appointment after discussion at length with Colonel Mathieu, deciding that Triquet was efficient at training and "satisfactory" at administration.

82 LAC, RG 24, Triquet Personnel File, 2nd folder, Department of Veterans Affairs file.

83 Boissonnault, *Royal 22e*, 347: On 10 January he visited Allard and his friends in the R22eR. When Allard asked him to say a few words, he congratulated them on their work and said he wished he could stay longer.

84 R22eR archives, Paul Triquet Collection, FPA-43, Letter from an Italian Girl, no date: "To the Triquet's boys ... Be sure boys, Paul does not forget you; he is with you."

85 "Reinforcements Permit Higher Leave Quotas, McNaughton Reports," *Globe and Mail*, 13 March 1945.

86 LAC, RG 24, Triquet Personnel File, 1st folder, "Reports – Periodic and Special" for 6 February–12 March 1945, Colonel Paul Mathieu, 27 March 1945: "This

officer organized 17 Cdn Inf Trg Bn to my complete satisfaction. He is a first class instructor and standard of trg of rfts has improved tremendously under this officer's direction ... His promotion to the acting rank of Lt. Col. has been recommended by me." See also LAC, RG 24, Triquet Personnel File, 1st folder, "Reports – Periodic and Special" for 6 February–12 March 1945, Brigadier K.G. Blackader, T/Comd, Cdn Rft Units, 22 March 1945.

87 Maurice Desjardins, "Triquet Finds No Friction between Volunteers, Draftees," *Montreal Star* and *Globe and Mail*, 19 April 1945. He added later that the performance of NRMA men was "marvelous. We found them well disciplined, with a good knowledge of soldiering and their weapons" (quoted in Dick Ryder, "Triquet Returns on Ship," *Halifax Herald*, 21 June 1945).

88 R22eR archives, Paul Triquet Collection, FPA-43, Letter from Major Placide Labelle, PR Services, to Triquet, 19 April 1945; Letter from Triquet to Comd, 9 CITR, 24 April 1945; Letter from F. Geo. Triquet to Paul Triquet, 4 May 1945: "Que ta bonne étoile te protège et amitiés à ta chère tante de notre part." See also letter from Colonel D.F. Spankie, Canadian Reinforcement Units, to Triquet, 8 May 1945.

89 R22eR archives, Paul Triquet Collection, FPA-43, Letter from Major Léo Gratton, padré, Hutte des Aûmoniers, Valcartier to Triquet, 7 May 1945: "Mon Paul, sois toujours bon Soldat, bon Chrétien, et n'oublie pas que tout le Canada français est fier du héros de Casa Berardi ... Je t'assure, mon cher, que la mentalité des soldats, pour ne mentionner que celle-là, est ici bien différente de celle de nos 'boys' outre-mer. Quelle affaire que la maudite politique dans l'armée ... Oublie ça ... comme on disait chez nous, au Régiment."

90 Henri Bélanger, interview, 4 January 2006; Auguste Côté, interview, 4 January 2006; André Courtemanche, interview, 8 August 2007.

91 Allard, *Memoirs*, 119.

92 R22eR archives, Paul Triquet Collection, FPA-43, Triquet to Comd, 9 CITR, 16 May 1945. He noted that he was a soldier of the Permanent Force with eighteen years of service, thirty-five years old, and physically fit.

93 LAC, RG 24, Triquet Personnel File, 1st folder, Letter from Brigadier E.W. Haldenby, Comd 14 Cdn Inf Trg Bde to HQ Cdn Rft Units, 2 June 1945.

94 LAC, RG 24, Triquet Personnel File, 1st folder, Letter from Brigadier K.G. Blackader, A/Commander Cdn Reinforcement Units, to CMHQ, 4 June 1945: "The most suitable type of emp for Lt. Col. Triquet is in the capacity of CO of a French Cdn Inf Trg Bn. As a result of the present re-org there is now only one such unit within CRU and the appointment of CO is held by another offr. There are vacancies for Lt. Cols. within various Repat Depots, but Lt. Col. Triquet is not in my opinion suitable for that type of emp. It is, therefore, recommended

that as he is surplus to requirements and is desirous of serving in the Far East, that he now be returned to Cda."

95 LAC, RG 24, Triquet Personnel File, 2nd folder, Department of Veterans Affairs file, from 23 June to 22 July 1945.

96 Trent Frayne, "Paratroop Unit Given Tumultuous Welcome during Halifax Parade," *Globe and Mail*, 21 June 1945; Frank Miller, "War Heroes Welcomed by Citizens," *Halifax Herald*, 21 June 1945.

97 Dick Ryder, "Triquet Returns on Ship," *Halifax Herald*, 21 June 1945: "'Aged 35: I'm just within the age limit for the Pacific' he chuckled. [The top priority he says is training men in tactics employed against Japan. That will take six months but Hoffmeister is] 'one of the best' Cdn army leaders."

98 Ibid.

99 LAC, RG 24, Triquet Personnel File, 7th folder, Comments by Brig W.A. Bean, 6 July 1945, on letter from Brigadier E. Blais, DOC, MD no. 5 to CMHQ, 29 June 1945.

Chapter Six

1 Vanier, quoted in Bernier, *Royal 22e*, 439.

2 Morton, *A Military History*, 227; Stacey, *Six Years of War*, 3: "Canada is an unmilitary community. Warlike her people have often been forced to be; military they have never been."

3 *Shorter Oxford English Dictionary*, vol. 1, 1944, 895.

4 Dean F. Oliver, "Awaiting Return: Life in the Canadian Army's Overseas Repatriation Depots, 1945–1946," in Peter Neary and J.L. Granatstein, eds., *The Veterans Charter and Post-World War II Canada*, 54.

5 Ian Mackenzie, *The Veterans Charter*; Neary and Granatstein, eds., *The Veterans Charter*, 3–12.

6 Desmond Morton, "The Canadian Veterans' Heritage from the Great War," in Neary and Granatstein, eds., *The Veterans Charter*, 28; Desmond Morton and Glenn Wright, *Winning the Second Battle*, 222.

7 Quoted in Durflinger, *Fighting from Home*, 195. Durflinger adds that "only the veterans themselves seemed to understand war's full brutality, and many of their experiences and much of their pain remained internalized."

8 Bernier, *Royal 22e*, 181–5. The regiment went through a period of reorganization in late 1945.

9 Durflinger, *Fighting from Home*, 199.

10 Rudin, *Founding Fathers*, 232. When a public opinion poll asked on 21 October 1944 if Canadians approved of extra money for soldiers who had volunteered

for active service, 69 per cent in the rest of Canada did; in Quebec only 39 per cent did, with 54 per cent opposed (Neary and Granatstein, eds., *The Veterans Charter,* 240). See also André Laurendeau, *La crise de la conscription, 1942.* Morton and Granatstein in *Victory 1945* quote the French-Canadian Committee of the Youth Commission concerned with signs of less interest in homemaking, "which strikes at the very heart of French-Canadian culture" (205). See also Dominique Foisy-Geoffroy, "Le Rapport de la Commission Tremblay," 292–4; Tremblay, *Volontaires*, chapter 5.

11 R. Scott Sheffield, *The Red Man's on the Warpath*, 43. On English-Canadians not recognizing Quebec's contribution, see Stacey, *Age of Conflict,* 372; Granatstein, "A Half Century On," 230.

12 Chester Bloom, *Winnipeg Free Press*, 8 November 1944.

13 Rudin, *Making History*, 210–21.

14 Vanier, quoted in Bernier, *Royal 22e*, 439. Bernier points out that the regiment had its own personality in 1945 (176).

15 Florence Triquet, *La famille Triquet,* 84: "Pauvre lui, il se fait insulter dans les hôtels à Québec et partout où il va," and "Voilà Cabano, la patrie de ce voyou de Triquet."

16 Ibid., 85: "Enlevez ça d'ici, nous avons mieux que cela à proposer à notre jeunesse."

17 Claude Triquet, in an interview on 31 January 2006, emphasized that he has never been aware of any hostility in the community and that those opposed to the war did not mix in the same circles with the family.

18 "Triquet's Father Given Back Job," *Windsor Star*, 3 October 1944; Claude Triquet, interview, 31 January 2006. On the election of 1944, see Durflinger, *Fighting from Home*, 181.

19 See for example Forbes, *Fantassin*, part 2, "Les tribulations d'un militaire en temps de paix," particularly 379–81, on his struggle with alcohol.

20 Claude Triquet, interview, 31 January 2006: "Pour lui il était en terrain où il faisait ce qu'il veut. En dehors de l'armée on fait ce qu'on veut. Il a fallu qu'il apprenne à vivre dans le civil ... Quand il est revenu de la guerre il s'est mis les pieds dans le plat souvent. Même avec la police à un moment donné ... Il s'attaquait à tout le monde."

21 Ibid.: "Il y avait les gens dans l'armée, plus senior par rapport à lui, des gens très pausés, avec un bon jugement, et quand on lui disait quelque chose il le prenait. Il était conseillé par les monseigneurs, surtout les gens de l'armée, encore là. C'étaient surtout des gens de l'armée dont il prenait conseil." He adds "Une autre caractéristique, qui est assez évidente, il avait son franc-parler. Il disait ce qu'il avait à dire à n'importe qui, n'importe quand ... Un monseigneur, un

homme haut politiquement. Il faisait attention parce qu'il était obligé de se corriger de ça ... Il s'est fait dire de surveiller ça. Et il le contrôlait un peu mais il n'était jamais capable de le contrôler complètement."

22 Ménard, in his diary of 18 April 1944, quoted in Vennat, *Général Dollard Ménard,* 165: "Stuart dit qu'on a fait un trop gros héros de moi. Il me donne des compliments sur toutes mes jobs. Il dit que j'ai un beau futur, faudrait pas le ruiner."

23 Jean Pariseau and Serge Bernier, *French-Canadians and Bilingualism in the Canadian Armed Forces,* 145: of seventy-five officers in 1947 at the level of colonel and above, nine were francophones. See also Vennat, *Général Dollard Ménard,* 168.

24 LAC, RG 24, Triquet Personnel File, 2nd folder, Department of Veteran's Affairs files. His service in Italy was from 15 June 1943 to 23 March 1944 and 16 July to 31 January 1945; in the UK from 17 December 1939 to 22 October 1940, 18 September 1941 to 15 June 1943 and 5 February to 10 July 1945. Boissonnault, *Royal 22e ,* 401–4, lists medals awarded to the R22eR during the war.

25 Ibid., 7th folder, Major A.E.T. Paquet to Records, 5 December 1946: after noticing a hole of a few days in Triquet's record, from 1 to 4 February 1945 while he was held over in France, Triquet's friend asked if it would be possible to "stretch the point" and allow Triquet to wear the France-Germany star. But this was not allowed, and the earlier decision that he not wear the award remained (Daily Orders, 4 October 1945; and Major A.C. Chadwick, Secretary, Service and Campaign Awards Committee, to DOC, MD no. 4, 19 September 1945).

26 Ibid., Public Relations Release, 27 August 1945. "Triquet Given Training Post," *Hamilton Spectator*, 27 August 1945.

27 "4,000 Service Personnel Arrive on Britannic," *Globe and Mail*, 15 August 1945; "20-Gun Salute Greets Pasteur, 4,500 Aboard," *Globe and Mail*, 13 August 1945; Allard, *Memoirs*, 121; R22eR archives, Paul Triquet Collection, FPA-43, Triquet to Major B. Langelier, Department of Veterans Affairs, 18 December 1945; letter from organizers in Hamilton, 27 June 1945, and reply by Triquet, 6 July 1945. See also "VC Winner's Boots to Help Stamp Drive," *Globe and Mail*, 14 July 1945, for the War Savings Stamps Committee campaign in September. The boots were probably the prize in a draw.

28 LAC, RG 24, Triquet Personnel File, 6th folder, Adjutant General to DOC, MD no. 5, 3 August 1945, requesting Triquet attend Canadian Legion War Memorial Building Ceremonies in Moncton on 7 September.

29 R22eR archives, Paul Triquet Collection, FPA-43, Triquet to M.J.A. Bilodeau, Maire, 11 September 1945: "Comme je suis présentement sous les ordres du Dis-

trict Militaire No. 4, il m'est impossible d'accepter de prendre part à ces cérémonies sans y être autorisé par mes supérieurs."

30 LAC, RG 24, Triquet Personnel File, 7th folder, Maurice d'Hont to Lt Col Paul Mathieu, Deputy Minister, DND, 2 November 1946: "It is my understanding that you have to issue permission for Col. Triquet to be present at this function." Brigadier W.H.S. Macklin added on the letter on 6 November that he approved, "provided no expense to public." Also (7th folder), Major General E.G. Weeks, adjutant general to GOC Central Canada, 31 October 1946, accepted another case, "provided this interview is at no expense to the public." See also 8th folder, Lt Col J.E.M. Archambault, Commandant, A-12 CITC, Farnham, to HQ, MD no. 4, Montreal, 15 November 1945.

31 R22eR archives, Paul Triquet Collection, FPA-43, Triquet to Simon Paradis, Quebec City Legion, 16 October 1945.

32 LAC, RG 24, Triquet Personnel File, 8th folder, Triquet speech, 7 September 1945 in Moncton, attached in letter from Lt Col M. Archambault, Commandant A-12 CITC Farnham to HQ, MD no. 4, 31 October 1945; R22eR archives, Paul Triquet Collection, FPA-43, Lt L.B. Peterson, Radio Liaison Officer, Army Public Relations to Triquet, 15 October 1945.

33 Douglas How, "Canada VC's Form Typical Cross-Section: Fade into Canadian Life like Comrades," *Montreal Daily Star*, 9 March 1946.

34 Colonel of the Regiment E.W. Hamber in "Seaforths' Honor Regimental Hero," *Vancouver Sun*, 19 January 1945.

35 R22eR archives, Paul Triquet Collection, FPA-43, H.N. Robson, VC, organizer, to Triquet, 9 October 1946, and reply on 11 October; LAC, RG 24, Triquet Personnel File, 7th folder, Adjutant General to DOC MD no. 2, 8 March 1946.

36 "Leafs Invite VC Winners to First Game," *Sudbury Star*, 3 October 1945: "More than usual interest is attached to one of Major Smythe's first post-war announcements."

37 R22eR archives, Paul Triquet Collection, FPA-43, Conn Smythe to Triquet, 27 September 1945; Triquet to Conn Smythe, 3 October 1945, and Frank Selke to Triquet, 13 October 1945; Triquet to Frank Selke, 20 December 1945.

38 "The Victoria Cross: The Stories of the Winning of the VC," available at CWM archives. Michael Ashcroft in *Victoria Cross Heroes*, xiv and 301, explains that 1,351 VCs have been awarded to individuals, with three receiving bars and one going to the American "Unknown Warrior," for a total of 1,355 awards.

39 Crook, *Victoria Cross*, 258–63.

40 Boileau, *Valiant Hearts*, 255. John Hundevad in "The V.C. Centennial," 4–6, writes that of the seventy Canadian VCs of the First World War, twenty-seven were posthumous.

41 Peters survived his action but was killed before he received his award. Merritt and Foote both were elected to Parliament, and Currie, Tilston, and Topham went into business.

42 Blatherwick, *1000 Brave Canadians*; Sweetenham, *Valiant Men*. Of the ninety-four, eighty-one were awarded to men in Canadian uniform.

43 Jean Brillant, 8–9 August 1918 (born at Assametquaghan, 15 March 1890); Joseph Kaeble, 9 June 1918 (St Moise, 5 May 1893); Richard Turner, 7 November 1900 (Quebec, 25 July 1871, died 1961); Campbell Mellis Douglas, 7 May 1867 (Quebec, 5 August 1840, died 1901); Thomas Holmes, 26 October 1917 (Montreal, 17 April 1898, died 1950); Okill Learmonth, 18 August 1917 (Quebec, 22 February 1894); Thain MacDowell, 9 April 1917 (Lachute, 16 September 1890, died 1960); Francis Scrimger, 25 April 1915 (Montreal, 10 February 1881, died 1937).

44 Boileau, *Valiant Hearts*, 253.

45 Blatherwick, *1000 Brave Canadians*; Sweetenham, *Valiant Men*; Douglas, *Great Canadian War Heroes*; Bishop, *Our Bravest*. See also the website of the Department of Veterans Affairs.

46 Phillips in *Victoria Cross Battles*, 10, lists 109 British VCs, 30 Indian, 17 Australian, 12 Canadian, 9 New Zealand, and three South African, and one each from Rhodesia, Denmark, and Fiji.

47 *The Victoria Cross*, 6.

48 Machum, *Canada's VCs*, 205.

49 Stacey, *Six Years of War*, 51. The five were Merritt, Mahony, Currie, Tilston, and Osborn.

50 Blatherwick, *1000 Brave Canadians*; Sweetenham, *Valiant Men*.

51 LAC, RG 24, vol. 12738, file 21/recommendations/Triquet, folio 53-100: doc. 82, Letson to Montague, 3 March 1944; doc. 79, Montague to Letson, 3 March 1944; and Letson to Montague, 2 March 1944. For citations see the website of the Department of Veterans Affairs.

52 Boileau in *Valiant Hearts*, 254, calculates that of ninety-eight Canadian VCs, eighty-eight have been in the Army, four in the Navy and six in the Air Force.

53 Ibid., 254: "An officer could often decide whether or not he was going to be brave, while a man in the ranks was often carried along in an action to whatever fate awaited him."

54 Percival, *For Valour*, 11: "Also highly esteemed were those who rallied a small party of men against overwhelming numbers of the enemy." He adds that most have a strong sense of responsibility and were willing to take calculated risks (237–9). Smyth in *Great Stories of the VC*, xiv, says in addition to sharing the common characteristic of being "prepared to sacrifice their lives" on that day,

they also had in common "a degree of obstinacy … a refusal to be beaten or pushed around." He adds that they also all lacked conceit and that many were small men but "tough as they come" (127). Also Claude Triquet, interview, 31 January 2006; Raymond Pelletier, interview, 31 December 2005.

55 Boileau, *Valiant Hearts,* 255.

56 Smokey Smith, quoted in *MacLean's*, 15 August 2005, 15–16.

57 Claude Triquet, interview, 31 January 2006.

58 LAC, RG 24, Triquet Personnel File, 7th folder, Col F.J. Fleury, Director of Personnel Services memo, 25 January 1946. Adjutant General to CO MD no. 2, 20 February 1946; Col F.J. Fleury to Major General E.J. Renaud, 11 February 1946: "The CGS has issued instructions for the H.W.E. of the Canadian School of Infantry to be amended by the addition of an Associate Comd in rank Lt. Col.," to be filled by Triquet.

59 R22eR archives, Paul Triquet Collection, FPA-43, Triquet to Lt Col Gilles Turcot, 26 February 1946: "Je suis présentement au Camp Borden comme Associé du Commandant à l'École d'infanterie [Canadian School of Infantry]. Je suis ici dans le but d'aider à l'organisation de l'instruction militaire à nos soldats de langue française. La représentation française n'est pas très forte ici présentement et je t'écris pour te demander si tu ne pourrais pas nous venir en aide." Triquet to Lt. Col. Gilles Turcot, 14 March 1946: "C'est pourquoi j'ai demandé l'autorisation 'qui m'a été accordée' de me rendre dans le District 4 et 5 afin de trouver le 'Staff' qu'il nous faut ici."

60 R22eR archives, Paul Triquet Collection, FPA-43, Triquet to Lt Col Gilles Turcot, 14 March 1946: "Gilles, je suis très heureux de cette occasion d'aller faire une courte visite au Bataillon, car je me sens un peu perdu ici. Borden est un vrai lieu d'exil pour un Québécois, mais si cela peut aider les nôtres, je ferai mon possible pour leur être utile."

61 LAC, RG 24, Triquet Personnel File, 7th folder, 12 September 1946, permission granted to transport wife and two children to Camp Borden.

62 Claude Triquet, "Autobiographie," November 2001. Yolande Triquet, interview, 31 January 2006: "It was an immersion into the English language and culture. For the first time I was allowed to go to the movies on Saturday afternoon. One day we were allowed to exchange comic books – we didn't know this before. It was a big change in culture. More than now."

63 R22eR archives, Paul Triquet Collection, FPA-43.

64 Triquet, quoted in "Triquet Lauds Cadet Training," *Montreal Star*, 11 November 1946. Cadet training, Triquet said, "helps youth become better Canadians." Also "Faits Divers au Camp Boren," *L'Amicale du 22ième* 1, no. 1 (May 1947): Triquet "passe en revue le corps des cadets du collège Ridley, Ste-Catherines

... L'entraînement militaire n'est pas une préparation à la guerre mais plutôt une mesure nécessaire pour se porter à la défense du sol paternel en cas d'agression."

65 *Le Canada*, 6 September 1946.

66 R22eR archives, Paul Triquet Collection, FPA-43, Triquet to L.T. Pallascio, president, *Amicale du 22ième* (29 May 1946).

67 Paul Triquet, "Lettre ouverte," *L'Amicale du 22ième* 1, no. 1 (May 1947): "Soyez assurés que ceux qui, comme nous sont éloignés de l'unité, serons très heureux de ce mouvement qui nous permettra de se tenir en contact avec les camarades de l'Amicale du Régiment."

68 Jacques Castonguay, *Les Bataillons et le dépôt du Royal 22e Régiment,* 17. The Molson family made the presentation.

69 Tremblay, in *Volontaires,* describes how only a small number of vets sought psychiatrists as "l'alcool est un refuge plus classique" (103).

70 LAC, RG 24, Triquet Personnel File, 3rd folder, Brigadier F.J. Fleury, Commander Eastern Quebec Area, to HQ, Quebec Command, 12 December 1951.

71 Ibid., 2nd folder, Medical Exam, by MO G.H. Raymond, 17 October 1947; Medical Exam, 20 May 1946.

72 Claude Triquet, interview, 31 January 2006: "Il avait aussi les défauts de ses qualités. Il a brûlé la chandelle par les deux bouts. Autrement dit, il avait une soif de vie tellement forte qu'il brûlait les étapes, il prenait un coup et toutes les choses de la vie, il en a abusé, incluant le travail. Il avait un très mauvais caractère, évidement surtout quand il prenait un coup." "Il n'était pas pire qu'un autre et il était moins pire que bien d'autres. Quand je vois ça je dis que mon père était correct dans le fond. Surtout après avoir vécu l'expérience de la guerre ... À Camp Borden mon père prenait un coup. C'était orageux, à tel point qu'il a fallu qu'on parte de là rapidement en cachette un soir en taxi de Camp Borden jusqu'à Cabano ... C'était à ce moment là que mon père était obligé de laisser l'armée parce qu'il prenait un coup et ça a créé des problèmes au point de vue de l'armée. Ils lui ont demandé de quitter."

73 LAC, RG 24, Triquet Personnel File, 6th folder, Brigadier W.H.S. Macklin, acting Adjutant General, to HQ Central Command, 13 June 1947: "The question of the retirement of Lt. Col. Paul Triquet, VC, was recently raised by GOC Central Command in a discussion with the Chief of the General Staff. It is understood that Lt. Col. Triquet has discussed the matter with the Officer Commanding the Royal Canadian School of Infantry as well as with the GOC personally, and that he will make no protest against retirement under KR (Can) 267(c)."

74 *King's Regulations and Orders, 1939.* Paragraph 267 (a) specifies that the officer is removed "on account of misconduct or manifest inefficiency."

75 LAC, RG 24, Triquet Personnel File, 6th folder, Brigadier W.H.S. Macklin, acting Adjutant General, to HQ Central Command, 13 June 1947; Major General Chris Vokes, GOC Central Command to Army HQ, 18 June 1947. Macklin then recommended Triquet's retirement to the minister on 21 June.

76 Ibid., Brigadier W.H.S. Macklin, acting adjutant general, to HQ Central Command, 13 June 1947. The adjutant general had this power under KR (Can) 1119 (a); 4th folder, AP&R no. 54, dated 23 December 1947: Triquet was retired to pension with rank of Lt Col as of 12 November 1947.

77 A question that was not raised, but had been earlier for VC recipients accused of serious crimes, was whether they would keep the VC. The original warrant had specified that a member could be expelled from the Order if "convicted before a Court Martial of cowardice, mutiny or desertion." However, this was subsequently modified so the penalty followed the recipient into civilian life and he could be expelled for "any infamous crime." In the first decades of the twentieth century there was "a softening in attitude towards holders of the VC who committed offences ... on 24 Nov 1921 a letter was sent from Buckingham Palace concerning their decision in the case of a recipient convicted of common assault. 'The King ... while regretting that a man with such a fine war record should have been convicted of such a horrible crime, is glad that the Army Council do not propose to recommend a submission for the forfeiture of the VC'." See Crook, *The Evolution of the Victoria Cross*, 64–5, 142, 258.

78 "Faits Divers au Camp Borden," *L'Amicale du 22ième* 1, no. 3 (July 1947): "Il est connu de tous et l'exploit qui lui a valu la plus haute décoration de l'Empire l'a rendu immortel dans l'histoire de notre glorieux Régiment." See also subsequent articles such as Lt Gov Eugene Fiset's tribute in *L'Amicale du 22ième* 1, no. 5 (August 1947). The MP for Rimouski, M. Gleason Belzile, noted in the *House of Commons Debates*, 4 July 1947, 5071, that the *Ottawa Citizen* reference to Triquet as the first French-Canadian to receive the VC was inaccurate, as Brillant and Kaeble had also received the VC, and French-Canadians were very proud of all three.

79 "Coin des Officiers," *L'Amicale du 22ième* 1, no. 4 (August 1947); "Visiteurs," *L'Amicale du 22ième* 1, no. 7 (November 1947).

80 R22eR archives, Paul Triquet Collection, FPA-43, Triquet interview, by Mme Bouchard, for CJAD radio series *Personalities in the News*, 8 April 1948; Florence Triquet, *La famille Triquet*, 83.

81 Mary McRoberts, letter to author, 14 June 2006. McRoberts and Douglas Delaney are preparing a book on Bert Hoffmeister's business and military careers.

82 LAC, RG 24, Triquet Personnel File, 8th folder, memo of 13 August 1947, confirming that there was no rule against starting work while on leave waiting to retire.

83 R22eR archives, Paul Triquet Collection, FPA-43, Triquet interview, by Mme Bouchard for CJAD radio series *Personalities in the News*, 8 April 1948, 5.

84 Triquet, "Farewell Message," *L'Amicale du 22ième* 1, no. 3 (July 1947).

85 "Farewell to Lt. Col. P. Triquet, VC from the Royal Canadian School of Infantry," *L'Amicale du 22ième* 1, no. 3 (July 1947).

Chapter Seven

1 DHH, 72/10, Suttie Report; also DHH 112.043 (D2), 2.

2 Campbell, *The Hero*, 391.

3 Charles Taylor, *Modern Social Imaginaries*, 19–20: "This individualism signifies a rejection of the previously dominant notion of hierarchy."

4 Charles Taylor, *The Ethics of Authenticity*, 4–18. He notes that such concerns have been expressed for several centuries as individuals have acquired more freedom to choose their own lives (seen by most as a positive development). Allan Bloom in *The Closing of the American Mind* presents a more critical view of the trend.

5 Dumont, *La société québécoise*, 307, 324.

6 Michael Behiels, *Prelude to Quebec's Quiet Revolution*; Robert Bothwell, *Canada and Quebec*, 79–87; Gérard Bouchard, *La nation québécoise au futur et au passé*; Rudin, *Making History*, 5, 72, 173, 191; Taylor, *Reconciling the Solitudes*, 137, 156; Rudin, *Founding Fathers*, 4, 230; Fernand Harvey and Paul-André Linteau, "L'évolution de l'historiographie dans la RHAF, 1947–72," 18; E. Catela de Bordes, ed., *Le Mémorial du Québec*, vol. 2, 181. Paul-Émile Borduas's 1948 manifesto, *Refus global*, is identified as liberating people from the restrictions of the Catholic Church and others: "Il est, au Québec, le symbole de la liberté."

7 John Ralston Saul, *Reflections of a Siamese Twin*, 356–7; Lucien Dumais, a French-Canadian veteran, published his war experiences in 1970 in *Un Canadien Français face à la Gestapo*, lamenting that his story and those of many Second World War veterans were not of more interest to the general public (9).

8 LAC, RG 24, vol. 20692, CSC Minutes, 5 February 1951; "Disciplined People," *Globe and Mail*, 15 June 1956; "Conscription, It Depends on Quebec," *Toronto Evening Telegram*, 20 January 1955; "A Compulsory Standing Army," *Calgary Herald*, 21 April 1979 (Minister of Defence Barney Danson favours conscription). See also many stories in February and March 1980, in LAC, RG 24, vol. 20126.

9 "Conscription Gets Support in Quebec," *Winnipeg Free Press*, 22 February 1964; "Réal Caouette, Leader of Créditiste Parti Supports Conscription," *Ottawa*

Journal, 2 November 1970; "Army Draft Opposed by Quebec Liberals," *Montreal Gazette*, 16 February 1971.

10 LAC, video, VI-8708-0004, Triquet interviewed by France Fortin and André Jean on the show *Camera Verité*, 1970.

11 Igartua, *The Other Quiet Revolution*, 5, 14, 164–92.

12 J.L. Granatstein, "A Half Century On," 230.

13 *L'Amicale du 22ième* 2, no. 1 (May 1949).

14 R22eR archives, Paul Triquet Collection, FPA-43, Triquet interview by Mme Bouchard, for CJAD radio series *Personalities in the News*, 8 April 1948.

15 DHH, 000.9 (D70), biographical file, Triquet, "Brigadier-général Paul Triquet, VC, CStJ, CD,"

16 "Chez les officiers," *L'Amicale du 22ième* 2, no. 14 (10 February 1949). "Nous avons eu l'agréable surprise de voir un véritable marchand de bois, un véritable civil, le Lt. Col. Paul Triquet, VC. Il semble aimer pouvoir dire 'nous les civils.' En tous cas, nous espérons le voir plus souvent dans nos murs; au fond, il est encore un peu beaucoup militaire."

17 LAC, RG 24, Triquet Personnel File, 4th folder, Lt Col P.M. Desautels, Quebec Command, to HQ, Eastern Quebec Area, 24 October 1950. The reply was translated into French and forwarded to Triquet from Lt Col L.A. Gagnon, Secteur de l'Est du Québec, 28 October 1950.

18 LAC, RG 24, Triquet Personnel File, 6th folder, an unsigned and undated note, states: "As this officer is a VC, it would not be good policy to make a recommendation at this time." VC recipient John Mahony, only one year younger than Triquet, did serve in Korea.

19 LAC, RG 24, Triquet Personnel File, 7th folder, Record of Service; LAC, RG 24, Triquet Personnel File, 7th folder, Recommendation form, approved by Major General R.O.G. Morton, Quebec Command, 17 November 1950. Papers were signed on 19 October 1950.

20 LAC, RG 24, Triquet Personnel File, 3rd folder, Brigadier F.J. Fleury, Commander Eastern Quebec Area, to HQ, Quebec Command, 12 December 1951. *L'Amicale du 22ième* 3, no. 6 (December 1949), reports that Triquet visited St-Jean for a Halloween party and made a big dent in the ginger ale supply. He had gained about forty pounds from his army days and now weighed 190 pounds.

21 Jacques Castonguay, Armand Ross, and Michel Litalien's *Le Régiment de la Chaudière, 1869–2004*, lists the commanders of the regiment since 1863: Lt Col R. Guenet was Triquet's immediate predecessor (481).

22 LAC, RG 24, Triquet Personnel File, 6th folder, Brigadier George Kiching, Director General of Army Personnel, replying to Major General Morton's request, 18 April 1951: handwritten note "Spoke with CGS – not to be accepted."

23 LAC, RG 24, Triquet Personnel File, 3rd folder, Brigadier F.J. Fleury, Commander Eastern Quebec Area, to HQ, Quebec Command, 12 December 1951. The mayor of Levis and other local civilian and military people also favoured the appointment.

24 *Quebec Chronicle Telegraph*, 14 January 1952; "Le Lieutenant-Colonel Triquet au Régiment de Lévis," *L'Amicale du 22ième* 9, no. 9 (January 1952): "Tous ses amis, et il n'a que ça des amis, se réjouissent de tout cœur. Il a compris qu'on avait encore besoin de ses services"; R22eR archives, Paul Triquet Collection, FPA-43, Bernatchez to Triquet, 29 January 1953, informs Triquet that the portrait painted by Adam Sherriff Scott, on loan from the National Art Gallery to the R22eR, would be lent to Le Régiment de Lévis. It was returned to the Citadelle in 1957.

25 LAC, RG 24, Triquet Personnel File, 7th folder, Record of Service. He attended Valcartier summer camp 22–8 June 1952 and 21–7 June 1953.

26 "Chez les officiers," *L'Amicale du 22ième* 2, no. 14 (10 February 1949): Triquet was named the third member for life of l'Amicale à Montréal; the two others were vets of the First World War, Raoul Taillefer and Emile Saintes. The article refers to a recent presentation by Triquet to youth.

27 Michael Gauvreau, *The Catholic Origins of Quebec's Quiet Revolution, 1931–1970*; reviews in Ferretti, Lucia, et al., "The Catholic Origins of Quebec's Quiet Revolution, 1931–1970," 373–88.

28 Claude Triquet, interview, 31 January 2006: "Il était très respectueux mais il n'était pas croyant. Avec les padres dans l'armée, il s'en servait beaucoup. Quand il avait des problèmes avec ses hommes il s'est servi beaucoup des padres pour aider à différents problèmes psychologiques ou autres avec ses hommes ... Il voyait que l'église avait un forte influence sur les gens. Il était très ami avec Mgr Roy, qui était archevêque de Québec. Il l'avait connu dans l'Armée. Il y avait aussi Mgr. Jobidon, c'était un prêtre qui a fait l'armée."

29 Gilles Turcot in an interview of 3 August 2007 remembers Triquet's reply in 1945 to words of congratulations from a priest who had earlier penalized him for his involvement in the army: "Mgr., you didn't think that in 1938!" However, all in the regiment liked Roy and would apologize if they swore in his presence.

30 "Camarades et amis du Royal 22e Régiment," *L'Amicale du 22ième* 6, no. 1 (May 1952). He asked for $2,000 and soon after reported that $1,640 had been raised and made another appeal: "Pour ceux du 3e bataillon," *L'Amicale du 22ième* 6, no. 11 (March 1953).

31 Castonguay et al., *Le Régiment de la Chaudière*, 483: "Fusion d'une unité à une autre est difficilement acceptée par les intéressés, peu importe l'excellence des

formations en cause ... Néanmoins, la bonne volonté des uns et la compréhension des autres aidèrent à aplanir les difficultés."

32 "Tiré des dépêches," *L'Amicale du 22ième* 8, no. 4 (August 1954): "Le Régiment de Lévis avait 90 ans d'existence et naturellement ce fut un choc pour le Lieutenant-Colonel Triquet d'apprendre la malencontreuse nouvelle, mais il se remit vite de sa surprise en commentant qu'il n'y avait certainement pas de place pour deux régiments d'infanterie sur la côte sud dans le district de Québec."

33 LAC, RG 24, Triquet Personnel File, 7th folder, Record of Service: 1 September 1954, moved from Régiment de Lévis, to 8 (Mil) Group HQ as Acting Colonel. Also 3rd folder, Brigadier F.J. Fleury, Commander Eastern Quebec Area to HQ Quebec Command, 3 August 1954. Col J.F. L'Espérance had thought that as commander of 12th Infantry Brigade he would have taken command of the newly reorganized 8th Militia Group (as the previous commander of 11th Infantry Brigade had received command of 7th Militia Group). Fleury recommended Triquet because of his "really outstanding job for the past two years as OC Le Regt de Lévis." On the militia reforms of 1953 to 1964, see Michel Litalien, *Le 51e Bataillon des services du Canada et ses origines, 1901–2005.*

34 Archives du musée de la Chaudière, Fonds L'Espérance, Louis St.-Laurent to J. Fafard, 17 September 1954; "compenser pour la disparition du Régiment de Lévis."

35 Archives du musée du Régiment de la Chaudière, Fonds L'Espérance, Col L'Espérance to Louis St.-Laurent, 7 October 1954. He argued that Triquet had retired in 1954, was not a resident of Lévis, and as the victim of this injustice, his social position and economic opportunities would be harmed. See also Col L'Espérance to Area Commander, Eastern Quebec Area, "Grievance," 15 October 1954; Fleury to Maurice Bourget, MP, 3 December 1954; Major J. Grenier, Eastern Quebec Area, in a memo on "Brigade Commanders-Reserve Force Policy," 9 June 1949, describes the policy on promotions to Brigade Command in the Reserve Force. See Fleury to Col L'Espérance, 18 October 1954: "You realize, of course, that the recommendation for Triquet to command Headquarters, 8 Militia Group, originated with me and has the 'blessing' of your superiors and mine in the chain of command up to and including the Minister of National Defence." See also L'Espérance to Lt Gen G.G. Simonds, 13 December 1954; L'Espérance to GOC Quebec Command, 26 November 1954; and Triquet to L'Espérance, 10 December 1954, thanking him for the excellent cooperation and asking for some files and forms.

36 LAC, RG 24, Triquet Personnel File, 3rd folder, Fleury to Bernatchez, 9 August 1956; ibid., Brigadier F.A. Clift, DCAP, Army HQ, to Quebec HQ, 29 October 1956: Clift noted that the CGS was concerned that Col L'Espérance was

opposed and "CGS does not want to go ahead" at this moment. H.D. Graham wrote on notes for files of 31 August 1956 that he had told GOC QueCom that "the minister was away and would probably not deal with this until end of Sept." H.D. Graham added to the notes for files of 11 September 1956, "There is a feeling that the time for the promotion of Col. Triquet is not now opportune."

37 LAC, RG 24, Triquet Personnel File, 3rd folder, Bernatchez to Allard, 9 October 1956: after noting that he agreed with Allard's recommendation of 28 September to confirm Triquet as colonel and make acting brigadier (and with Fleury's similar recommendation of 9 August), Bernatchez wrote, "however, AHQ pointed out that there are certain circumstances surrounding this case which must be taken into consideration before finalization of Triquet's case. I do not wish to discuss these circumstances on paper but will do so on the occasion of my next telephone conversation with you."

38 Ibid., 5th folder, D. Ménard, GOC, HQ, Quebec Command, memo to confirm rank, 6 March 1958: "During this period, my predecessor was entirely satisfied with Triquet's service and has noted that the units of 8 Militia Group have increased in efficiency and effectiveness during the tenure of his appointment. Accordingly, I have no hesitation in recommending that this officer be confirmed in his rank effective 1 March 58." Ibid., 7th folder, Record of Service, shows that Triquet attended Valcartier summer camp 20–26 June 1954 and 24–30 July 1955. His main administrative duties for which he billed the army included eight days just before and six days just after a conference in Montreal on 17–18 February 1956.

39 Ibid., 7th folder, Record of Service, *Nouvelles illustrés*, 28 February 1959, 11: "Triquet, le légendaire héros du 22ième abandonnera l'armée l'an prochain." The effective date was 30 June 1959; "Triquet Retires," *Quebec Chronicle Telegraph*, 30 June 1959; *Globe and Mail*, 1 July 1959. See also ibid., 5th folder, Triquet to Commander, Eastern Quebec Area, 13 March 1959: "In view of increased activities and responsibilities in the civilian field, I consider that very soon I shall not be able to devote as much time to the Militia as is required."

40 *Canada Gazette* 93, no. 50 (12 December 1959). There were two major generals (Ganong and Foster) and one other brigadier, and the others were lieutenant colonels and colonels. See LAC, RG 24, Triquet Personnel File, 5th folder, telegram to HQ Eastern Quebec Area, 26 October 1959: "The Gov Gen has approved the appt as hon adcs of Brig Triquet." See also DHH, 000.9 (D70), Biographical File, Triquet, "Brigadier-général Paul Triquet, VC, CStJ, CD."

41 LAC, RG 24, Triquet Personnel File, 5th folder, D. Ménard, GOC, HQ, Quebec Command, to Triquet, 16 June 1959: "Je ne puis pas laisser passer l'occasion de

ta 'deuxième' retraite de l'Armée, sans te dire combien j'ai apprécié la collaboration étroite que tu m'as toujours donnée et de te dire aussi l'admiration que j'ai pour toi tant au point de vue personnel que pour le travail que tu as fait au 8e Groupe de Milice depuis que tu le commandes." He added that Triquet put in much more time than the number of authorized pay days and that his work showed: "Encore une fois, merci, et comme disait St-Paul, lui aussi centurion, on pourrait dire de toi: 'il a combattu le bon combat, il a fini sa course, il a gardé la foi'" (from 2 Timothy, New Testament).

42 LAC, RG 24, Triquet Personnel File, 5th folder, D. Ménard, GOC, HQ, Quebec Command, to Triquet, 16 June 1959: "Comme tu disais l'autre soir à la fête d'adieu en ton honneur, tu seras toujours près de l'Armée, et si on a besoin de toi, tant pour des conseils que pour autres choses, je sais que je puis compter sur toi."

43 DHH, 72/10, Suttie Report. Also DHH 112.043 (D2), iv: "Recommend to the Minister of National Defence the best means of fulfilling the Militia requirements of the Canadian Defence Policy and the changes which should be made in the organization of the Militia to carry out its revised roles more efficiently and realistically." The commissioners were named in January 1964.

44 DHH, 72/10, Suttie Report. The other six participants at the rank of brigadier were J.P. Carriere, D.G. Cunningham, E.G. Eakins, F.T. Jenner, I.S. Johnston, and V.de B. Oland. Lt Col B.J. Legge was the ninth member. For a summary of the recommendations, see x–xv.

45 DHH, 72/10, Suttie Report; also DHH 112.043 (D2). The commission also recommended that federal funds be provided to establish a national program "competent in its field" and abolish the present "costly and ineffective" system of one PR officer per unit.

46 DHH, 72/10, Suttie Report; also DHH 112.043 (D2), 2.

47 Ibid., 3–4.

48 LAC, video, VI-8708-0004, Triquet interviewed by France Fortin and André Jean on *Camera Verité*, 1970.

49 Gilles Turcot in an interview of 3 August 2007 says he preferred talking to individual soldiers rather than to groups. Léonide Ouellette (interview, 4 January 2006) remembers being surprised when he drove the older, higher-ranking hero in his jeep in 1944 that Triquet spoke as a friend and came across as very nice and unaffected.

50 Archives de la Société d'Histoire de Rivière-du-Loup, dossier 177, pièce 9, "Fusiliers du St-Laurent," news clips on walk of 17 July 1967: "La Marche du Grand-Portage est un merveilleux exercice de formation pour nos jeunes."

51 Chauveau, *Royal 22e*, 326: Docteur ès Science Militaire, honoris causa, on 20 May 1977.

52 R22eR archives, Paul Triquet Collection, FPA-43, Triquet's reply to Luc Bertrand.

53 Claude Triquet, "Autobiographie," November 2001. He joined the Corps des ingénieurs militaires and later, at the start of the 1970s, was named commander of the Thetford Mines 775 squadron of Royal Canadian Air Cadets. He left the reserves to study for an MBA and then worked with the Ministry of Natural Resources in Quebec City until 1992.

54 Claude Triquet, interview, 31 January 2006: "C'est un chose qui m'a enmerdé pendant toute mon existence ... 'êtes-vous le fils de ...' J'ai toujours eu de la misère avec ça et mon père le sentait d'ailleurs. Il était correct de ce côté là. Il aurait pu insister pour que je sois plus impliqué dans ses affaires mais il m'a laissé m'occuper de mes affaires à moi. Alors de ce côté, là nous avions une très bonne entente ... On s'est parlé pas beaucoup mais il m'a donné un coup de main pour faire mes études. Il respectait ce que j'avais à faire et moi aussi. Ça a très bien été."

55 Yolande Triquet, interview, 31 January 2006; *Nouvelles illustrés*, 28 February 1959, 11.

56 LAC, RG 24, Triquet Personnel File, 6th folder, Jugement dans la cour superieure, Québec, Québec (Division des divorces), Paul Triquet requérant vs Dame Alberte Chenier, intimée (September 1969?). He paid $150 monthly to Mme Chenier: "Il allègue qu'à cause de circonstances spéciales, il serait d'intérêt public que le jugement soit rendu irrévocable avant le délai de trois mois prévu par l'article 13 de la Loi du divorce ... il a fait du service militaire comme brigadier, qu'il est maintenant à sa retraite, et qu'il s'occupe activement des organismes de bienfaisance pour les vétérans du Royal 22ième Régiment. Il est en relation directe et continuelle avec le public."

57 LAC, RG 24, vol. 20106, Ceremonies – Press Clippings of 11 November ceremonies during the 1970s. Triquet received his pension, which he had been collecting since his retirement on 12 November 1947: LAC, RG 24, Triquet Personnel File, 6th folder, Paul Mathieu, Associate Deputy Minister, to Treasury Board, 20 June 1960, notifying them of an increase from the annual amount of $1,789.89 to $1,879.39, based on Triquet's time in Les Fusiliers du St-Laurent from 30 September 1925 to 27 November 1927. There was also an annuity for VC recipients (Clarke, *Gallantry Medals,* 16). See also Crook, *The Evolution of the Victoria Cross*, 186–97: VCs received a tax-free annuity of £50, raised to £100 in 1957 and later to £1,300, irrespective of need.

58 Armand Gagnon, interview, 8 August 2007.

59 Claude Triquet, interview, 31 January 2006; Florence Triquet, *La famille Triquet,* 83. He also had kidney problems.

60 R22eR archives, Paul Triquet Collection, FPA-43, Triquet to M. et Mme. Guichard, 17 November 1975, informing them that he visited the grave of their son, Cpl Joseph Guichard, that June: "Des fleurs appropriées qui se renouvellent chaque année décorent chaque tombe." Triquet wrote to Mme Jules Brillant, 3 September 1974: "Lt. Brillant a toujours été pour nous un exemple de courage surhumain et d'une insurpassable grandeur d'âme." He wrote to thank his family for giving his medals to the museum and on 23 July 1975 wrote to the museum, noting that he had a ceremony in Toronto and needed "mes grosses médailles."

61 DHH, 84/126, Fonds Allard, file 89, Allard to Triquet, 28 September 1965. After accepting an invitation for an event 15–17 October 1965, he wrote: "En attendant le plaisir de te revoir, permets-moi d'abord de te féliciter pour le travail que tu accomplis comme Président de l'Association du Régiment ainsi que pour le grand dévouement que tu as pour ceux qui de près ou de loin s'intéressent aux affaires régimentaires." Triquet asked Allard for a contribution to *La revue de la Citadelle* (DHH, 84/126, Fonds Allard, file 89, Triquet to Allard, 16 November 1965; R22eR archives, Paul Bernatchez Collection, "Message du Colonel du Régiment," New Year's, 1965. Triquet was also involved when Queen Elizabeth visited the Citadelle on 10 October 1964.

62 On 28 April 1966 he was named commissaire provincial de l'ambulance St-Jean pour le Québec (DHH, 000.9 (D70), Biographical File, Triquet, "Brigadier-général Paul Triquet, VC, CStJ, CD," LAC, MG 28 I 100, Order of St. John file, vol. 3). In August 1973 he was awarded La croix du combattant de l'Europe from French Vets of Quebec (*Le Soleil*, 8 August 1973). In October 1976 he received La médaille du très vénérable (ordre) de St Jean de Jerusalem. In March 1977 he was given keys to the city of Fort Lauderdale by the mayor (Chauveau, *Royal 22e*, 323, Mayor E. Clay Shaw, Jr).

63 DHH, 84/126, Fonds Allard, file 89, "Procès-verbal de la première réunion du comité d'aide à la réadaptation à la vie civile," 9 March 1965: "Du fait de leur longue période de service, ces militaires ont perdu contact, dans une certaine mesure, avec les pratiques courantes dans le monde des affaires, de l'industrie et de la fonction publique." The committee was the idea of Colonel L.F. Trudeau.

64 John Hundevad, "The V.C. Centennial," in *The Legionary* 30, no. 8 (January 1956): 4; CWM archives, Thain MacDowell File, 58A-1-171 (contains the schedule of events, invitations and list of Canadians attending) and *The Victoria Cross: The Stories of the Winning of the VC*.

65 LAC, RG 24, Triquet Personnel File, 3rd folder, Lt Col L.F. Trudeau (AA and QMG), announcement with details of the ceremony, 5 June 1956; "Honneur

à deux héros qui ont mérité la Croix Victoria," *L'Amicale du 22ième* 10, no. 2 (June 1956); "Le centenaire de la Croix Victoria," *L'Amicale du 22ième*, 10, no. 5 (September 1956).

66 Jane Armstrong, "No Wheel Chair for VC Aged 85," *Toronto Evening Telegram*, 26 June 1956.

67 As the VC cannot be awarded to civilians, King George VI instituted in 1940 the George Cross for civilians and members of the services who performed "acts of the greatest heroism or of the most conspicuous courage in circumstances of extreme danger." See Swettenham, *Valiant Men*, xiii; Boileau, *Valiant Hearts*, 178. On his being active, see R22eR archives, Paul Triquet Collection, FPA-43, VC & GC Association to General Dextraze, 15 August 1980; Programs for meetings, Windsor Castle on 21 April 1976 with 61 VCs and 90 GCs; LAC, RG 24, vol. 20152, Honours and Awards – 1943–1970, "Canada's Winners of the VC and GC."

68 Yolande Triquet, interview, 31 January 2006: "We met the Queen. It was quite something ... It was an emotional time for him ... After the ceremony in London we went to Casa Berardi, with a military driver but not a delegation. He must have been shook up." And: "I saw a DND newsreel film with Dad during the war, during the Italian campaign. That was quite nice. The Italian campaign was not usually presented very much."

69 The 1960s was an important decade for the consolidation of regimental institutions and traditions: Serge Bernier, *Royal 22e*, 282–6. *L'Amicale du 22ième* 7, no. 5 (December 1953); "Soldier, VC to Be Feted by Comrades," *Montreal Star*, 12 December 1963.

70 DHH, 84/126, Fonds Allard, file 127, Triquet to Allard, 2 July 1964; Triquet to G.G. Crean, 7 July 1964. The "remembrance trip" was to "rendre hommage à nos camarades qui sont morts au Champ d'Honneur," Triquet told Allard, and he invited ten officers of the R22eR in Cyprus to join the group. Allard asked DND to pay for their flight. See also ibid. for Allard speech at Casa Berardi ceremony, 9 August 1964.

71 Claude Châtillon, "25e anniversaire de Casa-Berardi – Souvenir de voyage," in Chauveau, *Royal 22e*, 294–9; R22eR archives, Paul Triquet Collection, FPA-43, Triquet to Captain J.B. Goulet, 30 October 1971.

72 CWM Archives, Triquet file, J.D. MacFarlane, "Valour Revisited: The Battlefields of Italy, 30 Years After," clipping from *Canadian Magazine*, 1974: "A gold medal is the best an Italian soldier can get, so who's to quibble." The regiment had agreed to pay $800 for a plaque to "commemmorer les nôtres qui y sont morts." See also R22eR archives, Jean Allard Collection, 172/17/1/80 and 81: Letters from Maria Teresa Berardi to Triquet and their replies, April–June 1969. See photos in Eric McGeer, *The Canadian Battlefields in Italy*, 42.

73 DHH, 000.9 (D70), Biographical File, Triquet, "Brigadier-général Paul Triquet, VC, CStJ, CD." The other VC recipients died in the following years: Currie 1986, Foote 1988, Mahony 1990, Tilston 1992, Merritt 2000, Smith 2005. See "VC Winner a Career Army Man," *Globe and Mail,* 5 August 1980; also, with other clippings, in LAC, RG 24, vol. 20155.

74 Florence Triquet, *La famille Triquet,* 107–8. Their father died 28 April 1962; probably Paul insisted on the military funeral. Their mother died in 1966.

75 R22eR archives, Paul Triquet Collection, FPA-43, Lt Col Georges Bernier to Major General Bernatchez, 2 October 1973.

76 R22eR archives, Paul Triquet Collection, FPA-43, Gilles Lamontagne to Triquet 17 April 1980: "Ne lâche pas – il y aura encore de bons moments"; "L'ultime hommage au Brig. Triquet," *Journal de Québec,* 8 August 1980. There was a parade: "La fanfare régimentaire exécuta les marches funèbres de Beethoven et de Chopin ("Les funérailles du Général Triquet," *L'Amicale du 22ième* 16, no. 4 (August 1980).

77 "Les funérailles du Général Triquet," *L'Amicale du 22ième* 16, no. 4 (August 1980).

78 Ibid.: "Tout le Régiment, que dis-je, tout un peuple, sous le coup de l'émotion et de l'étonnement, conduisait à son dernier repos celui qui au cours de la Deuxième Grande Guerre fit tellement honneur à son unité le Royal 22ième Régiment et à son peuple tout en demeurant bon, simple, serviable. Il fut un grand et un véritable soldat."

79 Archives, Paul Triquet Legion Hall, Cabano, "Paul Triquet tel que nous l'avons connu," *Le Touladi,* 13 August 1980, quoting Lionel Côté: "Je n'ai jamais connu un homme aussi brave."

80 Soldat Laurent-Eug. Savard, "Témoignage d'un ancien de Casa Berardi," *L'Amicale du 22ième* 16, no. 5 (Octobre 1980): "Il s'est conduit en héros et c'est dans des moments pareils que se manifestent la force de caractère, le sens de la discipline et le sens du devoir de nos supérieurs. Je suis très fier d'avoir servi sous lui."

81 "Transfert des cendres du Général Triquet," *L'Amicale du 22ième* 16, no. 5 (October 1980).

82 R22eR archives, Paul Triquet Collection, FPA-43, Lt Col Georges Bernier to Major General Bernatchez, 2 October 1973; Bernatchez to Triquet, 4 October 1973, Brig François Richard to Triquet, 13 July 1979 (confirms letter of colonel of regiment of October 1973).

83 LAC RG 24, vol. 20155, Honours and Awards/Triquet, magazine clipping of 1966.

84 Yolande McArthur, interview, 31 January 2006.

85 Claude Triquet, interview, 31 January 2006: "Le contraire m'aurait surpris. C'était sa famille, le 22. Quand il fut enterré il y avait une foule énorme" and "Ce n'était pas un type qui pouvait se restreindre à une vie de famille. D'ailleurs, comme il disait, sa famille, c'était le 22. C'était sa vrai famille pour lui, c'était la 22 et ses enfants aussi, évidement il nous aidait mais ce n'était pas le même chose. Même quand il est sorti de l'armée il continuait à faire la réserve et il était encore dans l'armée."

86 Rudolphe Bélisle, interview, 4 January 2006. He added that some people did not like Triquet, finding him "bossy," but that those people did not understand well the role of a sergeant major in a military formation.

87 R22eR archives, Paul Triquet Collection, FPA-43, Capitaine Louis René Drapeau to Allard, 16 December 1963: "Les discours des 'VIP' en cette soirée mémorable furent très bien, sauf que les gens ont semblé oublier le fameux, vaillant et brave Major Ovila Garceau décédé qui entre nous fut le seul responsable avec sa Cie de l'avance et la réussite de la prise de Casa Berardi par le présent Brigadier P. Triquet V.C., car d'où nous étions (Cie de Garceau et étant dans le temps son 'CSM') nous sommes les seuls à avoir vu, suivi et supporté (de nos armes) visuellement chaque étape de l'avance de la Cie de Triquet du lever du jour au coucher du soleil." Drapeau added that he was happy and proud that Triquet had received the VC he so well deserved.

88 Châtillon, *Carnets de guerre,* 97, describes how D Company successfully completed its mission and was not lost, as the official history and others have claimed. On page 148 he writes that he had recommended an award for Ovila Garceau. He was proud of Triquet "et de l'honneur qui rejaillit sur tout le régiment; mais cette décoration suffira-t-elle, sera-t-elle l'unique récompense pour symboliser tant de souffrance, de bravoure, de blessés et de morts en ce coin d'Italie?"

89 He occasionally visited Cabano (he organized a celebration for his parents' fiftieth anniversary in Cabano, on 23 August 1955): Florence Triquet, *La famille Triquet,* 103. The Legion at Cabano celebrated its twenty-fifth anniversary in May 1969 (R22eR archives, Paul Triquet Collection, FPA-43). The Hon. J.E. Dubé, minister of Veterans' Affairs, noted that Triquet had "brought new glory to the R22eR and the Canadian Armed Forces" (LAC RG 24, vol. 20155, Honours and Awards/Triquet, text of speech by the Hon. J.E. Dubé, Minister of Veterans' Affairs, "25th anniversary of the VC to Brigadier Paul Triquet" Cabano, 11 May 1969). Triquet was moved, announcing that he still considered himself a citizen of Cabano and that the day reminded him of the reception he had received in 1944: "Je suis toujours un citoyen de Cabano," *Le St. Laurent,* 11, 14 May 1969.

90 "Cabano célèbre le 25e anniversaire des exploits militaires d'un de ses fils, le brigadier Paul Triquet," *Le St. Laurent*, 11 May 1969; "Hommage de Cabano à Paul Triquet," *Le St. Laurent*, 7 May 1969.

91 LAC, RG 24, vol. 15238, War Diary of the Royal 22e Régiment, 31 December 1943.

92 Fort Ingall Archives, Fonds Paul Triquet, "Musée militaire," Triquet to Mayor Guy Michaud, 26 November 1976; Triquet to Guy Hudon (president, Société d'histoire de Cabano), 22 March 1977; Triquet to Marc-André Leclerc (president, Société d'histoire de Cabano), 10 March 1978.

93 Triquet to Chauveau, 31 March 1980, in Chauveau, *Royal 22e*, 399.

94 LAC, RG 24, vol. 20155, Honours and Awards, copy passed by press censor for UK's *Daily Herald*, 7 March 1944.

95 Triquet to Chauveau, 31 March 1980, in Chauveau, *Royal 22e*, 399: "Pour ce qui est de Casa Berardi, je suis à écrire exactement ce qui est arrivé afin de donner crédit à ceux qui le méritent. Nous avons eu à Casa Berardi, deux commandants, Bernatchez et Allard ... La victoire fut surtout possible grâce à l'effort des Commandants de Cies Garceau et Yvon Dubé. Je retourne à l'hôpital demain pour une opération assez sérieuse et retournerai au Canada fin de mai ou début de juin, où j'ai l'intention de compléter le récit de Casa-Berardi afin de prévenir que ce soit raconté par quelqu'un d'autre, car il est assez difficile de raconter les choses telles qu'elles se sont passées sans les avoir vécues."

96 Armstrong, *Myth*, 4: "Myth is not a story told for its own sake. It shows us how we should behave." Campbell (*The Hero*, 11) writes that the function of myth is to carry human spirit forward and adds that heroes are "the world's symbolic carriers of the destiny of Everyman"(36) and are not ends in themselves "but guardians, embodiments, or bestowers of the liquor, the milk, the food, the fire, the grace, of indestructible life" (173). Northrop Frye in *The Critical Path*, 169, notes, "Myths of concern enable members of a society to hold together, to accept authority, to be loyal to each other and courageous against attack. Such myths are verbal constructions designed for specific social purposes."

97 LAC, video, VI-8708-0004, Triquet interviewed by France Fortin and André Jean on the show *Camera Verité*, 1970: "C'est pourquoi c'est absolument nécessaire que les troupes soient entraînées dans leur propre langue." He added that good progress had been made with more French-language schools and the appointment of francophones, notably Jean Allard, to high ranks.

98 LAC, RG 24, vol. 20100, Director General Information – Valcartier: news clips of 1 May 1980, "Referendum Discussion a 'Non-Non' in Military." Another clip from 28 January 1971 quoted René Lévesque as saying "Nowhere is there a bigger proportion of Parti Québécois guys than in the French-speaking R22eR." See also news clips in vol. 20,109.

99 Paul Triquet, "Casa Berardi – 13 décembre 1943, " in Chauveau, *Royal 22e,* 60–1: "Unis dans un même effort, dirigés vers un même objectif, rien alors n'a pu nous [anglophones et francophones] arrêter, et il n'est que logique de présumer que, quelque soit l'obstacle qui nous barrera la route, si nous restons unis, rien ne nous arrêtera. C'est la leçon qui se dégage de cet épisode, et au cas ou cette leçon pourrait être de quelque utilité à l'heure ou un certain courant, au défi de l'histoire, tend à nous isoler, à nous 'séparer' de nos frères canadiens, j'ai bien voulu écrire 'Casa-Berardi.'" The account is approximately 6,000 words. It was originally printed in "Casa Berardi," *L'Amicale du 22ième* 16, no. 10 (April 1962) and reprinted in *La revue de la Citadelle* 1, no. 6 (December 1965). It was also reproduced in the brochure *Casa-Berardi* published by La Société d'Histoire et d'Archéologie du Témiscouata in 1993.

100 Gordon, in *Making Public Pasts,* emphasizes that social groups are not individuals and public memory is not understood as the memory of the public but memory disputed by individuals in the public sphere.

Epilogue

1 John Bassett, Chairman of Baton Broadcasting, "We Cannot Ignore the Past When Charting a Course for the Future," Speech to the Empire Club of Canada, 28 June 1990, in Mary R. Byers, ed. *The Empire Club of Canada Speeches, 1990–1991.*

2 Both Henri Tellier and Gilles Turcot, who rose to the rank of lieutenant general, spoke of this in interviews. See also Sébastien Vincent, "Les frères d'armes, le Royal 22e Régiment et l'Armée canadienne dans les témoignages publiés par des combattants québécois francophones ayant participé à la campagne d'Italie (1943–1945)," 190. In Vennat, *Général Dollard Ménard,* 168, General Ménard recalled, "Vaincus lors de la bataille des Plains d'Abraham de 1759, nous étions toujours, même dans l'armée de 1939–1945, considérés comme des êtres inférieurs, donc incapables de commander une formation supérieure, où, bien sûr, il y aurait des anglophones." See also Pariseau and Bernier, *French-Canadians and Bilingualism.*

3 My italics. "Impressions d'un ancien," *L'Amicale du 22ième* 3, no. 9 (October 1949): "Le 22e bataillon fut formé en 1914 afin de grouper les Canadiens de langue française dans une même unité, les entraîner et aller au combat sous les ordres de chefs qui parleraient leur langue et sauraient les comprendre. Cette expérience prouva aux Canadiens des autres nationalités la valeur des nôtres et leur courage comme soldats … (1939–45) … Ils ont prouvé une fois de plus les qualités guerrières et le courage des nôtres quand ceux-ci pouvaient aller au feu sous les ordres de Canadiens qui parlaient la même langue qu'eux."

4 Igartua, *The Other Quiet Revolution*, 13.

5 Laurendeau, *Conscription*; Taylor, *Reconciling the Solitudes*.

6 Igartua, *The Other Quiet Revolution*; Richard Gwyn, *Nationalism without Walls*, 268–89.

7 Cook, *Clio's Warriors*, 250; Vance, *Death So Noble*; Frye, *Fables of Identity*, 53: "We notice that when a historian's scheme gets to a certain point of comprehensiveness it becomes mythical in shape, and so approaches the poetic in its structure." See media coverage from 1 to 9 April 2007 on the ninetieth anniversary of the battle of Vimy Ridge, particularly Michael Valpy, "The Making of a Myth," *Globe and Mail*, 7 April 2007, F4–5; Hillmer and Granatstein, *Empire to Umpire*, 181–209; Alvin Finkel, *Our Lives*, 6.

8 Morton and Granatstein, *Victory 1945*, 254. There was a reunion Christmas dinner in Ortona in 1998 on the fifty-fifth anniversary. See Brandon, *Art or Memorial?*, 51–3, 69–70; Maxime Saint-Laurent, "La couverture journalistique québécoise des commémorations du Débarquement de Normandie: Le cas des journaux *The Gazette* et *La Presse*," *Bulletin d'histoire politique* 16, no. 2 (winter 2008), studies the evolution.

9 Michael Valpy, "The Making of a Myth," *Globe and Mail*, 7 April 2007, F4: "Vimy was recognized as a Canadian victory in places that mattered to Canadians then, as now – the American and British press." Valpy quotes historian Geoffrey Hayes: "Mythology is a funny thing. We don't need to know what happened, we simply need to know what the myth tells us is significant … Vimy Ridge has become so closely associated with Canada as a nation that in some ways it almost doesn't matter what happened there." J.D.M. Stewart in "In the Political Trenches, Vimy Ridge Fights for the Issue of the Day," *Globe and Mail*, 3 April 2007, A13, describes the uses of Vimy for unity messages by Prime Ministers L.B. Pearson and Brian Mulroney.

10 The CWM has his radio and the Adam Sherriff Scott portrait of him in their collection, as well as the "Action at Casa Berardi" painting by Charles Comfort (AN 19500008-001: CWM – radio receiver: wireless set, "This radio may have been used by PT when he won his VC at CB"; AN 19710261-5841 Portrait; and Action at Casa Berardi: AN 19710226-2162, by Charles Comfort). The portrait travelled around Quebec City and Lévis: see 29 January 1953, Bernatchez to Triquet, painting by Adam Sherriff Scott lent by National Gallery to R22eR, who lent it to Régiment de Lévis: R22eR archives, Paul Triquet Collection, FPA-43.

11 John Bassett, chairman of Baton Broadcasting Inc, "We Cannot Ignore the Past When Charting a Course for the Future." Speech to the Empire Club of Canada, 28 June 1990, in Mary R. Byers, ed. *The Empire Club of Canada Speeches, 1990–1991*.

12 From www.valiants.ca, downloaded on 25 April 2007. See also Boileau, *Valiant Hearts,* 27. Canada Post issued a series of Canadian stamps on 21 October 2004 to honour the 150th anniversary of the VC.

13 Cliff Chadderton, chairman of the National Council of Veteran Associations in Canada, open letter of 13 June 2001, available at www.waramps.ca/news/valiant.

14 Taylor, *Reconciling the Solitudes,* 195–6. He adds, "It is hard to generate a widespread sense in Quebec today that Canada is a threat. The real fuel for independentism is now elsewhere, in the discourse of recognition." See also Dumont, *La société québécoise*; Michel Bock, *Quand la nation débordait les frontières*; Igartua, *The Other Quiet Revolution;* Jacques Mathieu and Jacques Lacoursière, *Les Mémoires Québécoises,* 328–41; Jocelyn Létourneau, "La production historienne courante portant sur le Québec et ses rapports avec la construction des figures identitaires d'une communauté communicationnelle," *Recherches sociographiques* 36 (1995): 9–45. Also, when pain and suffering were so great, there is an added hesitancy to speak of these events and an additional incentive to forget.

15 Robert Comeau, Serge Bernier, et al., *Dix ans d'histoire militaire* (see particularly the introduction by Jean-Pierre Gagnon); Rudin, *Making History,* 210–21; Jocelyn Létourneau, "Québec d'après guerre et mémoire collective de la technocratie," *Cahiers internationaux de sociologie* 90 (1991): 67–87; Marjolaine Saint-Pierre, *Léo Gariépy,* 11: "La grande majorité des Normands connaissent 'Monsieur Léo,' le citoyen d'honneur de Courseuilles-sur-mer." See also Pierre Vennat, *Les héros oubliés;* Louis Brosseau, *Le cinéma d'une guerre oubliée*; Cook, *Clio's Warriors,* 3; Tremblay, *Volontaires,* 111–23.

16 "100 Québécois qui ont fait le 20e siècle," *Actualité* (February 1999). See also "25 jeunes de 25 ans construisent l'avenir dans 25 coins du monde," *Actualité* (15 September 2000); Roch Légault, *Une élite en déroute,* 163.

17 Jean Cournoyer, *Le Petit Jean: Dictionnaire des noms propres du Québec* (Montreal: Stanké, 1993); Michel Veyron, *Larousse: Dictionnaire canadien des noms propres* (Quebec: 1989); Jean Provencher, *Chronologie du Québec* (Montréal: Boréal, 1991). Luc Bertrand, in "Seulement trois francophones ont reçu la Croix de Victoria," *La Presse,* 4 July 1993, A7, writes that Quebecers have "depuis longtemps effacé de leur mémoire" the story of Triquet.

18 Journal des débats, Débats de l'Assemblée Nationale, 11 November 1999: "Le nom du capitaine Paul Triquet n'est pas inconnu pour les gens de Québec, puisque le Centre de soins de longue durée pour anciens combattants porte son nom"; ibid., 7 November 2002, Bernard Landry refers to Triquet: "Pensons à des individus: le major-général Tremblay, dans les tranchées de Vimy,

1914–1918; au Colonel Paul Triquet, 1939–1945, croix Victoria, un des militaires les plus décorés de ce qu'on appelait autrefois l'Empire britannique."

19 CWM Archives, Triquet file, "Maison Paul-Triquet, VC," Department of Veterans' Affairs newsletter, May 1987; Henri Bélanger, interview, 4 January 2006; Réal Théberge, interview, 4 January 2006.

20 Paul Edgar Dumont, interview, 31 December 2005. In another interview, on 25 April 2007, Richard Blanchette, former president of the Legion at Cabano, explained that the hall is regularly rented for local dances and events.

21 Fort Ingall Archives, Fonds Paul Triquet 1993, File "Letters"; Archives, Paul Triquet Legion Hall, Cabano, "Cabano Fête Paul Triquet" (1–3 October 1993); the speaker was Raymond Sirois, honorary colonel of the Fusiliers du St-Laurent: "La stratégie du dépassement quotidien ou comment faire de chaque journée un jour héroïque." General Dollard Ménard spoke on another day. On the forty-fifth anniversary of Casa Berardi, Pierre Vennat had a short article on Triquet, "La Croix Victoria du Brigadier-Général Paul Triquet," in the *Legion Magazine* (December–January 1988–89): 5.

22 Jacques Fournier, president of La Société d'Histoire et d'archéologie du Témiscouata, *Casa-Berardi*, 1.

23 Fort Ingall Archives, Fonds Paul Triquet 1993, File "Letters." See particularly messages from Governor General Ramon Hnatyshyn and from Robert Champagne of the Department of Veterans Affairs.

24 *Casa-Berardi*, published by La Société d'Histoire et d'Archéologie du Témiscouata, 1993. The lines were also removed from the 1965 version published in *La Citadelle* (Paul Triquet, "Casa Berardi – 13 décembre 1943," in Chauveau, *Royal 22e*, 60–1: "Unis dans un même effort, dirigés vers un même objectif, rien alors n'a pu nous [anglophones et francophones] arrêter, et il n'est que logique de présumer que, quelque soit l'obstacle qui nous barrera la route, si nous restons unis, rien ne nous arrêtera. C'est la leçon qui se dégage de cet épisode, et au cas ou cette leçon pourrait être de quelque utilité à l'heure ou un certain courant, au défi de l'histoire, tend à nous isoler, à nous 'séparer' de nos frères canadiens, j'ai bien voulu écrire 'Casa-Berardi.'"

25 The *Shorter Oxford English Dictionary*, 1944, defined a hero as "a man of superhuman qualities, favoured by the gods; demigod," as did the *Concise Oxford Dictionary*, 6th ed., 1976. However, in the *Canadian Oxford Dictionary*, 1998, this definition, which had been the first, was now the third, behind: "a person distinguished by courage ... outstanding achievements."

26 John Ralston Saul, *Reflections of a Siamese Twin*, 138: "It is difficult to think of a country where the modern idea of Hero is less celebrated." He adds that Canadian literature is largely anti-heroic: "Heroic acts are admitted to, but invariably put down to accident or misadventure" (140).

27 Christie Blatchford, "Losing the PR War at Home and Abroad," *Globe and Mail*, 30 October 2006, A8, regretted that the media had not provided sufficient coverage of "the awarding of prestigious Canadian military decorations and honours" to soldiers serving in Afghanistan: "In a world where the word 'hero' has all but lost its meaning – attached as it is to almost anyone who endures a mild trauma without mental collapse or meets the now low threshold of nominal good citizenship – about forty gallant Canadian soldiers went almost entirely unrecognized by the press, and thus by their countrymen. It is little short of disgraceful." See also Blatchford's "Soldier Stories Deserve to Be Heard," *Globe and Mail*, 28 April 2007, A19: "This week, the story lost in the headlines over the Afghan detainee issue, Pte. [Jess] Larochelle was awarded the Star of Military Valour, in prestige second only to the Canadian Victoria Cross."

28 Jessica Lynch in Nancy Gibbs, "As the Congress Tangles with President Bush over Iraq, a Lesson on Truth," *Time*, 7 May 2007, 9. Lynch said she was no "little girl Rambo from the hills of West Virginia who went down fighting." Gibbs adds that NFL star Pat Tillman's brother Kevin revealed Tillman had died from friendly fire "and in both cases, the chain of command told a different story." On the banner see Hughes-Hallett, *Heroes*, 14.

29 Taylor, *Sources of the Self*, 23–4. Frye writes in *The Critical Path*, 167, "It appears that the idea of equality forms the nucleus of most myths of concern in our day, in both Marxist and democratic countries. It is not itself a myth of concern, but a concerned feeling entering into every serious myth, whatever its reference."

30 John H. Frost, president, Royal Canadian Legion, in the *Globe and Mail*, 6 March 2007, A12. The same day the paper's editorial "Our Victoria Cross" strongly supported the plan as "the long overdue patriation of the country's pre-eminent honour. The VC has an important place in Canadian history ... it is impossible to imagine this country without the Victoria Cross, and all that it represents." On the making of the first twenty Canadian VCs, see Canada, *Canada's Victoria Cross*.

31 Christopher McCreery in the *Globe and Mail*, 7 March 2007, A12. The following day in the *Globe* Jonathan Vance wrote to oppose the idea in "He's Just a Common Warrior," A17: "The unknown soldier doesn't stand for the remarkable – he stands for the common soldier ... He is the every-Canadian."

32 On the war memorial see Alan R. Young, "We Throw the Torch," 5–28. He describes the "mythology ... evident in the imagery of Canada's National War Memorial," unveiled in 1939 (16–17).

33 Cook in *Clio's Warriors*, referring to the recent controversy surrounding Ben Greenhous's excellent but critical study of Billy Bishop (as a brave flyer but a

bold liar), describes the reaction of Bishop supporters and asks, "Is that how history is viewed by the public? Is history to be the celebration of heroes or the dispassionate study of the available records?" (251).

34 Psychological wounds suffered by Triquet would not be hidden or considered unsuited to a hero today. If anything, empathy and admiration for Lieutenant General Roméo Dallaire's actions in Rwanda and after have increased since it became public that he suffered post-traumatic stress disorder (see Dallaire, *Shake Hands with the Devil*, xii).

35 Hughes-Hallett, *Heroes*, 7.

36 Brian Nolan, *Hero: The Buzz Beurling Story*, 83.

37 LAC, RG 24, Triquet Personnel File, 6th folder, DND message form, "Subject: Death of Brigadier-General Paul Triquet, VC, C St-J, CD," 6 August 1980: "It was General Triquet's wish that rather than flowers, donations be given to La Fondation General Vanier, c/o La Régie du R22eR, La Citadelle."

BIBLIOGRAPHY

PRIMARY SOURCES

Archives

Archives, Fort Ingall, Cabano.

Archives du Musée de la Chaudière, Lévis.
Fonds L'Espérance.

Archives, Légion Paul Triquet, Cabano.

Archives du Royal 22e Régiment, La Citadelle, Quebec.
Fonds Paul Triquet: FPA-43; Fonds J.P.E. Bernatchez: no file number; Fonds Jean Allard: 172/17/1/67; Paul Triquet Collection, FPA-43, unknown author, "The Biography of Paul Triquet, VC Chevalier de la Légion d'Honneur," ca. 1946.

Archives de la Société d'histoire et de généalogie de Rivière-du-Loup.
Dossier 177, pièce 9, "Fusiliers du St-Laurent."

Canadian Postal Museum Archives, Ottawa.
Triquet Collection–G15-25.10.

Canadian War Museum Archives, Ottawa (CWM).
Triquet file; Oral History Project interviews; Thain MacDowell file; brochure *The Victoria Cross: The Stories of the Winning of the VC, Which Are Represented in the Exhibition* (Marlborough House: Centenary Exhibition, 15 June–7 July 1956).

Directorate of History and Heritage Archives, Department of National Defence, Ottawa (DHH).

Reports of the Canadian Military Headquarters: No. 92, "General Activities, Canadian Army Overseas, June 1942–April 1943," 27 April 1943; No. 112, "Policy with Respect to Honours and Awards, Canadian Army Overseas, 1939–44"; No. 129, "Canadian Operations in Italy, September–December, 1943"; No. 135, "Canadian Operations in Sicily, July–August, 1943"; No. 144, "Canadian Operations in Italy, September 1943"; No. 161, "Canadian Operations in Italy, October–November 1943"; No. 165, War Diary, HQ, Eighth Army, 7 December 1943; No. 182, "The Strategic Role of First Canadian Army, 1942–1944," 23 May 1949.

Other files of use include: DHH, 96/47, Honours and Awards; DHH, 713.065 (D2), Honours and Awards, 1939–45; DHH, Allard Fonds, 84/126; DHH, Tellier Fonds, 91/235; DHH, Triquet file DHH, 000.9 (D70); DHH, 72/10, Suttie Report; also DHH 112.043 (D2).

Library and Archives Canada, Ottawa (LAC).

Manuscript Group.

W.L.M. King Papers, MG 26 J1-18.

King Diary, MG 26 J13.

Ernest Lapointe Papers, MG 27 III B10.

Chubby Power Papers, MG 27 III B19.

J.L. Ralston Papers, MG 27 III B11.

LAC Record Group.

Cabinet War Committee minutes (Privy Council, RG2).

External Affairs, RG 25.

National Defence, RG 24.

Triquet's Personnel File is located here, as are the following that were useful: War Diary of 3rd Canadian Infantry Brigade, reel T-11078; War Diary of 1st Canadian Division, reel T-1876, December 1943; War Diary of the Royal 22e Régiment, vol. 15235-8, 1–31 December 1943; War Diary of 1st Canadian Division, reel T-1876, November 1943, and vols. 10, 917, 20, 152, "Honours and Awards," and vol. 12738, file 21/Recommendations/Triquet, folio 53-100.

LAC Audio-Video.

Video, V1-8708-0004, Triquet interviewed by France Fortin and André Jean on the show *Camera Verité*, 1970.

Video, "Their Springtime of Life: The Italian Campaign," CBC documentary with Triquet and Allard interviews, 5 September 1972, at CBC archives, www.archives.cbc.ca.

Radio broadcast C-9352-acc.1984-0164, "Into Battle," broadcast 27 April 1944. Text also at LAC, RG 24, vol. 20155, file Honours and Awards /Triquet, written by Gordon Boshell, produced by Brigid Maas.

Radio broadcast 132875 C-09315 "Biography of Paul Triquet, VC" (1 April 1944) audio clip; also available at CBC archives, www.archives.cbc.ca.

Radio broadcast C-02609-1968-33, "Triquet Meets the King to Receive VC" (March 1944); also at CBC archives, www.archives.cbc.ca.

Radio broadcast LAC, C-10106-1967-0032-143680, interview with Triquet after meeting King, with Marcel Ouimet (27 March 1944); also available at CBC archives, www.archives.cbc.ca.

Radio broadcast "Put Victory First: Triquet and Loan Campaign" (24 April 1944); also at CBC archives, www.archives.cbc.ca.

Royal Military College of Canada Archives at Kingston.

Queen's University Archives.

Chubby Power Papers, box 67, file D-1109.

Grant Dexter Papers, vol. 2142.

Interviews

Family members

Claude and Louise Triquet, Paul Triquet's son and daughter-in-law, 31 January 2006.

Yolande McArthur, Paul Triquet's daughter, 31 January 2006.

Soldiers

Major Jean-F. Lacombe helped arrange interviews during the summer of 2007 with veterans of the R22eR and provided helpful insights. Réal Théberge helped arrange the interviews of 4 January 2006 with veterans at La Maison Paul Triquet and provided helpful insights.

Lieutenant General (ret.) Henri Tellier, 6 September 2006.

Lieutenant General (ret.) Gilles Turcot, 3 August 2007.

Corporal (ret.) Armand Gagnon, 8 August 2007.

Warrant Officer (ret.) André Courtemanche, 8 August 2007.

Léonide Ouellette, 4 January 2006.

Henri Bélanger, 4 January 2006.

Antoine Bourget, 4 January 2006.

Auguste Côté, 4 January 2006.
Rudolphe Bélisle, 4 January 2006.

Soldiers and friends from Cabano

Richard Blanchette, former president of the Legion at Cabano, 25 April 2007.
Lucie Latulippe of Cabano, 31 December 2005.
Georges Fraser of Cabano, 31 December 2005.
Raymond Pelletier of Cabano, 31 December 2005.
Paul Edgar Dumont, 31 December 2005.
Roch Belzile, 3 October 2007.
Réjean Gagnon, 6 August 2007.

PUBLISHED SOURCES

Parliamentary Publications

Canada Gazette.
Canadian House of Commons Debates.
Canadian Senate Debates.
London Gazette.

Newspapers and Magazines

L'Amicale du 22ième (regimental newspaper), 1941–80.
Legion Magazine.
Le St. Laurent, 1943–45.
Maple Leaf.
Clippings of Canadian newspaper articles on Triquet were available in large quantities in three places: (1) LAC files on VC recipients and Army PR, containing many articles of the period 1939–45; (2) the archives of the R22eR, in the Triquet collection, with many articles on his career, 1930–1980; (3) the well-indexed collection from the Second World War at the CWM.

Secondary Sources

Allard, Jean, with Serge Bernier. *The Memoirs of General Jean V. Allard.* Vancouver: University of British Columbia Press 1988.
Armstrong, Karen. *A Short History of Myth.* Toronto: Vintage 2006.

Ashcroft, Michael. *Victoria Cross Heroes.* London: Headline 2007.

Balzer, Timothy. "In Case the Raid Is Unsuccessful: Selling Dieppe to Canadians." *Canadian Historical Review* 87, no. 3 (September 2006).

Beauregard, Claude, *Guerre et censure au Canada, 1939–1945.* Sillery: Septentrion 1998.

Behiels, Michael, *Prelude to Quebec's Quiet Revolution.* Montreal and Kingston: McGill-Queen's University Press 1985.

Bernier, Robert. *Un siècle de propagande? Information, communication et marketing gouvernemental.* Quebec: PUL 2001.

Bernier, Serge. "Participation des Canadiens français aux combats: Evaluation et tentative de quantification." *Bulletin d'histoire politique* 3, no. 3 (spring 1995).

– *The Royal 22e Régiment, 1914–1999.* Translated by Charles Phillips. Montreal: Art Global 1999.

Bishop, Arthur. *Our Bravest and Our Best: The Stories of Canada's Victoria Cross Winners.* Toronto: McGraw-Hill Ryerson 1995.

Bizimana, Aimé-Jules. "Les correspondants de guerre canadiens-français de 1939 à 1945." *Bulletin d'histoire politique* 16, no. 2 (winter 2008): 163–78.

Blatherwick, F.J. *1000 Brave Canadians: The Canadian Gallantry Awards, 1854–1989.* Toronto: Unitrade 1991.

– *Canadian Army: Honours, Decorations, Medals, 1902–1968.* New Westminster, BC: FJB Air Publications 1993.

– *Canadian Orders, Decorations and Medals.* Toronto: Unitrade 2003.

Bloom, Allan. *The Closing of the American Mind.* New York: Simon & Schuster 1987.

Bock, Michel. *Quand la nation débordait les frontières: Les minorités françaises dans la pensée de Lionel Groulx.* Montreal: HMH 2004.

Boileau, John. *Valiant Hearts: Atlantic Canada and the Victoria Cross.* Halifax: Nimbus 2005.

Boissonnault, Charles-Marie. *Histoire du Royal 22e Régiment.* Quebec: Pélican 1964.

Borduas, Paul-Émile. *Refus global.* Montreal: Mithra-Mythe 1948.

Bothwell, Robert. *Canada and Quebec: One Country, Two Histories.* Vancouver: University of British Columbia Press 1995.

Bouchard, Gérard. *La nation québécois au futur et au passé.* Montreal: VLB 1999.

Brandon, Laura, *Art or Memorial? The Forgotten History of Canada's War Art.* Calgary: University of Calgary Press 2006.

Brennan, Patrick. *Reporting the Nation's Business: Press-Government Relations during World War II.* Toronto: University of Toronto Press 1994.

Brosseau, Louis. *Le cinéma d'une guerre oubliée*. Montreal: VLB 1998.

Byers, Mary R., ed. *The Empire Club of Canada Speeches, 1990–1991*. Toronto: Empire Club Foundation 1992.

Cameron, Craig B. *Born Lucky: RSM Harry Fox, MBE, One D-Day Dodger's Story*. St Catherines: Vanwell 2005.

Campbell, Joseph. *The Hero with a Thousand Faces*. 1949. Reprint, New York: Meridian Books 1969.

Canada. Department of National Defence. *The Canadians in Britain, 1939–1944*. Ottawa: King's Printer 1945.

– *Canadian Honours and Awards Bestowed upon Members of the Canadian Forces*. Ottawa: DND 2005.

Canada. Department of National Defence and Rideau Hall. *Canada's Victoria Cross*. Ottawa: DND-Rideau Hall 2008.

Canada. Department of National Defence, Public Affairs, Press Releases, available in Archives du R22eR, Paul Triquet Collection, FPA-43.

Casa-Berardi. Cabano: La Société d'Histoire et d'Archéologie du Témiscouata 1993. This 37-page booklet includes a reprint of a 16-page account of the battle written by Triquet in 1961, as well as contemporary accounts.

Castonguay, Jacques. *Les bataillons et le dépôt du Royal 22e Régiment: Vingt ans d'histoire, 1945–1965*. Quebec: Régie du Royal 22e Régiment 1974.

Castonguay, Jacques, Armand Ross, and Michel Litalien. *Le Régiment de la Chaudière, 1869–2004*. Lévis: Le Régiment de la Chaudière 2005.

Catela de Bordes, E., ed. *Le mémorial du Québec*. Vol. 6, *1939–52*. Quebec: Mémorial 1979.

Chapnick, Adam. *The Middle Power Project: Canada and the Founding of the United Nations*. Vancouver: University of British Columbia Press 2005.

Châtillon, Claude, *Carnets de guerre: Ottawa-Casa Berardi, 1941–1944*. Ottawa: Visages 1987.

Chauveau, Charles, *Soixante-cinq ans d'histoire: Notes historiques sur le Royal 22e Régiment*. Vol. 2. Quebec: 1983.

Clarke, John D. *Gallantry Medals and Decorations of the World*. London: Leo Cooper 2001.

Clarkson, Stephen, and Christina McCall. *Trudeau and Our Times*. Vol. 1. Toronto: McClelland & Stewart 1990.

Comeau, Robert, and Serge Bernier, with Mourad Djebabla, Béatrice Richard, and Stéphane Roussel. *Dix ans d'histoire militaire en Français au Québec*. Montreal: UQAM 2005.

Comfort, Charles. *Artist at War*. Pender Island: Remembrance Books 1995.

Cook, Tim. *Clio's Warriors: Canadian Historians and the Writing of the World Wars.* Vancouver: University of British Columbia Press 2006.

Crook, M.J. *The Evolution of the Victoria Cross.* Turnbridge Wells, Kent: Midas 1975.

Dagenais, Michèle, and Christian Laville. "Le naufrage du projet de programme d'histoire 'nationale': Retour sur une occasion manquée accompagné de considérations sur l'éducation historique." *Revue d'histoire de l'Amérique française* 60, no. 4 (spring 2007): 517–50.

Dallaire, Roméo. *Shake Hands with the Devil: The Failure of Humanity in Rwanda.* Toronto: Random House 2003.

Delaney, Douglas E. *The Soldiers' General: Bert Hoffmeister at War.* Vancouver: University of British Columbia Press 2005.

Dornier, François, and Marie-Claude Joubert. *Soldats de la côte: Les Fusiliers du St-Laurent d'hier à aujourd'hui.* Rimouski: Les Fusiliers du St-Laurent 1992.

Douglas, Tom. *Great Canadian War Heroes: Victoria Cross Recipients of World War II.* Canmore: Altitude Publishing 2005.

Dumais, Lucien. *Un Canadien français face à la Gestapo,* Montreal: Du Jour 1970.

Dumont, Fernand. *Genèse de la Société québécoise.* Montreal: Boréal 1993.

Durflinger, Serge Marc. *Fighting from Home: The Second World War in Verdun, Quebec.* Vancouver: University of British Columbia Press 2006.

English, John A. *The Canadian Army and the Normandy Campaign: A Study of Failure in High Command.* New York: Praeger 1991.

Evans, Suzanne. *Mothers of Heroes, Mothers of Martyrs: World War I and the Politics of Grief.* Montreal and Kingston: McGill-Queen's University Press 2007.

Fahrni, Magda, and Robert Rutherdale, eds. *Creating Postwar Canada: Community, Diversity and Dissent, 1945–75.* Vancouver: University of British Columbia Press 2007.

Ferretti, Lucia, Yvan Lamonde, Denyse Baillargeon, and Michael Gauvreau. "The Catholic Origins of Quebec's Quiet Revolution, 1931–1970." *Revue d'histoire de l'Amérique française* 60, no. 3 (winter 2007): 373–88.

Finkel, Alvin, *Our Lives: Canada after 1945.* Toronto: Lorimer 1997.

Foisy-Geoffroy, Dominique. "Le Rapport de la Commission Tremblay (1953–1956): Testament politique de la pensée traditionaliste canadienne-française." *Revue d'histoire de l'Amérique française* 60, no. 3 (winter 2007): 257–94.

Forbes, Charly. *Fantassin: Pour mon pays, la gloire et ... des prunes.* Sillery: Septentrion 1994.

Frye, Northrop. *Fables of Identity: Studies in Poetic Mythology*. New York: Harcourt, Brace and World 1963.
– *The Critical Path: An Essay on the Social Context of Literary Criticism*. Bloomington: Indiana University Press 1971.
Gagnon, Jean-Pierre. *Le 22e Bataillon (canadien-français) 1914–1919: Étude socio-militaire*. Quebec: Presses de l'Université Laval 1986.
Galloway, Strome. *The General Who Never Was*. Belleville: Mika 1981.
Gauvreau, Michael. *The Catholic Origins of Quebec's Quiet Revolution, 1931–1970*. Montreal and Kingston: McGill-Queen's University Press 2006.
Gillis, John. *Commemorations: The Politics of National Identity*. Princeton: Princeton University Press 1994.
Gordon, Alan. *Making Public Pasts: The Contested Terrain of Montreal's Public Memories, 1891–1930*. Montreal and Kingston: McGill-Queen's University Press 2001.
Gouin, Jacques. *Lettres de guerre d'un Québécois (1942–1945)*. Montreal: Éditions du jour 1975.
Granatstein, J.L. "A Half Century On: The Veterans' Experience." In *The Veterans Charter*, edited by Peter Neary and J.L. Granatstein, 230. Montreal and Kingston: McGill-Queen's University Press 1998.
– *Canada's Army: Waging War and Keeping the Peace*. Toronto: University of Toronto Press 2002.
Granatstein, J.L., and J.M. Hitsman. *Broken Promises: A History of Conscription in Canada*. Toronto: Oxford 1977.
Graves, Donald E. *Century of Service: The History of the South Alberta Light Horse*. Toronto: Robin Brass 2005.
Greenhous, Brereton. *The Making of Billy Bishop*. Toronto: Dundurn 2002.
Grimal, Pierre. "Man and Myth." In *Larousse World Mythology*, edited by Pierre Grimal. London: Hamlyn 1973.
Groulx, Lionel. *Dollard: Est-il une mythe?* Ottawa: Fides 1960.
Guérin, Jean-P. "Mission à Casa Berardi." Brochure. Montreal, April 1944.
Gwyn, Richard. *Nationalism without Walls: The Unbearable Lightness of Being Canadian*. Toronto: McClelland & Stewart 1995.
Halliday, Hugh, *Valour Reconsidered: Inquiries into the Victoria Cross and Other Awards for Extreme Bravery*. Toronto: Robin Brass 2006.
Harvey, Fernand, and Paul-André Linteau. "L'évolution de l'historiographie dans la RHAF, 1947–72." *RHAF*, vol. 26, 1972
Hillmer, Norman, and J.L. Granatstein. *Empire to Umpire: Canada and the World to the 1990s*. Toronto: Copp Clark 1994.
Hughes-Hallett, Lucy. *Heroes*. Toronto: Viking 2005.

Hundevad, John. "The V.C. Centennial." *The Legionary* 30, no. 8 (January 1956).

Igartua, Jose E. *The Other Quiet Revolution: National Identities in English Canada, 1945–1971*. Vancouver: University of British Columbia Press 2007.

Jung, Carl G. *Dialectique du moi et de l'inconscient*. 1933. Reprint, Paris: Gallimard 1964.

Keshen, Jeffrey. *Saints, Sinners, and Soldiers: Canada's Second World War*. Vancouver: University of British Columbia Press 2004.

Laurendeau, André. *La crise de la conscription, 1942*. Montreal: Les éditions du jour 1962.

Lefebvre, Florent, Elizabeth Armstrong, and R.B. Oglesby. *La Presse canadienne et la Deuxième Guerre mondiale*. Ottawa: National Defence 1997.

Légault, Roch. *Une élite en déroute: Les militaires canadiens après la Conquête*. Montreal: Athéna 2002.

Létourneau, Jocelyn. "Québec d'après guerre et mémoire collective de la technocratie." *Cahiers internationaux de sociologie* 90 (1991): 67–87.

– "La production historienne courante portant sur le Québec et ses rapports avec la construction des figures identitaires d'une communauté communicationnelle." *Recherches sociographiques* 36 (1995): 9–45.

Litalien, Michel. *Le 51e Bataillon des services du Canada et ses origines, 1901–2005*. St Hubert, Quebec: Le Bataillon 2005.

Lowenthal, David. *The Heritage Crusader and the Spoils of History*. Cambridge: Cambridge University Press 1997.

MacFarlane, John. "Quebec and Conscription: The Death of Ernest Lapointe and a Fateful Change of Policy." *The Beaver* 75, no. 2 (April–May 1995): 26–31.

– "Double Vision: Ernest Lapointe, Mackenzie King, and the Quebec Voice in Canadian Foreign Policy, 1935–1939." *Journal of Canadian Studies* 34, no. 1 (spring 1999): 93–111.

– *Ernest Lapointe and Quebec's Influence on Canadian Foreign Policy*. Toronto: University of Toronto Press 1999.

Machum, George C. *Canada's V.C.'s: The Story of Canadians Who Won the Victoria Cross*. Toronto: McClelland & Stewart 1956.

Mackenzie, Ian. *The Veterans Charter: Acts of the Canadian Parliament to Assist Canadian Veterans*. Ottawa: King's Printer 1947.

Mathieu, Jacques, and Jacques Lacoursière. *Les mémoires québécoises*. Quebec: PUL 1991.

Mayo, James. *War Memorials as Political Landscape: The American Experience and Beyond*. New York: Praeger 1988.

McAndrew, Bill. *Canadians and the Italian Campaign, 1943–1945*. Montreal: Art Global 1996.

McCreery, Christopher. *The Canadian Honours System*. Toronto: Dundurn 2005.

McGeer, Eric. *The Canadian Battlefields in Italy: Ortona and the Liri Valley*. Waterloo: Laurier Centre for Military, Strategic and Disarmament Studies 2007.

McNairn, Alan. *Behold the Hero: General Wolfe and the Arts in the Eighteenth Century*. Montreal and Kingston: McGill-Queen's University Press 1997.

Melville, Douglas A. *Canadians and the Victoria Cross*. St Catherines: Vanwell 1987.

Mitchell, G.D., with Brian Reid and W. Simcock. *RCHA – Right of the Line: An Anecdotal History of the Royal Canadian Horse Artillery from 1871*. Ottawa: RCHA History Committee 1986.

Morgan, Cecilia. *Heroines and History: Representations of Madeleine de Verchères and Laura Secord*. Toronto: University of Toronto Press 2002.

Morton, Desmond. *When Your Number's Up: The Canadian Soldier in the First World War*. Toronto: Random House 1993.

– *A Military History of Canada*. 4th ed. Toronto: McClelland & Stewart 1999.

Morton, Desmond, and J.L. Granatstein. *Victory 1945: Canadians from War to Peace*. Toronto: HarperCollins 1995.

Morton, Desmond, and Glenn Wright. *Winning the Second Battle: Canadian Veterans and the Return to Civilian Life, 1915–1930*. Toronto: University of Toronto Press 1987.

Neary, Peter, and J.L. Granatstein, eds. *The Veterans Charter and Post-World War II Canada*. Montreal and Kingston: McGill-Queen's University Press 1998.

Neatby, H. Blair. *William Lyon Mackenzie King*. Vol. 3: *1932–1939, The Prism of Unity*. Toronto: University of Toronto Press 1976.

Nelles, H.V. *The Art of Nation-Building: Pageantry and Spectacle at Quebec's Tercentenary*. Toronto: University of Toronto Press 1999.

Nemni, Max, and Monique Nemni. *Young Trudeau: Son of Quebec, Father of Canada*. Toronto: McClelland & Stewart 2006.

Nicholson, Adam. *Seize the Fire: Heroism, Duty and the Battle of Trafalgar*. London: HarperCollins 2005.

Nicholson, G.W.L. *The Canadians in Italy, 1943–1945: Official History of the Canadian Army in the Second World War*. Vol. 2. Ottawa: Queen's Printer 1957.

– *The Gunners of Canada: The History of the Royal Regiment of Canadian Artillery*. Vol. 2: *1919–1967*. Toronto: McClelland & Stewart 1972.

Nolan, Brian. *Hero: The Buzz Beurling Story.* Toronto: Lester and Orpen Dennys 1981.

Owram, Doug. *The Government Generation: Canadian Intellectuals and the State, 1900–1945.* Toronto: University of Toronto Press 1986.

Pariseau, Jean, and Serge Bernier. *French-Canadians and Bilingualism in the Canadian Armed Forces.* Vol. 1, *1763–1969: The Fear of a Parallel Army.* Ottawa: Supply and Services 1986.

Percival, John. *For Valour: The VC, Courage in Action.* London: Thames 1957.

Phillips, C.E. Lucas. *Victoria Cross Battles of the Second World War.* London: Heinemann 1973.

Pierce, John. "Constructing Memory: The Vimy Memorial." *Canadian Military History* 1, nos. 1–2 (autumn 1992) 5–8.

Pouliotte, Jean-François. "Le Royal 22e Régiment pendant la Deuxième Guerre mondiale: Une étude socio-militaire." Montreal: UQAM 1996.

Powell, George. "Funny How the Word Arrived." *Legion Magazine*, March/April 1998.

Richard, Béatrice. *La mémoire de Dieppe, radioscopie d'un mythe.* Montreal: VLB 2002.

– "La mémoire collective de la guerre au Québec: Un espace de résistance politique?" *Canadian Issues/Thèmes canadiens* (winter 2004): 17–20.

Riddle, David, and D. Mitchell, eds. *The Distinguished Service Order to the Canadian Expeditionary Force and Canadians in the Royal Naval Air Service, Royal Flying Corps and Royal Air Force, 1915–1920.* Winnipeg: Kirby-Marlton 1991.

Roy, Reginald H. *For Most Conspicuous Bravery: A Biography of Major-General George R. Pearkes, V.C., through Two World Wars.* Vancouver: University of British Columbia Press 1977.

Rudin, Ronald. *Making History in Twentieth-Century Quebec.* Toronto: University of Toronto Press 1997.

– *Founding Fathers: The Celebration of Champlain and Laval in the Streets of Quebec, 1878–1908.* Toronto: University of Toronto Press 2003.

Saint-Laurent, Maxime. "La couverture journalistique québécoise des commémorations du Débarquement de Normandie: Le cas des journaux *The Gazette* et *La Presse.*" *Bulletin d'histoire politique* 16, no. 2 (winter 2008): 197–211.

Saint-Pierre, Marjolaine. *Léo Gariépy: Un héros récupéré, célébré en France ignore ici.* Montreal: ADP 1993.

Saul, John Ralston. *Reflections of a Siamese Twin: Canada at the End of the Twentieth Century.* Toronto: Viking 1997.

Schragg, Lex. *History of the Ontario Regiment, 1866–1951.* Published by the Regiment, 1951.

Sheffield, R. Scott, *The Red Man's on the Warpath: The Image of the "Indian" and the Second World War*. Vancouver: University of British Columbia Press 2005.

Smyth, John. *Great Stories of the VC*. London: Arthur Barker 1977.

Speaight, Robert. *Vanier: Soldier, Diplomat and Governor General*. Toronto: Collins 1970.

Stacey, C.P. *Six Years of War: The Army in Canada, Britain and the Pacific; Official History of the Canadian Army in the Second World War*. Vol. 1. Ottawa: Queen's Printer 1955.

– *Arms, Men and Governments: The War Policies of Canada, 1939–1945*. Ottawa: Queen's Printer 1970.

– *A Very Double Life: The Private World of Mackenzie King*. Toronto: Macmillan 1976.

– *Canada and the Age of Conflict*. Vol. 2: *The Mackenzie King Era*. Toronto: University of Toronto Press 1981.

Stacey, C.P., and Barbara M. Wilson. *The Half-Million: The Canadians in Britain, 1939–1946*. Toronto: University of Toronto Press 1987.

Swettenham, John. *Valiant Men: Canada's V.C. and George Cross Winners*. Toronto: Hakkert 1973.

Taylor, Charles. *Sources of the Self: The Making of the Modern Identity*. Cambridge: Harvard University Press 1989.

– *The Ethics of Authenticity*. Cambridge, Mass.: Harvard University Press 1992.

– *Reconciling the Solitudes: Essays on Canadian Federalism and Nationalism*. Montreal and Kingston: McGill-Queen's University Press 1993.

– *Modern Social Imaginaries*. Durham and London: Duke University Press 2004.

Tremblay, Yves. *Volontaires: Des Québécois en guerre (1939–1945)*. Montreal: Athéna 2006.

– *Instruire une armée: Les officiers canadiens et la guerre moderne, 1919–1944*. Montreal: Athéna 2007.

Triquet, Florence. *La petite histoire de la famille Triquet, 1840–1995*. Montreal: Les Éditions Francine Breton 1997.

Vance, Jonathon. *Death So Noble: Memory, Meaning, and the First World War*. Vancouver: University of British Columbia Press 1997.

Vanier, Georges. *Paroles de guerre*. Montreal: Beauchemin 1944.

Vennat, Pierre. *Les héros oubliés: L'histoire inédite des militaires canadiens-français de la Deuxième Guerre mondiale*. Montreal: Méridien 1997.

– *Général Dollard Ménard: De Dieppe au référendum*. Montreal: Art Global 2004.

Vincent, Sébastien. *Laissés dans l'ombre: Quatorze Québécois racontent leur participation volontaire à la Seconde Guerre mondiale.* Montreal: VLB 2004.

– "Les frères d'armes, le Royal 22e Régiment et l'Armée canadienne dans les témoignages publiés par des combattants québécois francophones ayant participé à la campagne d'Italie (1943–1945)." *Bulletin d'histoire politique* 16, no. 2 (winter 2008): 179–96.

Vokes, Chris, with J. MacLean. *Vokes: My Story.* Ottawa: Gallery Books 1985.

Wilson, Edmund, ed. *The Crack-Up*, by F. Scott Fitzgerald. New York: New Directions 1945.

Winter, Jay. *Sites of Memory, Sites of Mourning: The Great War in European Cultural History.* Cambridge: Cambridge University Press 1995.

Young, Allan. "'We Throw the Torch': Canadian Memorials of the Great War and the Mythology of Heroic Sacrifice." *Journal of Canadian Studies* 24, no. 4 (winter 1989).

Young, William Robert. "Making the Truth Graphic: The Canadian Government's Home Front Information Structure and Programs during World War II." Ph.D. thesis, University of British Columbia, 1978.

Zuehlke, Mark. *Ortona: Canada's Epic World War II Battle.* Toronto: Stoddart 1999.

INDEX